LEICESTERSHIRE

AND

RUTLAND

The King's England

A New Domesday Book of 10,000 Towns
and Villages

Edited by Arthur Mee

Complete in 41 Volumes

NOTHING like these books has ever been presented to the English people. Every place has been visited. The Compilers have travelled half-a-million miles and have prepared a unique picture of our countryside as it has come down through the ages, a census of all that is enduring and worthy of record.

THE MEDIEVAL GUILDHALL, PRIDE OF LEICESTER

THE KING'S ENGLAND

LEICESTERSHIRE AND RUTLAND

EDITED BY
ARTHUR MEE

With 280 Places
and 138 Pictures

THE KING'S ENGLAND PRESS
1997

First published 1937 by
Hodder and Stoughton Ltd

This edition published 1997 by
The King's England Press
21 Commercial Road
Goldthorpe Industrial Estate, Goldthorpe
Rotherham, South Yorkshire S63 9BL

© The Trustees of the Estate
of the late Arthur Mee

ISBN 1 872438 02 4

Printed and bound in Great Britain by
Woolnough Bookbinding, Irthlingborough, Northants.

The Editor is greatly indebted to

EDWIN SHARPE GREW
and
SYDNEY WARNER

for their valuable help with this book

For the pictures to
SIDNEY TURNER, ART EDITOR,
And to the following photographers :

Messrs W. A. Call, the late Brian Clayton, Fred Crossley, Country Life, J. Dixon-Scott, G. C. Druce, Herbert Felton, F. Frith, Photochrom, H. J. Smith, E. W. Tattersall, W. F. Taylor, and to the City of Leicester Publicity and Development Department

PICTURES OF LEICESTERSHIRE

Where the pictures are not on or facing the page given
they are inside the set of pictures beginning on that page

PICTURES OF RUTLAND

LEICESTERSHIRE

Busy Towns and Green Pastures

LEICESTERSHIRE is a land of green pastures and running waters, 820 square miles of pleasant country in the heart of England. It belongs to those Midlands which stand out in England for nothing in particular, but are famous for being typically English, the ordinary England of ordinary folk—rather like a Constable picture, just England.

Yet in history this Leicestershire is far from being an ordinary English place: run quickly down its 20 centuries and it is a romantic tale. Its capital was the chief town of Central Britain in Roman days. Its glory passed away and it was nothing until there came a Norman lord who married the Earl of Leicester's sister; his name was Simon, and from this alliance sprang that Simon de Montfort who married the King of England's sister but put himself on the side of Magna Carta and the Barons, and founded the first Parliament in the world before he fell on the battlefield of Evesham. Then came the bloodstained Richard on his way to Bosworth, perishing there to be first buried in Grey Friar's Church and then thrown into the river to pollute its waters. One noble man and one ignoble man the rivers of Leicestershire have received in death—it was the Swift that carried the ashes of John Wycliffe to the sea, and the Soar that was stained with the dust of the last Plantagenet. Then Wolsey came, begging a little earth for charity, and then Jane Grey came into that pathetic page of history which as long as England lasts must bring a tear to the eyes of men.

It was just before these days that Henry the Eighth meant to make a bishopric of Leicester, restoring that of Saxon days, but he spent the money on something else and the bishopric went to Peterborough. We may wonder what the fortunes of Leicester would have been if the king had been less extravagant, for the town would have gathered about a great cathedral. As it was, the long hair of the sheep in these green pastures was found to be good for fine woollens, and the 17th century built up the

3

reputation of the county for fine hose. Agriculture and industry grew hand in hand, and today everywhere in Leicestershire we see a chimney and green fields, and Leicester is growing to greatness once again, with its Roman walls reappearing before our eyes, and its commercial prosperity unsurpassed in either England or the British Empire.

William Cobbett had much to say in praise of the towers and spires of this county of modest hills, flowing rivers, and winding streams, and since his day an endless procession of travellers has walked along these hundreds of miles of roads shaded with trees, never failing to find much interest in a county whose first town sends its boots across the world and whose second town sends its bells to ring in steeples everywhere.

The county is divided into two almost equal parts by the chief river running through it. The Soar, flowing northward into the Trent, separates east and west Leicestershire by a broad valley, flowing like a silver ribbon through historic Leicester in the very heart of the county, gathering to itself the Rothley, the Blackbrook, the Fishpool, and other streams, and becoming the Nottinghamshire boundary before it meets the Trent. It has another river (the Mease) forming the Derbyshire boundary and still another (the Welland) separating it from Northants. The Witham runs below the Wolds, and the Anker flows from Charnwood Forest to the Trent. The Swift runs into Shakespeare's Avon (it would carry Wycliffe's ashes there). Among the many streams which play so great a part in the agricultural prosperity of Leicestershire are the Wreak, flowing into the Soar near Melton Mowbray; the Anstey Brook, gathering its waters on the high ground of Charnwood Forest; the Eye Brook running into the Welland; the Devon; and the Smite. Eight rivers run along the boundary of this well-watered county, which, though of course entirely inland, is surrounded by 70 miles of water and 94 miles of land.

There are a few lakes. Groby Pool is the best natural sheet of water in the county. Charnwood Forest has four beautiful lakes: the reservoirs at Thornton, Bradgate, Blackbrook, and Swithland, two of them alone holding more than a thousand million gallons, and one of them described as so picturesque with its rugged hills behind that Central England has no landscape to beat it.

The two halves of Leicestershire east and west of the Soar are characteristic divisions of the county, the east with the small hills called the Wolds, the west with the more industrial area and Charnwood Forest in the midst of it. The open hilly country of the Wolds rises near Loughborough and runs for 16 miles to the north-eastern corner of the county. From Belvoir another ridge of the Wolds goes south to the valley of the Wreak, and from there a higher range with Burrough Hill, Billesdon Coplow, and the charmingly-named Robin-a-Tiptoe, ends in the Welland Valley near Market Harborough. In the west the Charnwood Forest ridges run in a line of heights from Bradgate Park (outside Leicester) to the neighbourhood of Ashby-de-la-Zouch, from near the tower in which Lady Jane Grey sat reading Plato to near the castle in which Mary Queen of Scots spent part of her captivity.

The Forest area is ten miles long and six miles wide, but the little mountain region has lost much of its woodland, though its heights are clothed with trees. Among the heights are Birch Hill, Whittle Hill, Cliffe Hill, and Beacon Hill, and from them we may look far over the Midlands and see Belvoir Castle, Lincoln Cathedral, the Derbyshire hills, the Clee Hills of Shropshire, and the blue line of the Malverns.

Except for its industrial capital, crowded with one of the most energetic populations in the Midlands, Leicestershire has no great crowds of people. Leicester itself is one of the remarkable cities of the world. It has a historic memory of proud significance in our history, and it has the proud satisfaction in our own day of having been declared by the League of Nations the most prosperous city in the British Empire and the second most prosperous community in the world. It is proving worthy of its great repute, for it is setting up an admirable group of buildings. It has one of the noblest of all the memorials to the men who never came back from the war. It has bought for its people the great park of Bradgate with Lady Jane Grey's tower still standing, and has, besides, a thousand acres of green space. It threw the worthless dust of a king into its river, and nobly guards the dust of Cardinal Wolsey. It traces its birth back to the Romans, and is proud of the Roman pavements and the Roman walls that all may see in its streets. Its great Earl of Leicester was the founder of our first Parliament, and his castle was the scene of one of Parliament's first meetings. Citizens of no mean city are the hard-working and plain-thinking people of Leicester.

Nearly half the county lives in this busy capital town. Not one of Leicestershire's towns is over 20 miles from Leicester; the rest of its people are in over 200 villages. Everywhere on the hills are countless flocks, and always as we ride about this county of green fields we are reminded that Leicestershire holds an unrivalled place for the quality of its sheep. It was Robert Bakewell who gave it this proud place. On his Leicestershire farm he raised the standard of agriculture for all England. He made the flocks of sheep on these hillsides famous for their long wool. He introduced the scientific breeding of sheep and cattle which has so vastly improved our farming. The farmer of Dishley Grange is little known, but the quiet work he did has made him one of the benefactors of the world. The county was famous in his day for its village industry, and the whirr of William Iliffe's stocking-frame was heard in thousands of its cottages. From Hinckley the hosiery works of Leicestershire have spread far and wide, and the stocking-frame has been replaced by amazingly complicated machinery working all day long in factories at Leicester and Loughborough and many busy little towns.

Men and women tramp about the earth in every part wearing shoes and stockings from Leicester, and often enough as they walk about they hear the bells that came from Loughborough, where bells have been made for a hundred years, and where stands the first grand carillon set up in our land. There are iron works at Leicester and Market Harborough. Coal was worked at Coleorton in medieval days and in our time has made a village into a great mining town. Coalville, Swannington, Snibston, Hugglescote, Moira, Ibstock, Nailstone, Bagworth, and Ellistown are all busy mining villages. The local tiles and terracotta are always in demand, and the hard bricks made in Leicestershire are much used in London. We may see them in St Pancras Station. The county's granite is famous; it comes from the well-known Mountsorrel, from Groby with its familiar pool, from Enderby and Croft and Brandon Hill. It wears marvellously well, being used for paving-stones and kerbs as far north as Scarborough and as far south as Dorset; there are places where after half a century of traffic there is little wear in this hard stone. It is stirring to think that the roadmakers of the 20th century use the same kind of stone as the Romans used for Ermine Street. Every year the county exports a million tons of granite, though it is so expensive for quarrying and transport that the million tons cost half a million pounds in labour. The huge machines crushing the great masses of rock are among the great sights of the county.

It is, of course, the favourite ground of those who hunt with hounds. No county in England has so many hunting-seats as Leicestershire, the huntsman's paradise with its hills and dales, its open views, its wide grassland and scattered woods. Charnwood Forest was a hunting ground in Saxon days, when the Forest Courts were held at Groby, Whitwick, and Shepshed. It shares with Rutland and Northants whatever glory there may be in this old sport, and its packs of hounds (the Quorn, the Belvoir, the Cottesmore, and the Pytchley) are famous, for it may be said that fox-hunting as we know it was born at the foot of the Charnwood range, where stands Quorn Hall, the home of Hugo Meynell for nearly half a century. For those who neither work nor hunt in Leicestershire it has a great appeal. Day after day we have journeyed through it, up hill and down dale, and day after day there have been new pictures for our delight, woods and parks and churches and lovely villages. We have stood among the earthworks at Breedon known as the Bulwarks, and have seen fragments of ramparts surviving on Beacon Hill from days older than England's history.

Mile after mile we may travel along Leicestershire's two Roman roads, and in Leicester we may follow in the footsteps of the Romans, where what is now called New Walk is one of the oldest in the land. Near Ratby and at Medbourne, Evington, Market Harborough, and Stonesby are traces of what are supposed to have been Roman defences. In the museums are countless fragments of Roman pottery, weapons, instruments, and ornaments found in the county. There is Saxon work in the tower of Tugby church, and still more in the church at Breedon, standing like a fortress on its north-west hilltop. There are Norman arcades at Allexton, Arnesby, Foston, Theddingworth, Bringhurst, Thurlaston, Hallaton, Kilworth, and Twyford. We do not wonder that Leicestershire has long been famous for its churches in village and town, for we have found scores of them with charm that only age can give, and many of them have a rare beauty which centuries have not destroyed. Spires have pointed heavenward above Saxelby and Hallaton since the 13th century, and there are noble spires at Market Harborough, Barkby, Gaddesby, Oadby, and Kirby Bellars. One of the finest is at St Martin's in Leicester; there are beauties at Belton, Queniborough, Shepshed, Wigston, and Stoke Golding; and at Bottesford the loftiest spire in the county keeps watch over the county's loveliest group of tombs. There are grand old towers at Higham-on-the-Hill, at Buckminster and Tugby, at Sproxton and Stonesby, and every traveller knows the tower that crowns the wonderful church at Melton Mowbray, which many believe to be the finest church in Leicestershire.

Indoors the churches are often rich in treasure. About forty of them have kept their ancient glass, as at Coston, Thornton, Kegworth, and Goadby Marwood. About thirty keep their medieval screens, and in village after village we come upon old woodwork. For centuries sermons have been preached from the pulpits of Rotherby, Shepshed, Loddington, Saxelby, Thorpe Langton, Peatling Magna, and, of course, John Wycliffe's Lutterworth. There are rare medieval benches at Gaddesby (where is also one of the very few equestrian statues in English churches), at Ragdale, at Saxelby, Dunton Bassett, Croxton Kerrial, Shearsby, Thornton, and Misterton, and a few other village churches have kept finely carved old chairs, notably Barkeston, Bottesford, Goadby Marwood, and Lutterworth. At Ashby-de-la-Zouch we come upon what is probably a unique finger pillory. There are heart shrines at Sibson and Sheepy Magna, a rare reredos carved in alabaster by a medieval craftsman at South Kilworth, and the earliest known brass inscription in English [prose at Wanlip. For monuments impressive or curious we should come to Prestwold, Belton, Noseley, Quorn, Skeffington, Thurlaston, and Bottesford, some of them with a noble array of knights and ladies in stone and alabaster. Fine fonts we may find in scores; there are at least a score made by the Normans, and another score that were made beautiful by English masons 700 years ago.

There are charming villages with a great variety of appeal. We remember Woodhouse for its fine views of Charnwood; Shackerstone for two miles of trees leading over the border to Gopsall Hall, where Handel used to stay with his friend Charles Jennens; and Newtown Linford for a beauty all its own and the historic interest of Jane Grey's tower in Bradgate Park. The only school known to have been built by Sir Christopher Wren is at Appleby Parva. Stapleford's old Hall has a marvellous array of sculpture out of doors. Kirby Muxloe has a ruined castle that has seen five centuries go by, and at Lockington, Redmile, Sibson, and Waltham-on-the-Wolds curfew still rings out as it has rung out for 20 generations of their people. Queniborough, Buckminster, Gumley, Cossington, and Prestwold are all delightful places. Wistow and Withcote have notable old halls. Ulverscroft Priory still has its old tower, and there are still standing the ruins of the Priory of Grace Dieu. And there is, of course, the incomparable Belvoir Castle. We may wonder if among all the spacious splendours of our countryside there is anything that surpasses Belvoir. It is a majestic spectacle set on a hill, setting us dreaming of hill-cities far away as we catch sight of it projecting in the sky, while as for the gardens we feel as we walk about them (as we may on many days) rather like children walking in a fairy tale.

All who know Leicestershire in bluebell time know Swithland Wood. All who love fine trees know the oak by the rectory at Burton Overy planted from an acorn of Boscobel, the oak in Donington Park 44 feet round and known as Chaucer's oak, and what is known as King Dick's Clump in Bosworth Park, a group of trees which is said to stand where Richard's banner waved in the last hour of the Plantagenet dynasty. Sutton Cheney has a small pyramid enclosing Richard's Well, from which tradition says the last Plantagenet took his last drink on the way to Bosworth Field. We may stand on one of Leicester's bridges and look along the road where King Richard went riding on his white horse to the Battle of Bosworth Field. That night he had 15,000 men to fight Henry Richmond, but his dark day was over; the day was done, the dog was dead. It is said that they carried his body head downwards into Leicester.

Leicester, growing more prosperous and more stately day by day, has, as we have seen, the memory of the last days of Richard and the last days of Wolsey, and it has the noble distinction of being the birthplace of the Idea of Parliament, for it has the name of Simon de Montfort, Earl of Leicester and founder of our Parliament, on its roll of fame. One of the first Parliaments met in its castle. It has one of the most superb of all our peace memorials, standing on a hill looking down on the town in memory of 12,000 men who fell in the war. The county's second town has also sent its name ringing through the world, ringing literally, for its bells have made Loughborough famous. The fame of Melton Mowbray is in its church and in its pies. Market Harborough attracts the traveller to its ancient grammar school, set on its wooden pillars soon after Shakespeare's day, and with a little marketplace beneath. Market Bosworth has the clump of trees marking the spot where Richard raised his standard, and it was at a school in this small town that Dr Johnson was master for a while. Ashby-de-la-Zouch has a castle renowned as the scene of the tournament in Ivanhoe and the scene of the imprisonment of Mary Queen of Scots. Rothley on the edge of Charnwood Forest has a Saxon cross and a Tudor house which was the home of the Trevelyans, and Rothley Temple is famous as the birthplace of Macaulay. He was a visitor here when he was born, for his mother was visiting the Trevelyans and he lived little here, but it is his shining name that brings Rothley into history. At Kibworth Harcourt was born Mrs Barbauld, whose lines are known to everyone:

> *Life! We've been long together,*
> *Through pleasant and through cloudy weather,*

and at Kegworth lived the Irish poet Tom Moore, who wrote some of his lovely melodies here. At Belton was born the famous Francis Beaumont who wrote over fifty plays in the days of Shakespeare and almost certainly shared some of the work with the master poet of the world. Lutterworth is immortal for all time for the church in which John Wycliffe preached; his monument in her streets describes him proudly as the Morning Star, though it was the evening of his life he spent in this small town on the River Swift. It is no mean claim for any county to have among its famous men so great a figure as Wycliffe, a founder of the tongue that Shakespeare spake and a champion of the faith that Milton held. At Thurcaston was born one of Wycliffe's successors, immortal Hugh Latimer, Bishop of Worcester; in this small place he made his first acquaintance with the world to which he was to say farewell in Oxford with those words on his lips which will never be forgotten:

Be of good comfort, Master Ridley; we shall this day light such a candle in England as I trust shall never be put out.

It is a noble roll of fame that Leicestershire has, and the county is not unworthy of it. Its story is twenty centuries old;

it has shared abundantly in the events that make up England's history; and it is a representative piece of England which is English to the core, with half a million people living in it of that plain honest type who do their work well day by day and never fail the country in its hour of need.

The Pure Soul of Everard Digbie

AB-KETTLEBY. High up on the windswept Wolds a medieval church stands in a field, with a few farmhouses and thatched cottages to keep it company, and in one of the gardens a vine on which may hang in one summer 250 bunches of grapes.

It is a lonely place, and in this solitude the traveller will find on the walls of the ancient church this pathetic epitaph to Everard Digbie:

When his pure soul from Holiwell did haste
Of light and life the eternal spring to taste
Within this stony casket was enclosed
The dust of Everard Digbie here deposed,
Whose name still fresh, like precious ointment finds,
A sweeter cabinet in good men's minds.
Whose goodness here in vain, ye readers, seek;
Tis writ in tears on many a neighbouring cheek,
And such sad drops do more adorn a herse
Than painted coats, or brass, or flattering verse.

Everard Digbie died in 1628 and must have sat on some of these old benches with traceried ends by 15th century carpenters. He may have been christened in this plain Norman font; he must often have looked up at the faces sculptured on the 700-year-old capitals of the south arcade.

The tower has a stone spire, and when we called the ivy was creeping over the chancel walls.

Content

ALLEXTON. The Eye Brook ripples past, bordering the county, and a narrow road winds up the hillside to the church, where limes stand as sentinels at each corner, and two grotesque lions, once adorning the Tudor porch, repose like pensioned guardians in the shadow of the 15th century tower.

Much of the church has been made new, but it still keeps its Norman arcade, one arch richly carved with zigzags and the other with diamonds. The capitals of the chancel arch are also Norman. In a window are a few fragments of 14th century glass, and near it is a monument to Richard Smith, 48 years rector in the 18th century, who used his store "Content with what he had, nor wished for more." Close by is the Elizabethan manor house which has been rebuilt this century, standing in grounds with magnificent firs.

Poor Ned Ludd

ANSTEY. It has a curious place in history, for it was put there by the village simpleton, poor Ned Ludd. His memory is almost all it has, yet it keeps something of its old-time charm in spite of industry creeping in. It has some old timbered cottages, a 14th century packhorse bridge with five arches astride the Rothley Brook, and the old tower keeping the new church company.

But we remember it because Ned Ludd, a half-witted apprentice, here broke up two stocking-frames, and all unwittingly gave his name to the movement of the Luddites, who set out to destroy the industry on which so much of Leicestershire depends.

The long war against Napoleon was a heavy drain on the resources of this country, and though it was the wealth produced by our commerce and industry that enabled us to win in the end, the final years proved very difficult. From 1792 to 1815 the National Debt rose from £240,000,000 to £860,000,000, and the masses had to bear a heavy share of the interest on this loan. Their bread and salt, their boots and clothes, were taxed. Prices of necessaries rose though wages went down, while in spite of the losses in the war the population increased by a quarter. The condition of the working classes was indeed unhappy.

Especially was this so in the Nottingham district, where machinery was rapidly taking the place of the workers by hand. The stocking-frame of Arkwright and Jedediah Strutt, and the lace-making machine of Joseph Heathcoat, had proved quite successful. These machines were regarded by the working classes as injurious to their livelihood. The frames worked so rapidly that in 1811 many Nottingham hosiers had to dismiss workmen because their market was overstocked. Then the Luddite Riots began, called so because Ned Ludd of Anstey smashed two stocking-frames at which he was working. The rioters worked at night and broke up the frames in the factories.

The lace-makers joined in and proved so destructive that Heathcoat left the district for Tiverton. Special constables and even soldiers failed to stay the organised destruction. The Luddites placarded the streets of Nottingham, offering a reward for the delivery of the mayor into their hands; they bribed the militia, seized their arms, and killed a manufacturer. In the end seven regiments had to be drafted into the district to preserve order, and Parliament passed an

Act imposing the death penalty on any who destroyed machinery used in manufactures.

By this time the movement had spread and affected the woollen and cotton industries, mills being burned down and militia depots stormed, and only a fall in prices led to a cessation of these riots.

The House in the Moat

APPLEBY MAGNA. Among its fields and orchards is a timbered manor house built five centuries ago, its moat still wet and its gatehouse well preserved. Over a kitchen mantelpiece it has quaint figures roughly carved on stone, among them an armed man, a woman leaning on a stick, and Michael with the dragon.

In the fine 14th century church is a marble tomb with an armoured knight and a lady with two dogs at her feet, believed to be Sir Edmund Appleby and his wife, lord and lady of the manor when the church was built. There are a few fragments of original glass showing a monk in a cloak, a woman in a close-fitting hat, two angels, and the head of the Madonna.

Dr Johnson Calls at Christopher Wren's School

APPLEBY PARVA. It is only a hamlet of Appleby Magna, but through its grammar school it has achieved a measure of fame denied to its elder brother.

This fine three-storeyed house of red brick was built by Sir Christopher Wren in 1697, and is believed to be the only school he designed. But it has yet another claim to immortality, for Dr Johnson applied for the mastership here and would have been elected could he have obtained his degree of Master of Arts. Johnson at that time was trying to emancipate himself from literary drudgery and the mastership at Appleby, with its £60 a year, seemed riches to him. His friend Pope did his best to help him, and another friend wrote to Dean Swift begging him to persuade Dublin University to confer upon him the necessary degree. He said that Dr Johnson was not afraid of the strictest examination, though he was afraid of the long journey to Ireland; but he would venture if necessary, choosing to die upon the road rather than be starved to death in translating for the booksellers. Luckily the degree was not forthcoming, and the Great Cham of Literature was saved from a life of comfortable obscurity.

In the school is a statue of the founder, Sir John Moore, a Leicestershire man who went to London and became Lord Mayor after making a fortune in the East India trade. Charles the Second knighted him, went with the queen to see his Lord Mayor's Show, dined with him at the Guildhall, and (we can scarcely doubt) borrowed money of him. His hall still stands close to his school, a stone house partly in ruins, but still with tenants of lower degree than the prosperous Sir John.

A Hero of Nonconformity

ARNESBY. It has a church, a chapel, and a windmill, all attracting the traveller's eye. The church goes back to Norman days, the arches in the nave having stood 800 years. For seven centuries the village children have been christened at the font, and for generations St Peter has been looking down from the chapel gable, blessing all who pass this way.

The little red chapel, made new when the 18th century was ending, is memorable among Nonconformists as the successor of the chapel in which Robert Hall first raised the voice which was to stir all Leicestershire and afterwards all England. His father was minister here and here his son preached his first sermon.

He was the youngest of the minister's 14 children, a poor weak boy in childhood and a martyr to physical suffering for 66 years. But he was brilliant, learning his alphabet from gravestones, writing hymns when he was eight, and preaching when he was eleven. From his earliest years he was dedicated to the ministry and at 14 became a member of the Baptist church. After three years at a Baptist academy the village congregation, seeing his rare promise, sent him to Aberdeen University.

At 19 he was invited to become assistant minister at Broadmead Chapel, Bristol, and his success as a preacher was phenomenal. All classes crowded to hear him and were spellbound; often they would be standing when the sermon ended, so absorbing was his eloquence. He repeated his successes at Cambridge, at Leicester, and again at Bristol, his ministry at Leicester continuing nearly 20 years. William Pitt compared him with Demosthenes.

His struggle with pain was a lifelong tragedy. The doctors of that time were unable to give relief, and his chief alleviations were opium, tobacco, and tea, in the drinking of which he surpassed even Dr Johnson, taking 30 cups a day.

Asfordby
The Wreak flowing by the Church

Ashby-de-la-Zouch
Memorial to Countess Loudoun

Anstey   The 14th Century Packhorse Bridge

Ashby-de-la-Zouch   The Ruined Castle

Ashby-de-la-Zouch   The Medieval Church

A great and good man, an honest thinker, a fine scholar, broad-minded when broad minds were few, Robert Hall would have been far more than the most brilliant orator of his age if he had had the blessing of health. Nonconformity counts him one of its heroes.

The Ancient Cross

ASFORDBY. Nature and Art have both been kind to this village on the Wreak. It has a delightful old bridge with three arches astride the river, an old stepped-cross, and a 14th century church which, seen across the river reflecting its venerable stones, is a charming picture of rural serenity.

It has some Norman masonry, and on an outside wall a curious figure with a cross believed to represent a Saxon bishop. The pinnacled tower has a band of quatrefoils below its battlements and is crowned with a slender spire. The south doorway is enriched with ballflower and the nave roof is held up by 12 wooden minstrels.

Among the numerous corbels dotted about the building many will notice the supercilious lady of the tower. The fine chancel screen, with its 15th century tracery and canopy, has been made new and its carvings of Calvary are the peace memorial. The transept window has figures of St John, the Good Shepherd, and Moses, as a memorial to John Cartmell, who ministered here for 40 years.

The Town of the Ruined Castle

ASHBY-DE-LA-ZOUCH. Plain Leicestershire folk call it plain Ashby, but when the first lord of the manor (Alain de Parrhoet la Souche) gave to it his high-sounding Norman name, he set it on the path to fame. History touched it with its magic in the days of Richard the Third, when William Lord Hastings built his castle here, and the castle and the manor lived in the bright glow of noble names for centuries after Hastings had gone to the headsman's block. Romance gathered about it like the ivy on the castle walls.

Today, as we walk up the busy market street between the comfortable houses, old and new, we can almost hear the clatter of the horses of medieval knights on the cobbles, we can almost see the sun glancing on the harness and the halberds of the men-at-arms. We can picture Lord Hastings with his ample train on his way to the proud castle which commanded the town at its foot. We can picture his son Edward riding from the castle to avenge his father on the famous Bosworth Field.

We shall need the imaginative genius of Sir Walter Scott to see the knights and their ladies riding to the joyous tournament of Ashby-de-la-Zouch, where the Black Knight who was Richard Lionheart tourneyed with Ivanhoe, where Isaac and Rebecca watched the conflict with such varying emotions, and where King John failed to quell the bold archer. Sir Walter invented it all, though at the neighbouring hamlet of Smisby there is in fact a field where tournaments were held.

But at the castle itself, though it is no more now than a splendid ruin, history takes us by the hand. Its great tower, like a Norman keep with four storeys, is standing. In a niche over its doorway two kneeling figures still support the Hastings arms. The Great Hall still opens its 17th century windows to the skies. The spacious quadrangle, once peopled by knight and squire and page and ladies walking in silk attire, is empty, but the kitchen tower, with the vaulted 14th century kitchen and the buttery, are intact. By one of Time's little ironies they are the least ruined. The buttery has its great mullioned window. The kitchen, one of the biggest known, is 52 feet long, 28 wide, and 34 high. What barons of beef, what haunches of venison, what flocks of capon, came from its two mighty firesides! From the kitchen tower to the keep is an underground passage, but we must assign to it no use more mysterious than that of forwarding the joints.

Two Tudor doorways, replacing earlier ones, lead us to the Great Hall, where hundreds of retainers could fall to when the viands were brought in from the kitchen. The hearth was once set in the middle, and the smoke escaped through a hole in the roof. In more dainty Jacobean days a chimney was built by the wall. It is there now.

From the hall another turning leads to the chapel, and this, though ruinous, has still four medieval windows. There are two smaller openings through which, glancing upward, we can see the Solar, the sunny room with the Tudor window through which the sun shone for a little while on Mary Queen of Scots. She was being taken from Tutbury to Coventry in 1569. Did she, looking on these castle walls, now so ruined but then so formidable, realise that she was a captive whom only death would set free?

George Hastings, first Earl of Huntingdon (grandson of Shakespeare's Lord Hastings), took part in the trials of Anne Boleyn and Sir Thomas More. Francis, who followed him, was in high favour with Edward the Sixth. Henry, his successor, who was for the brief period of Mary's sojourn here her keeper, was a power in Elizabeth's day; no sympathy would come from him for his Queen's enemy. George and Francis are made more real to us than some of the others of their name, for in the church we see them in their habit as they lived.

Other figures vivid or obscure, wise or foolish, rash or cautious, pass by us in these empty halls. To Elizabeth (who never was here) succeeded James the First, who cherished few sentimental memories about his ill-fated mother. He came to Ashby with all his Court to be entertained for many days in royal style. When dinner was served in the banqueting hall thirty poor knights in gold chains and velvet gowns attended as servitors, and the expense of the prolonged entertainment made the earl almost as poor as his impoverished knights. One of his descendants wrote:

> *The bells did ring,*
> *The gracious king*
> *Enjoyed his visit much ;*
> *And we've been poor*
> *Ere since that hour*
> *At Ashby-de-la-Zouch.*

We can hardly help wondering whether James, in the midst of all this extravagance and junketing, ever looked out from the mullioned window at which his mother stood at the beginning of her long captivity.

His own son Charles, with his queen Henrietta Maria, was entertained here in 1634, when the quarrel between King and Commonwealth had just received fresh fuel by the imposition of Ship Money but had not yet burst into flame. Charles came again, eleven years later, as a kingly guest whose kingdom was falling from him. He tarried for a few days on his way to Naseby, he stayed again for a night when the battle had been lost and won, following (all unknowing) in the footsteps of Mary the captive of the sunny room.

At that time Henry Hastings, brother of the earl, was holding the castle for the king. He was a stout fighter in the Civil War. From the castle he conducted a guerilla warfare against the Parliament, and when all hope of help from Charles was at an end, and Ashby Castle had to be surrendered, Hastings and his men were allowed to march out without molestation. Part of the outworks of the town and the castle were then demolished, and three years later it was mined and reduced to harmless ruins.

Such is the story of this castle whose battered walls are eloquent still. Standing by them we can make out the plan of the castle in its great days. West of the tower was the sunny room with the mullioned window looking south. Farther west was the banqueting hall and the kitchens. At the north-east corner among the trees the 19th century manor house is where Ashby House once stood.

In the later house lived Lady Edith Hastings, Countess of Loudoun, who when she died in 1879 was so gratefully remembered by the people of Ashby that they set up the memorial cross 70 feet high where three roads meet. Sir Gilbert Scott designed the cross and Disraeli wrote the inscription to his old friend, of whom he said that "sprung from an illustrious ancestry, she herself possessed their noblest qualities."

From castle and cross we may turn to the church, where the story of Ashby and its historic walls finds other echoes. Most of it is 500 years old, coming from the time of the Hastings who raised the castle, but time has changed it greatly and its antiquity is chiefly in its memorials. The pillars of the nave arcades, with panelled battlements instead of capitals, are an unusual architectural feature.

One very rare survival the traveller finds here, a thing unique as far as we remember. It is called the "finger pillory" and was used, according to tradition, to subdue those who were unruly in church. It has two posts about a yard high, supporting a beam with 13 grooves to take fingers of varying sizes. Over this, and hinged to it at the end, is another beam with corresponding grooves underneath, and when the two were locked together they formed an effective and somewhat drastic punishment. It is one of the strangest relics of the past that we have found in any church.

The oak reredos, with vines trailing down the sides and a cherub's head aloft, was carved in the 17th century and has been ascribed to Grinling Gibbons. There is an old ironbound chest and a screen of delicate ironwork decorated with crowns and the Tudor rose, separating the old south aisle from the Hastings Chapel. Here stands the tomb of the Second Earl of Huntingdon and his wife, the finest monument in the church. It shows the favoured statesman of Edward the Sixth resting in armour, coronet, and Garter insignia, with his feet on a curious lion, and his countess in robe and long girdled garment, by his side. On the sides of the tomb are their six sons and five daughters.

In this chapel is the sculptured head of another of the family who sleeps here, the famous Countess of Huntingdon who brought the Puritan spirit nearer to our own time. She was the friend of Wesley and patron of Whitefield, and was a leader among their followers. She died in 1791 and was brought here from London to be with her people. Rysbrack's sculpture of her is full of feeling and sympathy.

These are the most historic monuments but there are others commanding attention. Under an arch in the north aisle is a 15th century figure of a pilgrim in a long cloak, with his bare head resting on two tasselled cushions and a dog at his feet. On his right is the broad-brimmed pilgrim's hat, bedecked with the scallop shell to show that he had journeyed overseas, and the pilgrim's wallet; other scallop shells hang from his belt and his pilgrim's staff is by his side. Over the south door is a delightful wooden bust of Margery Wright, who died in 1623, and "who, being born in this towne, did (out of her charitable and pious disposition) give in her lifetime £43 to provide gowns yearly for ever to certain aged and poor people." She wears a tall Welsh hat and a broad ruff round her neck, and carries a red muff to warm her hands.

By the tower wall stands a stone with the engraved figures of Robert Mundy and his two wives, all in Tudor dress. He is extraordinarily tall, with a long loose-sleeved gown over a close-fitting doublet, and his wives, to whom the engraver has tried hard to give a touch of individuality, wear triangular hats, tight-waisted gowns, and gauntlets. In the south aisle is a wall monument declaring the many virtues of Rector Arthur Hildersham, a Puritan whom Queen Elizabeth deigned to speak of as Cousin Hildersham, and on another wall monument we found the name of Thomas Kirkland, the doctor who was called in to attend the steward Johnson after he had been shot by his master, Earl Ferrers, and who, in spite of many threats, aided the arrest and conviction of the murderer. Kirkland, who died in 1798, was one of a famous line of Ashby doctors. Not least among these notable memorials is the tomb, decorated with musical angels, of Edward Mammatt, organist here for 40 years. He lost his sight as a boy of six, yet not only became a musician and composer but educated himself to lecture on scientific subjects, and it is remembered of him that he wrote and printed and bound a book with his own hands.

In the east window is some old heraldic glass from the castle chapel, but more notable are the 11 modern windows of the Life of Christ, beautiful in colouring and admirable for their delicate draughtsmanship. There are many carved heads on the pillars of the new aisles, among them Martin Luther, the wife of Pontius Pilate, the Roman centurion, Mary Magdalene, Constantine, David, Solomon, and the Queen of Sheba. Outside are eight more heads, ranging from Elijah and Moses to Queen Victoria and Archbishop Tait.

In the churchyard, where many tombstones of the famous Swithland slate lie flat on the ground, sleep several French prisoners captured in Napoleon's wars.

A curious story is told here of the memorial to the men who did not come back from the war. On it is the name of Horace Smith among the fallen, and much interest was aroused by the arrival of a letter from India in which Horace Smith made enquiries as to what had happened to his kinsmen since the war, and later by the arrival of the hero himself, only survivor of five soldier brothers.

Lord of the Castle and Gaoler of a Queen

IT would have appealed to the ironic spirit of Mary Stuart could she have foreseen that the third Earl of Huntingdon, lord of Ashby Castle and one of her gaolers, was to be succeeded by a man who was to risk life and liberty and all his estates in defence of her grandson.

The Hastings family was of royal descent, and Mary thought it a special indignity that she should be committed to the custody of a man who was her rival for the succession to the throne of Elizabeth. But all such contentions and pretensions were forgotten in the Civil War, when Henry Hastings, younger son of the fifth Earl, held the castle for Charles against all the forces of Parliament.

Not only did he do so, but he was as a latterday Hereward in sallying forth to harass the opposition in the open; convoying munitions to Oxford, taking part in battles and successful sieges of Cromwellian cities; commanding the road to the North, and repeatedly despoiling the trains of carriers conveying supplies and riches along the main highway.

For three years he kept the royalist banner flying over the castle here; then, with the ruin of the King's cause, he capitulated, and the castle was destroyed. Hastings was given honourable freedom, which he employed in the second Civil War to prove himself once more one of the most resolute and audacious of the Cavaliers.

Although named in Parliament as one of the seven greatest delinquents in the realm, and marked down for banishment, he was saved from this fate and lived to see the Restoration, when he was rewarded with the Earldom of Loughborough and a generous pension for life. He died unmarried, and was buried in St George's Chapel, Windsor.

The Famous Countess of Huntingdon

IT was a Countess of Huntingdon (Selina) who was the foremost woman in the religious revival of the 18th century.

An heiress, married at 21 to the ninth Earl of Huntingdon, she was converted to Methodism soon after her wedding, to the great scandal of her friends. An indignant appeal being made to her husband, he induced a friendly bishop to have one talk on the subject with his wife, and then, content, he paid her the compliment of leaving her all his wealth at her entire discretion.

A fond and indulgent mother, she kept her expenditure within the narrowest bounds compatible with the health and happiness of her children, and devoted her fortune to the spread of religious teaching.

Caught up in the controversy between George Whitefield and the Wesleys, she espoused the cause of Whitefield and soon began to build her own chapels and appoint her own chaplains. She founded a college for the instruction of her ministers, and organised open-air preaching on the widest scale.

On his return from missionary work in America Whitefield became one of her chaplains, and her work extended from place to place in the provinces until the Countess of Huntingdon's Sect assumed significant proportions. All this time she had kept nominally within the established Church, but in the end she had to register her chapels as dissenting meeting-houses under the Act of Toleration.

Many of her ministers left her at this juncture, but her work grew and grew, and an association was formed to carry on the labours of her lifetime after her death. Prior to this she had directed and controlled the whole movement with signal skill and success.

To the end, unpopular as her religious ideas were with her aristocratic associates, she retained a unique circle of illustrious friendships, which included not only bishops, philanthropists, the leading

Nonconformists, and men of commerce, but minds completely at variance in spiritual matters with her own, such as Chesterfield and Bolingbroke.

She died in 1791 and was buried here, where she had for many years made her country home after leaving Donington. Her work survives, two centuries after she began it.

Standard Bearers

ASHBY FOLVILLE. Its old church has been restored with great understanding, making it a neat casket for many remarkable treasures. It has a lofty tower 500 years old.

Here are several Norman coffin lids, a Norman font, the base of a 15th century screen, and figures of a medieval knight and Stuart Cavaliers. Above them all soars the fine 15th century nave roof with angels playing musical instruments and stone faces smiling from the corbels. The 14th century knight Sir Eustace Folville sleeps in chain mail, his feet on a lion. On his breast is a piece of iron said to represent the point of the lance with which he was killed by a neighbour.

Long before that fatal quarrel Sir Michael Carington was standard bearer to Richard Lionheart, and fell fighting in Holy Land. From him and his great family of crusading warriors descend the Smiths, whose grand 17th century monuments are still here to pay them tribute. George Smith, lying in armour with gauntlets at his feet, has his placid wife at his side, and in niches on the altar tomb below are coloured figures of their four sons in doublets and seven daughters in tight-waisted dresses, one of them weeping. The eldest son, Sir Francis Smith, lies with his wife Anne on another coloured tomb, arrayed in his gilt armour, his head on a plumed helmet. Francis, who died in 1629, was no soldier, but his son John, who sleeps at Oxford, fought at Edgehill and was there knighted for recapturing the royal standard. A wall monument to Ralph Woodford of the 15th century has a shield-bearing angel on each side and another shield supported by quaint human figures.

Unhappy William

ASHBY PARVA. About this place so pretty and so peaceful lingers the shadow of the story of William Paul, who was born here when Charles the Second was king and grew up to link his fortunes with the Old Pretender.

Paul became a clergyman, with every flattering prospect of advancement till he was drawn into the net of Jacobite intrigue. When the standard of the Jacobite rebellion was raised he hastened with others from Lutterworth to join the lost cause. He was taken, brought to trial, and sentenced to death for treason, though he abjured the cause in the hope of saving his life. When that hope failed he recovered his courage and died a Jacobite.

The little 15th century church where the unhappy William sang his first hymns has a modern tower with two fearsome beasts looking out from a lofty perch. The chancel is also modern, but in the wall can still be seen the stairway which led to the old roodloft. The oldest possession of the church is the Norman font, with cable moulding below the bowl at which Paul was christened in 1678.

The Small Figure at Prayer

ASTON FLAMVILLE. It has a group of cottages and houses gathered about a shady churchyard, with a neat bed of roses opposite the porch. The small church, rebuilt last century, still has a small Norman window in its nave, and on a 16th century altar tomb are engraved figures of Sir William Turvil and his wife with their five children. A little alabaster figure in Cromwellian armour kneels in prayer under the chancel arch.

The modern font has the Evangelists on its corners and small panels showing Moses striking the rock and Elijah in the chariot.

What the Old Bridge Has Seen

AYLESTONE. One might linger here for an afternoon, leaning over the parapet of the medieval bridge, looking into the clear waters of the Soar, and seeing in fancy the long procession of those who have crossed it. Charles Stuart was among them after his flight from Naseby; he stopped at the Tudor manor house here while Leicester was besieged. Dorothy Vernon of Haddon Hall was married in the church, and may have crossed the bridge on the arm of her young lover John Manners. William Cobbett came this way, and gathered little comfort from the sight of Leicester's lofty spires two miles off, or from the pleasant meads through which the river flows, for his reforming eyes were fixed on the miserable hovels of the villagers.

That is changed now, and even Cobbett would be pleased, for Leicester has brought its new houses nearer, the old ones are well cared-for, and the churchyard, bordered on one side by 11 yews standing like aged mourners, is neat and trim.

The church has an unusual spire and an impressive 14th century chancel bigger than the nave, said to be the biggest in any village church. Over the modern porch is a fine figure of St Andrew, young guardian of ancient treasure, and in the nave are several roughly carved grotesques. The south aisle has two medieval stone screens, and one of its windows has a fragment of old glass showing a man standing by his house. It was brought from a church in Rouen, burned down when all France was caught in the red flames of Revolution.

There is a 17th century poor-box, some choir stalls with old fronts, and a splendid brass of William Heathcot, a 16th century rector who is said to have married Dorothy Vernon to John Manners. He is shown as they would have seen him in his gown, with pouchy sleeves and Bible in hand. One of his 17th century successors who also sleeps here was Nathaniel Tovey, one of Milton's teachers at Cambridge. Christopher Milton told John Aubrey that his brother was whipped by Mr Chappell, his first tutor, and afterwards came under the wing of this Mr Tovey.

In the field by the church is a long sandy hillock fenced and topped by a few trees; it marks the defence lines of an early British tribe and the British earthworks used by the Romans.

It is the records of this church which shatter one of the legends of Derbyshire, for here Dorothy Vernon was quietly and ordinarily married; she did not elope from Haddon Hall.

The Truth About Dorothy Vernon

ROMANCE has decided that Dorothy Vernon of Haddon Hall was the victim of a stern father's tyrannous insistence upon his right to dispose of her hand as he chose. The father, Sir George Vernon, a man of boundless wealth and of hospitable habits to match, was known from his lavish magnificence as the King of the Peak. He and his two daughters, of whom one was winsome Dorothy, are authentic figures of the 16th century; but, deplorable as it is to shatter a romantic illusion, Dorothy's elopement is an idle fable.

The story has many variants in novel, opera, and play, but essentially it is agreed that the masterful Sir George had made up his mind that Dorothy and her sister should each marry a Stanley, Margaret Sir Thomas Stanley, and Dorothy his younger brother Edward. Dorothy loved John Manners, a younger son of the Duke of Rutland, but the father furiously forbade the match and insisted on the carrying-out of his own scheme.

Dorothy, so the romance runs, was equally minded not to obey, and was sustained in her resolve by bold John Manners, who, in the guise of a forester, used secretly to visit Haddon Hall by night and breathe his vows beneath the window of her chamber. Finally, when the ball was in progress which was to celebrate her sister's wedding, Dorothy, we are told, stole from her father's hall, crept down the stone staircase which is still precious as being that by which she escaped, and fled with her lover.

There is not a word of support for the legend. So far as the family records tell, the lovely Dorothy married her lover in quite the ordinary way, except that, instead of choosing Bakewell for her wedding, she was married at Aylestone. She suffered no penalty from her father through her marriage, but inherited Haddon Hall from him in due course, and through this marriage the estate passed to the ducal house of Rutland, in whose possession it has ever since remained.

Trackways Before the Romans Came

BARDON HILL. It soars 900 feet, the highest point in the county, with glorious views over Charnwood Forest and the hills of Derbyshire and Shropshire. It is scarred by huge granite quarries, but trees still resolutely climb its slopes, descendants of the dense primeval forest where, as legend tells, a man could walk from Beaumanor to Bardon without seeing the sun.

The hill was the haunt of the early British people who knew the trackways through the forest long before Romans or Saxons came to disturb the glades. There was a stronghold here in the Bronze Age, and a bronze spearhead used by a Saxon has been found.

Charles Stuart's Soldier and His Books

BARKBY. It is set on a wooded hill with a stream flowing by the houses in its High Street, and in its church and on its hill comes the thought of Father Time. We see him in the church holding his scythe, on a fine 18th century monument to William Pochin, and on Round Hill is a tumulus in which have been found a Roman urn and many Saxon relics.

It may have been this ancient grave which set young Thomas Marshall thinking. He was born here in time to leave Oxford to be a soldier in Charles Stuart's garrison. He became a preacher to the

Merchant Adventurers in Holland, and came home to be Dean of Gloucester after the Restoration; but he is chiefly remembered as one of the first students of Saxon life and Saxon ways. He left Saxon grammars and dictionaries behind, and we may see them in the library of his old university with many of his manuscripts in Arabic and Coptic.

The 700-year-old church has a grand spire, but is chiefly notable for its windows, one above the chancel arch and eight in the aisles showing seven designs of tracery. In one are fragments of old glass.

The Lowing Herd Winds Slowly O'er the Lea

BARKESTON. Past its cottages every evening the lowing herd winds slowly o'er the lea, for it is a dairy-farming village in the rich vale of Belvoir.

The church, with its slender spire peeping above a lofty screen of sycamores, was made new 400 years ago and restored last century, but has kept a Norman doorway with zigzag ornament, an ancient tub front, a stone figure of a 14th century lord of the manor in a handsome tunic, and fine old woodwork.

It has one of Leicestershire's best 15th century screens, its doors forming a second screen in the tower arch. There is a fine Jacobean chair and a beam perhaps 300 years old, enriched with foliage and fruit such as Grinling Gibbons might have carved. Even more attractive are four 15th century stall-ends now fashioned into a reading desk and a sedilia, one pair with two kneeling monks, and the others with figures of Jesus with the lamb, and St James as a pilgrim.

In the churchyard are several yews (one near the porch with a girth of 12 feet) that have grown old watching generations of village folk go to and fro.

Outpost of the Stone Age Men

BARROW-ON-SOAR. From this busy town above the Soar there are enchanting views of the river and of Buddon Wood, and the granite hill of Mountsorrel on the other side.

Many have looked on that view because of the strength of the position, with the river as the first line of defence. This was an outpost of the men who fought with stone axes and of the Romans who bound their Empire with the bands of iron spear and shield. Both have left their traces. After the last legionary had gone the stronghold slumbered awhile, awaking again only in the dim Dark

Ages when it became part of the manor which held a third of Charnwood Forest in fee, with King Harold as its first lord.

The church was built in the 14th century, but its tower and chancel
are modern. There is an old wall monument to Martha Utber, a tiny
lady kneeling at a desk with a shield as witness to her gentility. A
Jacobean chest has a medieval one to keep it company.

The finely carved stalls with linenfold, the rich sedilia, and the
stone reredos with the Last Supper and eight saints, are all modern.
The beautiful transept panelling, adorned with flowers and fruit and
figures of St Mary and St John by the cross, with angels holding
candlesticks, is the peace memorial, the work of a local craftsman.

The east window of the Four Evangelists and Our Lord in
Majesty is a memorial to three of Barrow's benefactors. The first
was William Beveridge, who became Bishop of St Asaph, and, dying
in his lodgings in Westminster, was buried in St Pauls; the others
were Theophilus Cave and Humphrey Babington who founded the
almshouses, a charming picture in 17th century brick and stone.

The Faithful Toby Rustat

A BARROW man unremembered in the church was Tobias
Rustat, born at the vicarage in 1606, three years after the first Stuart
had reached the throne. He was to spend his 87 years serving them
and helping by gifts of statues to perpetuate their memory.

His father seems to have taught him nothing except his prayers,
and to have apprenticed him as a mere child to a London barber.
It was an unhappy lot for a country lad, and he soon entered the
service of Viscount Feilding, with whom he went on embassy to
Venice. In this pleasure city he remained "a sober person and
religious," as a surprised companion has recorded. Next he joined
the household of young George Villiers, second Duke of Buckingham, and attracted the notice of Charles Stuart. The king appointed
him a servant of his son Charles (then 14), and Tobias waited on the
young prince all through the Civil War.

Tobias loved the King unswervingly; Charles could do no wrong
in his eyes. After the king's capture the devoted servant went with
the queen and the prince into exile and risked his life carrying
messages. He took part in the disastrous rising of the Royalists in
Kent in 1648, saved Buckingham's life, and escaped with him over
the water again, there to spend the long years of exile until 1660.

At the Restoration Rustat was sworn into office as Yeoman of the Robes with a salary of £40 a year. He received another £40 as pension and was also made a Page of the Backstairs. John Evelyn described him at this time as very simple and ignorant, but honest and loyal. He was so thrifty that he saved money and made a small fortune. He never married and spent his riches on the poor and fatherless, remembering his own childhood and founding scholarships for the orphans of clergymen and pensions for their widows. The chief of his benefactions were given to Jesus College, Cambridge. In 1674 Cambridge gave him an honorary degree which must have delighted one who, uneducated himself, had helped so greatly to educate others.

His devotion to his royal master never flagged. In 1680 he gave Charles the Second the copper statue of himself on horseback by Strada, with the pedestal by Grinling Gibbons, on which it still stands at Windsor. The bronze statue of Charles at Chelsea is also his gift. The gallant Rustat honoured James the Second in the same way, erecting the fine statue of that king by Grinling Gibbons which stands in St James's Park by the Admiralty. He retired to Chelsea Hospital to spend his last years, and lived to be much grieved by the overthrow of the Stuarts. When he died (in 1693) they took him, with the inscribed monument he had prepared for himself, to Jesus College Chapel for burial, and there the University still holds him in remembrance, the faithful friend of two unfaithful kings. He was a good man in a bad Court, and he has left a very pleasant memory.

John Torksey Preaching

BARWELL. The Industrial Age has brought great changes here, and the church alone has preserved its ancient aspect. Standing on a hill in a churchyard with venerable yews, it is notable as a complete church of the 14th century, with lovely windows and a chancel beautiful with modern stalls, altar, sanctuary rails, and reredos, all carved with fruit and foliage by men of the village.

There are two splendid 17th century brasses, one showing Richard Breton with his wife and their seven children at prayer, the other John Torksey preaching from a pulpit to his wife and six children, five daughters kneeling in a line behind their mother and a sixth in swaddling clothes, blissfully unaware of the father's homily.

The Tub and the Well

BEEBY. It gave England a famous judge, the unbending Robert Catlin who refused to alter the ancient forms of the Court to please Queen Elizabeth when her favourite Dudley was on trial.

In the 13th century the church belonged to the rich Croyland Abbey, and it still keeps its elaborate font of those days. It has also a few fragments of ancient glass, and a 14th century screen enriched with new gates and old oak from the roof of a neighbouring church.

The churchyard has a fine border of yews, and near by is an ancient well with a stone cover set up by a 19th century vicar, and inscribed:

> *In summer's heat and winter's cold*
> *One constant temperature I hold :*
> *When brooks and wells and rivers dry*
> *I always yield a full supply :*
> *My neighbours say (I'm often told),*
> *I'm more than worth my weight in gold.*

The old church spire is so short that it has been called Beeby Tub.

The Ruins of Grace Dieu

BELTON. Not far from Belton's broad main street, with its tall maypole and its aged elm, are the ruins of Grace Dieu Priory. They are but fragments (even as Charnwood Forest is now but a fragment), and they lie rather lonely in a field beside a little brook. The priory was founded 700 years ago by Lady Roesia de Verdun, who sleeps in Belton's church.

Three hundred years later the ruthless agents of Henry the Eighth reported that it should share the Suppression of the Monasteries, and it was afterwards conveyed to one of the Commissioners, John Beaumont of Thringstone. The Beaumonts built their own Grace Dieu, a magnificent Tudor house, and here in 1582 was born Sir John Beaumont, poet and friend of Shakespeare. Two years later his brother Francis was born here, the Francis Beaumont who collaborated with Fletcher and so inscribed his name as one of an immortal band.

The glory of Grace Dieu has long departed, and all that remains are the fragments of two towers, the chapel, and the walls; Wordsworth gazed upon the ruins and endowed them with his magic:

Beneath yon eastern ridge, the craggy bound,
Rugged and high, of Charnwood's forest ground,
Stand yet, but, stranger, hidden from thy view,
The ivied ruins of forlorn Grace Dieu.

The modern manor house, a handsome place, with no such historic associations, was once the home of Charles Booth, eminent in our own times for his monumental volumes on the Life and Labour of the People in London.

Time has been kinder to Belton's church, and those years that dealt so harshly with Grace Dieu left it intact, so that it stands to this day, a finely proportioned 14th century building with a lofty spire and angels watching over its nave. It still has the 13th century font and the 15th century screen, and in its windows are a few fragments of ancient heraldic glass. The finest monument is that of Lady Roesia, restored a few years ago, and showing her in mantled gown, veil, and wimple, with mourning figures at her head and feet and two angels bearing her soul to its reward. Lady Roesia died in 1248, and nearly three centuries later, when her priory was doomed, a new resting-place for her remains was found within this church.

Here towards the end of the 16th century the two Beaumont poets stood by their father's grave, friends of Shakespeare in a sad hour.

Two Friends of Shakespeare

WHEN Francis Beaumont, judge of the common pleas, died in 1598 at Grace Dieu he had three young sons at Oxford. The Beaumont family, of Norman origin, had been conspicuous in Leicestershire for more than 400 years. The boys, Henry, John, and Francis, came home, and all were entered as students at Inner Temple. Henry succeeded his father, but died when he was 24; John, who succeeded Henry, was 23 and Francis 21, and the ambition of these two was to be poets.

Three years before their brother died they had each published a volume of verse. John's book was a mock-heroic poem on Tobacco, and Frank had contributed a poem to it. Frank's book had a classical theme, and John prefaced it with some brotherly lines. They had also ardently sought the society of the poets who were then following in the wake of Shakespeare, the idol of young Frank, and soon they knew Ben Jonson, Michael Drayton, young John Fletcher (the bishop's son) and were free to join the circle drinking and coruscating at the Mermaid Tavern.

Hallaton 13th Century Spire

Brentingby 13th Century Tower

Breedon-on-the-Hill
Old Village Lock-up

Cold Overton
The Medieval Church

Castle Donington   King's Mills by the Trent

Castle Donington   The Old Key House

They were welcomed there with open arms. Michael Drayton began to call them his dear companions and his bosom friends. When Francis Beaumont was only 22 Ben Jonson prefixed the young man's verses to his newly-published plays and Beaumont wrote to him the rhymed letter which ecstatically exclaims "What things have we seen done at the Mermaid !" It is plain that the seasoned poets gladly received the new beginners with the Norman name from the Charnwood mansion.

And that good feeling continued. Almost every reference made by contemporaries to the Beaumonts is complimentary, yet, strangely, there are no sure tests by which they can be confidently judged. It does not matter much about John. He began to write ambitiously. He looked hopefully to posterity. He felt that "No earthly gift lasts after death but fame." But later he slacked off, became a baronet, and was a most exemplary country gentleman. His poems took a strongly religious turn. They were smooth but not inspiring. The book on which he spent most time, The Crown of Thorns, is lost. His other considerable work, Bosworth Field, describing the battle, is tame. Sir John died at 44, when his younger brother Francis had been dead eleven years. Both of them lie in Westminster Abbey. It is Francis, who gave himself up entirely to poetry and the stage, who started the name of Beaumont on a new road to fame.

After some writing of little importance Francis Beaumont joined John Fletcher in a united authorship of plays, and they lived together as bachelors, apparently till about two years before Beaumont's death in 1616, when he was 32. Few of their plays were printed in their lifetime, or probably with their authority. After Fletcher's death, however, 52 plays were published as being by Beaumont and Fletcher. It cannot be said with certainty that any one of these plays was by Beaumont alone, or by Beaumont and Fletcher alone, for many of them were revised and largely re-written by other play-wrights, and other writers collaborated with Beaumont and Fletcher, when all worked jointly. There are not, therefore, any separate works that can be so confidently said to be by Beaumont that they make a basis for sure literary judgment. His writing is buried in a mixed mass. Specialist critics claim to unravel the twisted threads of half a dozen literary craftsmen, but the critics contradict each other. The Beaumont and Fletcher plays never reached the height of great drama. They came in a too shallow age. But they retain interest as significant illustrations of that age, and the two close friends may be left to share such fame as the plays confer.

The House of Great Splendour

BELVOIR CASTLE. High on an isolated spur of the Lincolnshire Wolds, its stately terraces, its battlemented walls and towers, command a prospect so wide that it seems to comprise the plain of England. Those who have lived on this height have seen 900 years of England's history pass by.

Below the terraces of this house of splendour, home of the Dukes of Rutland, beyond the timbered woodland girdling the castle, is the Vale of Belvoir, a level country picked out with villages, spires, and distant towns. Here are the 22 manors of the duke, and shadowy against the skyline are Nottingham Castle and Lincoln Cathedral.

This stately castle, with its round tower, battlemented gatehouse, and pinnacled chapel, has had a chequered story since Robert de Todeni, who bore the Conqueror's standard at Hastings, raised its first tower. In the Wars of the Roses it was shattered; in the Civil War it withstood a siege before Cromwell " razed it to the ground." With the restoration of the monarchy came the restoration of the castle, to the same plans and on the same foundations, but over the present small drawing-room, dining-room, and all the rooms on their floor, a whole bedroom-floor was built, so that Belvoir lost the aspect of a castle and looked like a house. When Elizabeth, wife of the fifth duke, came to it on her honeymoon at the end of the 18th century, fresh from her father's stately Castle Howard, she is supposed to have said that she must have a castle, and the young people set to work, took off the new roof, and turned the low bedroom-floor into a series of high and stately rooms. Sometimes turrets were added and other touches of Gothic, but the same great walls remain from Norman days. One of the most interesting modern parts of the castle was also left—the stables, untouched since they were set up in Charles the Second's day.

When Robert de Todeni received his liege lord he offered him a golden key to the Stanton tower, and to this day the custom is continued, the key having been given to more than one king who has come in peace or war. William de Albini, who lived here after its first lord had gone to his fathers, was one of the barons who signed

Magna Carta. King John, coming to visit him, seized him and his castle. James the First was more genially inclined. Staying here on his journey from Scotland to London, he celebrated the joyous pilgrimage by making 46 knights before breakfast, and left two valuable miniatures of his sons. King Charles was also hospitably entertained here in 1634.

There are a hundred other footnotes to history in the names of sons and daughters and kinsmen of this famous house who have come and gone within its walls. There are relics of the Marquis of Granby (heir of the house) who fought at Minden in the Seven Years War, and whose name adorns the signboard of many inns.

The picture galleries of the castle have scores of family portraits. Van Dyck painted the Duchess of Buckingham, a daughter of the house who married George Villiers; Reynolds painted the lovely Lady Tyrconnel, sister of the fourth duke; and Hogarth painted the Duchess of Somerset, whose daughter married the Marquis of Granby. Here also is one of the finest of the Holbein portraits of Henry the Eighth. There are many other paintings and portraits of famous men, a great altarpiece by Murillo of the Holy Family, priceless Gobelin tapestries, miniatures, furniture, and marvellous manuscripts.

A curious treasure much sought by sightseers is the silver punch bowl with the Rutland crest, so big that we remember Violet, Duchess of Rutland, telling us that her four children sat in it to be painted by Sir J. J. Shannon.

On the side of the hill where the castle stands (the summit of which was once reached by 55 steps cut in the red sandstone and still called the Jerusalem Stairs) are the gardens. The Duchess's Garden is full of terraces and stone statues of gods and goddesses and Father Time. The Duke's Walk to Spring Gardens is an entire valley filled with flower beds and trees. Lady Elizabeth's Garden is a little dell with a clear spring. The Water Garden (or Frog Hollow) is in sum_mer filled with azaleas and rhododendrons, a marvellous spectacle.

At the foot of the hill are the slight remains of the priory founded by Robert de Todeni when he built the castle; they are rather over-shadowed by the famous Peacock Inn. The ninth duke, when he was an Eton boy, was allowed by his grandfather to excavate the whole of Belvoir Priory with the help of two workmen. He took plans, and so, although most of it had to be covered again, the exact formation of the building is known. On Blackberry Hill an avenue of firs and trees leads to the mausoleum, a marble memorial to the Duchess of Rutland who died in 1825. From a low altar tomb the duchess rises with outstretched arms and looks up to the clouds, where are four cherubs, the children who died before her. All the Dukes of Rutland are buried in this mausoleum, the last being the eighth, whose fine bronze monument shows him in Garter robes.

There is one other name to be mentioned here of one who has a place in letters if not in history. It is that of the parson-poet Crabbe, who was chaplain here about 1785, and who was, as his letters tell, rather overpowered by the magnificence of his surroundings.

Two Boys at School

BILLESDON. It is so scattered that Leicestershire folk have a saying In-and-out like Billesdon. And its history is as scattered as its ways.

It has three springs called Billesdon Brooks which are older than all else. Yet the village itself begins before history was written, with Billesdon Coplow, a high wooded hill which may have served as a landmark among the ancient forests for the men who carved the primitive trackway running here. The story is continued with the high mound like a promontory fortress which Britons or Romans may have raised to defend the road. Then the Saxons take up the tale; a beautiful brooch that may have been buried with one of their chieftains was found here.

Much of the 13th century church has been made new, and its oldest possession is the plain font at which Billesdon children, rich and poor, have been baptised for 700 years. The free school, built in 1650, is the successor of one in which two famous men learned some of their lessons. One was George Fox the Quaker, whose life was a triumph over insults, persecutions, and imprisonment under King and Commonwealth; the other was George Villiers, Duke of Buckingham, royal favourite and proudest nobleman in Europe, who came to this school until he was 13 and was here "taught the principles of music and other slight literature."

Among the trees on the railed-in green are two crosses, one a slender fluted shaft which has been here since the Wars of the Roses, the other a sad memorial of our last Great War.

LEICESTERSHIRE

The Faithful Servant

BIRSTALL. Rail and Road and the River Soar all pass it by, but its black and white cottages and its church remain steadfastly rural, though Leicester is but a mile or two away and creeping closer.

The church is old enough to have a Saxon window, discovered in the chancel last century with part of the lattice which let in the light on monks to whom glass was something of a mystery and a miracle. Most of the church is 13th century and the plain old font has been here all the time.

Two old ladies are remembered here, Elizabeth White whose place in the pews for most of last century is marked with a brass, and Hannah Bond, who was one family's servant and friend for 75 years, almost unique as a record of service in one home.

BITTESWELL. It is a mile from Lutterworth, its houses and its church widely spread about the green. Much of the church is 600 years old, and in the old tower is a huge recess thought to have enshrined the founder's tomb. On the south arcade are sculptured eight heads of saints, and in the churchyard is a lychgate set up in memory of James Powell, who was vicar during the reigns of four sovereigns, dying in 1844.

The Blind Parson

BLABY. The spire of its 13th century church, decorated with three rows of grotesque heads, soars high above a churchyard guarded by two big yews.

In the venerable building is a plain font reputed to be Saxon, and a tablet to two 18th century parsons, father and son. Edward Stokes the younger, though blind from boyhood, bravely ministered here for 50 years after his father, sometimes riding to hounds, accompanied by a man who rang a bell when it was necessary for the blind parson to take a fence.

Richard Vines and the King

BLASTON. It has charming cottages with pretty roofs of wavy-patterned thatch, and two churches made new last century. One is St Giles, unwanted and forlorn in a wilderness of nettles; the other is St Michael's, a tiny place with a bell turret, keeping an old font outside and a rare medieval chalice within, engraved with a lovely Calvary.

37

In these tranquil surroundings was born a boy who was to come into close touch with one of the most poignant hours in English history. He was Richard Vines, a Puritan who, while minister at St Lawrence Jewry in London, was one of those who offered his services to Charles Stuart on the morning of his execution. Sir Thomas Herbert in his memoirs tells how "they presented their duty to the king with their humble desires to pray with him and perform other offices of service if his Majesty pleased to accept," but the king, in thanking them personally for their love and hoping they would be mindful of him at the last, said he had chosen Bishop Juxon and would have none other.

Cavalcade of Monuments

BOTTESFORD. To this fair corner where the River Devon winds through the lowlands the noble families of the Manners, lords of Rutland for 800 years, have brought their dead to lie. They laid them in this church with a tower and spire like a sentinel keeping watch over the northern marches, and their monuments crowned with beauty this noble structure set in a green churchyard. It is the biggest village church in the county, with a stream rippling through the churchyard in the shade of oaks, and elms, and sycamores; and the spire rising from the lovely tower is the highest in Leicestershire, 210 feet.

By the porch stands a little red brick house which has kept company with this great splendour for more than 200 years, and opposite the church is the white almshouse founded by an Earl of Rutland in the days of Shakespeare. In the marketplace is the stump of an ancient cross over 600 years old; it is raised on five steps, and by it stand the ancient stocks and the whipping-post.

There is no church for many miles around more appealing than this, its captivating walls crowned with cornices and pinnacles and adorned with canopied niches and fine turrets. Wonderful gargoyles and corbels look down on the churchyard. Indoors it is a scene of monumental splendour. The great nave of five bays, its pillars carved with kings, bishops, priests, lions, sheep, and griffins, leads us to a chancel filled with impressive tombs. Here is such an array of monuments to knights and lords and ladies of renown that we seem to be in the corner of some cathedral. They are like footnotes to the history of England, with the Crusades leaving a dim trace and men and women of Tudor, Stuart, and Georgian days silently coming and going.

We begin with Robert de Ros, although only half his black marble figure reveals the chain armour he wore and the sword he wielded before he joined his ancestors in 1285. From those far-off days comes the worn figure of an unknown lady engraved on a stone in the south aisle, and then we come to the 14th century with Margaret de Ros wearing a veil and a sleeveless gown. William and John de Ros are both from the 15th century, William with a peacock at his head and a dog at his feet, eight angels holding his shield, and John in flowing robes with a lion and eight angels; he fell at the Battle of Beaugé, one of the fights which followed Agincourt.

Next in order comes the fine tomb of Sir Thomas Manners, Lord de Ros and first Earl of Rutland. He occupied the perilous position of being a favourite of Henry the Eighth, his cupbearer, and was appointed later to be Lord Chamberlain to the unwanted Anne of Cleves. But it is not the earl in his Garter mantle, nor his countess with the coronet above her jewelled cap, who most commands attention, but one of the six sons who with nine daughters dutifully accompany their parents; it is the second son John, a slender lad in a tunic with a sword by his side, who grew up to be the hero of a never-forgotten romance. It was he who led away Dorothy Vernon from Haddon Hall and married her in Aylestone church. It is not true that he eloped with her; they were married in the ordinary way and the legend that everybody knows is legend and no more.

One of the best of all these monuments is to the second Earl of Rutland and his countess. He wears his coronet and armour and has a book and a sword; she has jewels in her hair and a lion at her feet. The tomb has a top like an Elizabethan Communion Table, with two sons and a daughter kneeling on the top, which rests on four beautifully carved pillars. Edward the third earl, one of the Commissioners appointed to try Mary Queen of Scots, is in armour, with a bull's head at his feet, and his wife at his side with their only daughter. It is remembered that when he travelled to London Edward took with him a retinue of 41, including a chaplain, a trumpeter, and an apothecary. John the fourth earl is with his countess in stately robes with eight children, and Roger the fifth earl shares with his Elizabeth the glory of one of the richest of all these monuments beautiful with colour. At his feet is a peacock and at hers a hedgehog; she wears an ermined mantle over her gown and has a horseshoe cap beneath her coronet.

It was Roger who endowed the white brick almshouse across the road, but Elizabeth has a more romantic claim to fame, for she was Sir Philip Sidney's only child. Here she lies in proud marble, but her body is not here; it rests in a grave at Shoreditch, in a churchyard which we found a blaze of colour like a garden. She was only three years old when he became immortal on the battlefield of Zutphen, and in his will it was found that he had left her £4000. She was blessed with good fortune, for Queen Elizabeth was her godmother and she grew up to become Countess of Rutland, marrying Roger Manners, a traveller and soldier like her father. Ben Jonson thought much of her, and declared that she was "nothing inferior to her father in poesie." But her promising life was cut short too soon, and she died still young.

A grand monument to Francis, the sixth Earl, portrays him in robes with a peacock at his feet, his first wife Frances in red robe and coronet on one side and his second wife Cecily in black robe and ruff on the other. Their daughters kneel at their heads and feet and we wish their sons were with them, but it is lamentable that both sons died in infancy, and still more lamentable that in that benighted day their death was attributed to wicked sorcery.

George the seventh earl, who died before the Civil War broke out, and John the eighth, who lived to see the waning of Charles the Second's popularity, stand upright, clad in Roman togas as Gabriel Cibber sculptured them. To John Manners, Marquis of Granby, Commander-in-Chief during the Seven Years War, there is no monument, though he was buried here, but as Sir Joshua Reynolds painted him a dozen times posterity hardly needs it. The twentieth century has added its own touch of grandeur with a white marble figure of John Manners, the seventh duke.

We turn from the cavalcade of monuments in this great place to the windows and the carving. One of the windows has the heads of a king and a monk in 14th century glass, and another has the Adoration of the Shepherds in memory of a Duchess of Rutland. The font is splendid and remarkable, an octagonal bowl on four richly carved pillars resting on a low base with eight queer heads round it. It is Jacobean, and the carving shows angels among oak leaves and

The Lovely Vale of Belvoir

The Stately Walls of Belvoir Castle

Nave Corbel   The First Earl of Rutland's Tomb   Nave Corbel

A Son of the Second Earl   The Jacobean Font

Monument of the Fourth Earl of Rutland
THE WONDERFUL CARVING AT BOTTESFORD

The First Earl and his Wife Eleanor

The Sixth Earl with his Wives Frances and Cecily

The Fourth Earl and his Countess
THE EARLS OF RUTLAND AT BOTTESFORD

A Frieze of Birds and Men and Beasts

St Paul on East Wall   Ornament on the North Wall

Arcaded Figures on the Porch
WONDERFUL SAXON SCULPTURE AT BREEDON-ON-THE-HILL

acorns and apples. Two ancient chairs with backs nine feet high are carved with the Tudor rose. There are 15th century brasses of two rectors, John Freeman headless but with an ornamental cope (on which his initials appear five times), the other in a magnificent cope richly decorated with eight saints about God the Father with a Crucifix. He is Henry de Codington, and stands below a triple canopy with a small Madonna and Child in the centre.

In the north transept is a neat brass medallion of Thomas White, once rector here and famous as one of the Seven Bishops who defied the wretched James the Second. He left £10 a year to be given to 20 poor people who could correctly say the Creed, the Lord's Prayer, and the Ten Commandments.

The iron gates of the chancel are of delicate 17th century craftsmanship, given to the church by the Duke of Rutland at the end of the Great War; they are worthy of the splendour to which they lead us. Beauty and history indoors, church and almshouse, river and bridge, and its marvellous steeple looking down on it all—Bottesford is a village richly blessed.

BRANSTON. It lies in the Wolds with the River Devon flowing by on its way past Knipton Reservoir and Belvoir Castle. Many thatched cottages line its long street, and in its churchyard a flight of 15 steps climbs up to the porch. The church comes from our three great building centuries, the round arches in the nave being 700 years old. There is a Norman font bowl finely arcaded, and a stone in the chancel floor with an engraved portrait of a 14th century priest, John Perkyn, worn with the footprints of countless passers by. The gilded wooden reredos, with its painting of the Last Supper, is watched over by four little angels with outspread wings.

BRAUNSTONE. It is one of busy Leicestershire's little neighbours, with a fine hall standing serene and sheltered in the park, and a medieval church. The church has kept its 15th century screen, and in the windows are some fragments of old glass, with a delightful figure of Cecilia with her violin.

The 1000-Year-Old Treasure on a Sacred Hilltop

BREEDON-ON-THE-HILL. It is matchless in its situation and outlook, with a history receding to a past when men fought and delved with flints, and a hilltop sanctuary enshrining in its walls a fragmentary masterpiece of Saxon craftsmen. This gem of ancient art is part of a stone frieze with foliage, birds, animals, and small human figures carved on it with unusual delicacy of form and invention, having survived in a remarkable way the passage of a thousand years. No work of the kind in Western Europe during the 8th or 9th centuries is its equal, and it is hardly necessary to say that it is unsurpassed in England.

We make our way to the church from the crescent-shaped village in the shadow of Breedon Hill, by a stony roadway winding round the steep rock. The road is so inaccessible in winter that the evening services are held down below. The narrow path to the summit has been trodden by unnumbered feet for thousands of years. The flattened hilltop is enclosed by an earthwork which must certainly once have swarmed with ancient dwellers who chose this height above the forest for their defence. As the ages went on and the Saxon succeeded the British heirs of the Romans, becoming themselves converts to the faith which conquered Rome, they built a minster, and Bede writes of a priest in the monastery here.

In another epoch of our island history a Norman priory was built where the Saxon monastery had been. That was in 1144, and the priory church received the villagers as well as the monks. When the Dissolution overthrew the monastery it was the villagers who took the eastern part of the church as their place of worship and let the nave fall into ruins. By some miraculous good fortune the most precious relic of its earlier days, the Saxon frieze built into the wall, remains.

Only an archaeologist can rightly understand the significance of these stones in the history of ornament or in sacred art, but it needs no such special knowledge to read the simple lesson of their beauty. There are no fewer than 30 fragments, great and small, built into all parts of the structure. By far the greater number are sections of carved friezes which, if they could be put together, would measure 80 feet. There are fragments of moulding and carving, a panel of the lion, two sculptured stones with figures under arches, and three stones of an entirely different character, with other figures of saints or apostles, each under his own arch. The lengths of the frieze on the walls of the chancel, some of strange beasts with a wonderfully interlaced pattern of curves and spirals, are the most astonishing in their revelation of a finished decoration at such an early period.

The panels of the sculptured figures on the outside walls of the south porch are less astonishing in their beauty, but not less remarkable.

The best preserved fragment is on the inside of the east wall, a perfect piece of vine decoration. Among the sections of friezes of birds and foliage in the tower is the figure of an angel, his robe thrown over his left arm, his right arm raised in blessing. The panel outside on the eastern wall may have been a figure of Paul, his hand raised to bless, an eastern cloth bound about his forehead and falling over his shoulders. Among the most interesting of the bird decorations is the continual appearance of the cock, the falcon, and the peacock.

When the Saxon tradition had almost faded into oblivion and even the misfortunes of the later priory were forgotten, the old dismantled church took on a new life with the coming of the Shirleys, whom we come upon again at Ragdale and at Staunton Harold. The chancel, aisles, and south transept were rebuilt in the 13th century and the Saxon fragments incorporated in the new walls. The 14th century gave the church its panelled font, the 15th century added a clerestory and the 16th century endowed it with fine monuments.

John Shirley lies in armour on his Elizabethan tomb, a book in his hands, a sword, a dagger, and gauntlets by his side, and a lion at his feet. His kinsman Francis Shirley, who soon followed him to the grave, is also here, an armoured figure with his wife Dorothy in a lace cap beside him, and two sons, an infant boy in a shroud, and four daughters below. Sir George Shirley and his wife kneel under arches in prayer, with two babies in cradles beside them, and two sons and a daughter behind. One of the two sons married a daughter of Elizabeth's Essex. Under this tomb is the figure of a skeleton to typify the vanity of it all. The north aisle, with an iron grille separating it from the Shirley tomb, is a private chapel belonging to Earl Ferrers. In it is an elaborate canopied Jacobean pew. In the last window is a small modern picture of this church on the hilltop.

Breedon is its church and the church is Breedon, but when we descend from the hill we find much to capture our interest in the irregular streets below, and may especially note an odd 18th century round house with a conical top and a nail-studded door; it is a village lock-up, a survival from the Bad Old Days.

Beowulf's Barrow

BRENTINGBY. It is a hamlet near the River Eye, watched over by the tiny spire of a 13th century tower. The rest of the church was refashioned 300 years ago, but still keeps two worn old benches. On a windowsill is a model font six inches high.

Near the church is a dignified 17th century farmhouse, but for other relics of Brentingby's antiquity we must find our way through the dim mists of tradition, which declares that its name comes from the northern tribe of Brentings, whose name is mentioned in a Saxon poem celebrating the deeds of Beowulf and giving instructions for the disposal of his body:

> *Command the war-chiefs*
> *to make a mound*
> *bright after the funeral fire,*
> *upon the nose of the promontory;*
> *which shall for a memorial*
> *to my people*
> *rise high aloft*
> *on Hronesness;*
> *that the sea-sailors*
> *may afterwards call it*
> *Beowulf's barrow,*
> *when the Brentings*
> *over the darkness of the floods*
> *shall sail afar.*

BRINGHURST. Its old thatched cottages are perched like a fortress on a lonely hilltop, and an imaginative traveller may easily visualise a baron's castle here with sentinels on the watch for any strange figure in the valley. It may well have been so, but most of Leicestershire's castles have long since vanished, and here only the cottage walls play the part of battlements, with the church tower as the castle keep.

Though the church has changed with the passing centuries it has kept its Norman tower arch and its simple Norman font. Some of the arches in the nave are also Norman, their capitals adorned with zigzag and flowing lines, and one with a Norman head. Over the arcades are six more faces, like death masks of the feudal age.

The peace memorial is a seat in the shade of a chestnut tree.

LEICESTERSHIRE

The Home of Buckingham

BROOKSBY. Though it is endowed with both charm and grace, Brooksby's chief pride is its hall. It stands handsomely in its park with the church as its companion and guide, and has stood so since it was built as an Elizabethan manor house. Here in 1592 George Villiers, high favourite of his king and of fortune, soldier and ambassador, was born. A soldier of another time who also lived here, a more successful figure in England's wars, was Lord Cardigan, leader of the Charge of the Light Brigade at Balaclava. He came here after the Crimean War, and often must have brooded on his memory of that fateful day in 1854. One of his hunters was buried under an elm in the garden, but Lord Cardigan himself lies in the Brudenell Chapel at Deene in Northants.

In spite of its tower and spire, the church is rather more like a nobleman's chapel than a villager's house of prayer. Shields form a frieze outside its nave and chancel, and old armorial glass fills the east window. It has an ancient font and two monuments of note— one a slab in the chancel floor, bearing engraved figures of a 15th century William Villiers and a wife on either side; the other a white marble monument with figures of an 18th century William Villiers and his wife, both in cloaks. Their death ended an association of Villiers and Brooksby that had lasted for 500 years, and the great house was for many years the home of Admiral Beatty.

English Dictator

CIRCUMSTANCES suggesting an Eastern court rather than St James's enabled George Villiers, younger son of a Leicestershire knight to take his place, when only 23, as virtually the master of the realm, to be transformed from a needy hanger-on at court into the possession of a dukedom and wealth and estates making him almost the richest man in the nation.

Polished in France, he added the perfection of shallow, showy brilliance to a handsome figure and unfailing aptitude, which enabled him to realise that audacity and arrogance were passports to the favour of James the First. To James he was Steenie; to the country he was a detested autocrat who dispensed all patronage, selling office for ignoble service and corrupt support. It has been well said of him that he treated events which determine the destinies of nations as though they were intrigues to gratify pride and passion.

The famous mission of Buckingham and Charles in quest of the hand of the Infanta of Spain was Buckingham's project; its fortunate failure sprang from his insolence. Undeterred by the fury of the nation against a Roman Catholic match, he engineered the ruin of Charles by arranging his marriage to Henrietta Maria.

Complete master of James, Buckingham gained an equal ascendancy over Charles on his accession, and plunged the country into profitless and dishonouring wars with Spain and France. An attempt to impeach him was averted only by the abrupt dissolution of Parliament with no supplies voted. His expedition against France ended in disaster, and again, this time with success, an impeachment was framed against him as the author of all the ills and humiliations of the realm.

Buckingham staked all on a second expedition and spent £60,000 of his own in furnishing the fleet for the relief of Rochelle, declaring that he would be the first to set foot upon the dyke, "to die or do the work." Before he could sail a man with a grievance, the melancholy Felton, slew him as he left his breakfast table at Portsmouth.

The crime fired the nation with a sort of joy, not horror; and songs were sung to celebrate it. It was necessary to bury the victim secretly lest his body should be dishonoured by the implacable mob.

The Man in His Leather Suit

BROUGHTON ASTLEY. George Fox was here about 300 years ago, addressing his first great outdoor meeting. He tells of it in his Diary, and it is easy to picture him in his famous leather suit opening the pages of his Bible and finding words to justify his fiery doctrine. "The Lord opened my mouth," he wrote of that day in 1647, " and the everlasting truth was declared among them. Several were convinced in these parts and were turned from darkness to light."

It is probable that he stood near the spot where two bridges cross the stream and lead to the medieval church. It was one of those "steeple houses" which the Quaker distrusted.

Most of the building is of the 14th and 15th centuries, but in its porch is a Norman stoup, its bowl hollowed out of a cushion capital and supported on a shaft carved with zigzag. In the nave are some old corbels, a mitred bishop's head, and one or two hideous grotesques; by a doorway in the chancel are two more comely 15th century faces.

Some of the windows have beautiful flowing tracery and fragments of 600-year-old glass, Peter with the keys and kneeling saints in blue and gold among them. The chancel has a modern screen with a rich canopy and four tiny angels kneeling like holy sentinels.

Like a Medieval Picture Book

BUCKMINSTER. High up in the Wolds it stands, one of the most charming places in the county, its dignified Georgian hall and park, its cottages and its green, the tree-lined roads and the new plantations, all conspiring to make it a village of delight.

The church of the 14th and 15th centuries has an earlier tower 700 years old, with a little vaulted chamber in one of its piers and a 14th century spire soaring over it, but curious for being at the east end of an aisle. By the chancel arch is an eight-sided turret of lovely white stone, richly panelled with quatrefoils, arcading, and foliage, which carries a staircase to the tower and probably once served also as the spiral roodloft stairway.

Among other stone carvings are some 40 heads looking from the walls as from a medieval picture book. The 15th century font has a panelled bowl and eight faces below, grave and gay.

Close to the well-kept churchyard is the mausoleum of the earls of Dysart, with a richly vaulted roof.

A Tribute by Sir Isaac Newton

BURBAGE. Here the River Soar rises to begin its winding journey to the Trent; here is the finest village common in the county; here are wide curving streets with handsome old houses and timbered cottages and a fine church with a buttressed tower and a slender spire rising in their midst. Many great people have known them all.

The first among them is the rector's son, Roger Cotes, who became first professor of astronomy at Cambridge, dying when he was only 34. Trinity College, Cambridge, has his tomb but his finest epitaph was spoken by Sir Isaac Newton, who said, "Had Cotes lived we might have known something."

Another man of that most fruitful period in scientific knowledge, was rector here, Dr James Duport. He was the tutor of John Ray, Father of English Zoology, and of that other great naturalist Francis Willoughby.

The third great man who lived here awhile was George Canning Minister for Foreign Affairs during the time when Napoleon's star had reached its zenith and was beginning to wane; and remembered also for his speeches against slavery.

Much of the church is modern, but it has kept its 13th century chancel and its 14th century tower. The nave arcades and the font are 600 years old, the south door has fine 17th century ironwork and carving, and there is a 16th century monument with engraved figures of Richard Wightman standing in armour with two wives, five sons, and three daughters.

Lost in the Storm

BURROUGH-ON-THE-HILL. We may still see the rampart lines of a stronghold set up on its lofty hill in some dim epoch of the past. Some of the mounds of this encampment are 20 feet high still, and from this ancient earthwork the Leicestershire countryside is seen in a vast panorama, with the higher hills of Billesdon, Whatborough and Robin-a-Tiptoe to the south.

Though young compared with these ramparts, the church has seen seven centuries. It still has its original font, with skulls and faces in its decoration, and two 15th century figures of William de Stockden in armour with his wife in her flowing gown and lions at their feet.

The village is associated with two great doctors. Here in 1688 was born William Cheselden, one of the fathers of English surgery, who attended Sir Isaac Newton on his deathbed; and here the famous Victorian physician Sir Benjamin Richardson went to school. In his memoirs he tells a strange story of a village schoolmaster who was lost in a snowstorm on Burrough Hill and was given up for dead when his fiddle was found two days later; but on the next day another search party was sent out and he was found rolled in snow, very little the worse for his adventures.

All is Vanity

BURTON LAZARS. It is a small red village on a hillside, taking its name from a leper hospital founded here by Roger de Mowbray, a valiant Norman knight safe home from the second crusade. All trace of the hospital has vanished, but the church with its pretty bell gable has still its 13th century arcades. The font is 500 years old, and up in the roof is an orchestra of ten old folk with musical instruments.

In the churchyard is a strange stone monument 20 feet high adorned with skulls and Passion symbols, serpents and eagles, and figures of Time, Faith, Hope, and Charity. When William Squire died in 1721 he left money that he might be thus remembered, the surplus to be used for the education of poor children. Alas for human hopes and vaunted charity! There was no money left for the children when this monument was finished, and we found it with ivy creeping over it, mournful witness of the ancient Preacher's words, Vanity of Vanities, all is Vanity.

Three hundred years ago there worshipped here Thomas Jacombe who became parson of St Martin's on Ludgate Hill, but was "put out for nonconformity." He comes into the diary of Pepys for making "a gracy sermon, like a Presbyterian."

Hugh Weston to Hugh Latimer

BURTON OVERY. It lies secluded in the valley with a humble medieval church still treasuring intact its beautiful 15th century screen of richly carved oak, and an old ironbound chest.

At the plain old font there was baptised over 400 years ago Hugh Weston, who grew up to be Dean of Westminster and preacher to Mary Tudor. He was confessor to the Duke of Somerset and Sir Thomas Wyatt at their execution, and presided at the trial of Cranmer. He also examined Latimer and Ridley, and to Latimer he said, "Your stubbornness is all vainglory, and that will do you little good when a faggot is in your beard. If you go to heaven in this faith, then I will never come thither."

Little he knew of the candle Latimer was to light in England, and little could he have imagined that Latimer's greatness would be the measure of his own smallness. Foxe called him, "this ruffling prolocutor, with his jug at his elbow," but in fairness it must be recorded that he was one of the best preachers of his time.

In front of the rectory is an oak planted at the Restoration from an acorn of the famous oak at Boscobel. It is a grand old veteran, keeping a watchful eye on one of its own children, a young oak grown from one of its acorns to celebrate the Diamond Jubilee of the Victorian Era.

CARLTON CURLIEU. It stands on a high ridge with Carlton Clump close by, looking across fair vistas as far as Charnwood Forest 20 miles away. Its stately hall, gleaming white in the sunshine, is perhaps the finest Elizabethan house in the county, although its front with five Dutch gables was added in the 17th century.

The church, though most of it has been made new in the last 200 years, has a 17th century tower raised up on the thick walls and the sturdy arch of the Normans. It has some old heraldic glass, a 14th century font, and a fine Jacobean monument of alabaster and black marble showing Sir John Vale in armour with his wife, five upright sons, a daughter, and a babe in swaddling clothes.

Old Village by the Trent

CASTLE DONINGTON. Its pleasant houses of yesterday, with here and there a gabled one of long ago, stand finely on a hill, dominated by an old church whose tower and slender spire have been a landmark in the wide Trent valley for about six centuries. Where the road pauses awhile in its long climb up the hill are some of the oldest houses, some of them thatched, one fine rambling one with timbered walls having a bay projecting quaintly on to the wayside. Under its gables are three dates, 1595, 1636, and 1899, and by the first and last hangs a key; it is known as the Old Key House. A windmill lends charm to the village, which is linked to Derbyshire by the 18th century Cavendish Bridge over the Trent at Shardlow. From many points there are magnificent views; on a clear day can be seen the towers of about a score of churches, and the dark rock of Nottingham Castle.

Once it had its own castle, and few dwellings can have a finer view than the house and cottages which stand on its site and have in their walls some of its old stones. Their steep-banked gardens are part of the old moat. Part of the old cellars are still in Castle House, and here, too, in one of the rooms is part of one of the old stone fireplaces.

Henry de Lacy, Earl of Lincoln, Counsellor of Edward the First and Lieutenant of England while the king was on a visit to France, built the first Norman castle here. From him Lincoln's Inn in London gets its name, because it was built on the site of his London house. When the Wars of the Roses mingled kings and nobles in a common ruin, the castle was held for a time by that Lord William Hastings who was Great Chamberlain of Edward the Fourth and whose high head was brought low by the bloodstained Richard Crookback. In 1595 Sir George Hastings, fourth Earl of Huntingdon "ruined the castle and built a fair house in the park."

Castle Donington : The fine 15th century brass of Robert de Staunton and his family

The church (with the rare dedication to Edward, King and Martyr) began as an aisleless building about 1200, of which time there remain the inner walls of the tower and the walling at the east end of the nave arcades. The south aisle was added soon after, but was made new before the century closed; its prettiest window is one with trefoils for tracery, and shafts with carved capitals. The chancel is 13th century, with lancet windows and two of a little later time. The north aisle is 600 years old, the clerestory and the porch are 15th century.

Over each arcade is a very quaint row of old heads. There are sedilia and a piscina in the chancel and also in the south aisle. The font is 15th century, and the oak lectern, carved with flowers, has a marble medallion with portraits of the first Marquis of Hastings and his wife. It is a memorial to the marquis, who was Governor of India for seven years after Waterloo.

Very interesting is the old stone pulpit, hiding its secret from the casual eye. It is made from old memorial stones removed from the floor, and a peep inside shows us the children of a family group, looking like ten little maids in a row.

The oldest memorial here is a tonsured figure of about 1320. Sculptured in stone, he lies in the chancel, wearing finely embroidered vestments. A lion is at his feet, and another is at each side of the canopy above his head.

From the middle of the 15th century comes the fine brass of Robert de Staunton and his wife, their figures engraved below a rich double canopy. The knight wears plate armour, the lady horned headdress, and at the feet of each is a dog. With them are small figures of four sons and three daughters.

For 400 years the fine figures of Robert Hesilrige and his wife have lain on their tomb enriched with sculptures of angels with shields, friars with staffs and beads, a sadly battered Trinity, and a Madonna and Child. The lady has an embroidered kennel headdress on her plaited hair, and three chains are round her neck; over her gown with belt and sash is a mantle, and at her feet are two dogs. Robert's armour is most interesting for its detail. His collar of SS passes over his lance-rest, and his praying hands rest on the strap which fastens his helmet to his cuirass, while the armour under his right arm is shaped for his lance to pass under freely.

Donington Park, the home of the Earls of Huntingdon when their castles here and at Ashby had become ruins, is two miles away to the west, the fine hall having been rebuilt in 1795 by William Wilkins, architect of the National Gallery. Among the grand oaks in the big park is one with a girth of 44 feet about which John Evelyn wrote; it is called Chaucer's Oak on the rather slenderly founded tradition that the poet came here with his patron, the Duke of Lancaster. But another poet who certainly came here and came often was Thomas Moore, who may have written some of his Irish Melodies in the shade of these trees. A recent memory of the hall is that of the German officers who were interned here, among them the Zeppelin Commander who was captured when his airship was brought down in 1916, and who, 16 years later, came back to England and broadcast an account of his experience. Some of the prisoners escaped, and there is still to be seen the opening of the tunnel they made, and the 50 tons of earth they removed. Now the hall is a hotel, and in the lovely park, with two herds of deer, is a motor racing track.

Under the woods of the park is King's Mills, a beauty spot by the Trent, where the stream rushes over weirs and by the great rusty wheel of the ruined old paper-mill, and eddies round many little islands. Here are white cottages in a row, and an old house (where we can take tea) said to be on the site of the monks' chapel. The bowery lane dropping down to King's Mills is spanned by an overhead bridge made of chains, hanging like a web among the trees.

Forerunner of Wordsworth

CATTHORPE. It is Leicestershire's Farthest South, a neat red hamlet with gay gardens set on a hillside overlooking Shakespeare's Avon, here an infant stream.

We come by a modern lychgate to the small church that has stood 500 years with bells in the tower that have been ringing since the days of Agincourt. High on the wall of the nave are six old carvings of angels and men, and set in the chancel wall is a curious figure of a 14th century lady holding a heart; she wears a veil and a wimple, and is engraved on an ancient coffin lid found last century in the chancel wall. She may have been baptised at this font, for it is 13th century. There is an old ironbound chest, and one of the rectors who must have opened it many times to put his papers in was John Dyer who married a lady claiming descent from Shakespeare, but had a greater claim on his own account, for he was a poet of whom Wordsworth wrote:

Though hasty Fame hath many a chaplet culled
For worthless brows, while in the pensive shade
Of cold neglect she leaves thy head ungraced,
Yet pure and powerful minds, hearts meek and still,
A grateful few, shall love thy modest lay.

Of one of his poems, The Fleece, a wit of the day was moved to write:

Adventurous Jason stole a Golden Fleece ;
Dyer's own wool produced a Silver Piece.

Wordsworth was attracted by Dyer's love of nature, much like his own, and the simple expression of it in his verses, as:

O may I with myself agree,
And never covet what I see ;
Content me with a humble shade,
My passions tamed, my wishes laid.

His simple love of nature amid the pompous dullness of the 18th century was like the solitary piping of the early-waking bird before the full chorus came with Wordsworth.

CHADWELL. At the end of a sloping country lane is a small church which seems to shepherd half a dozen cottages. The Normans built it plainly, but a little of their ornament appears in two comical heads and the chevrons on the capitals of blocked arches. The rough-hewn font is also Norman, and in the tower and the chancel are lancet windows seven centuries old.

A Group of Famous Men

CHURCH LANGTON. It is the chief of the five Leicestershire Langtons, and it is famous in the countryside for one of the best churches in the county. It has also a graceful rectory of Georgian red brick, finely ornamented with vases and plaster designs and facing the peace memorial on the green. It has near it the hamlet of West Langton, where was born the Walter Langton who, as Bishop of Lichfield and Lord High Treasurer, knelt by Edward the First as he lay dying. In a field at Tur Langton is what is called King Charles's Well, at which the King is supposed to have watered his horses on his flight from Naseby.

The church is a noble place with a lofty 15th century tower, and a magnificent clerestoried interior restored and beautified by a famous rector of the 18th century, William Hanbury, a forceful man who loved music and flowers, and came here still full of the hopes and dreams of youth. He dreamed of founding a collegiate church with all the splendour of a great cathedral. He would establish a musical festival there. Not all his hopes were fulfilled, but he had the rare experience of making money out of botany and spending it on Langton's Free School, and on benefactions for three churches, and in this church, where he lies, he ministered for a quarter of a century. He lies in a vault below the vestry, and on his memorial is a lovely cherub copied from one in Amiens cathedral.

Long after him came a Thomas Hanbury to be rector here for 57 years. A white angel guards his grave in the churchyard and a window keeps his memory green.

From the lofty arch of the tower to the lofty arch of the chancel runs a stately 15th century roof with elaborate beams, bosses, and carvings. It looks down on an interior with much that is attractive old and new. There is a stone ledge in the north aisle supported by heads with smiling faces, a 15th century font with a Jacobean cover, a 17th century almsbox, a battered figure of Richard Roberts, one of King Charles's knights, a new oak pulpit and a new chancel screen, and a sculpture of Leonardo's Last Supper in the sanctuary.

Long before William Hanbury came this way there had passed by a man with the strange name of Polydore Vergil, a rector sent to England by the Pope, an Italian historian of great repute. He liked our country very well and stayed here in the seclusion of Langton for 28 years, writing a history of England at the invitation of Henry the Seventh. From 1503 to 1535 Church Langton knew him, and as his scholarship kept him in touch with such men as Sir Thomas More, Hugh Latimer, and the great Erasmus, it is not improbable that some of these giants came to see him on his Leicestershire hillside.

In the end he went back, an old man, to Urbino, and spent his last years in his native land—happier than the rector who succeeded him, Lawrence Sanders, who was burned alive by Mary Tudor.

The Small Poets

CLAYBROOKE. It is both Great and Little, and embraces in its hospitable arms Wigston Parva and Ullesthorpe as well, but our praises are warmest for the corner where an elm-bordered pathway leads from the white cottages of Little Claybrooke to a 600-year-old church.

Its chancel can bear comparison with that of any small church in the land, and the beauty of its proportions is enhanced by the lovely flowing tracery of the seven windows which shed light so serenely upon it. The base of the medieval screen, with its sculptured foliage, has been preserved in the new, and the nave is remarkable for its ancient roof, with its great gallery of heads and figures of man and woman, saint and grotesque, all sculptured here in piety and fantasy. Six stone faces bear them company on the arches below, two grinning broadly as though to drive dull care away.

Some of the gentlefolk who worshipped here in the 18th century of grace are well remembered, and Hannah More contributed two epitaphs on her friends. The first to Cluer Dicey begins with the lines addressed to any "friend or stranger who shall tread these solemn mansions of the silent dead," and ends

> *O pause! reflect, repent, resolve, amend !*
> *Life has no length, Eternity no end !*

The other is on a wall tablet to Anna and Emma Dicey, who died at the beginning of the 19th century when both were young:

> *Sweet pair! from life, love, friendship snatched away*
> *When your fair dawn announced so bright a day !*

Another tablet has an inscription by Lady Craven, who also had a taste for versifying, paying a tribute to her friend Charles Jenner, an 18th century vicar,

> *One who only lived to make his friends*
> *And all the world regret he e'er should die.*

Jenner, who was a poet of rather more capacity than his admirer, left some verses which afford an entertaining picture of an 18th century vicar's recreations. He tells how he had:

> *Grown sick of liberty and country air,*
> *The morning saunter in the one-horse chair,*
> *The social pipe, the solitary muse,*
> *The bowling meeting, and the weekly news,*
> *The rustic Vicar quits his lone retreat*
> *To try what joys the London clergy greet.*
> *He mounts his mare, whilst Thomas at his back*
> *Conveys twelve shirts and his best suit of black,*
> *A half-year's tithes, to buy his way in town,*
> *His six best sermons, and his last new gown.*

A mile away at High Cross, where Roman Watling Street crosses the Roman Fosse Way, is a mouldering ivy-covered pillar, placed there a century before the "rustic vicar" set out for London and harking back some 1700 years from those leisurely days. For there the Romans set up their strong post Venones, and there, beneath the earth, were buried coins of the soldier's pay from the Augustan Age to the days of Caligula.

COALVILLE. As we hurry through this workaday place (which carries its story in its name) there are three things to see. One is the neat municipal building of brick and stone. Another is the century-old church with linenfold panels and coloured bands of vine and grape adorning its screen, and an inscription to 34 miners who lost their lives at Whitwick, leaving 27 widows and 84 children. The third is a striking clock tower of brick and stone, dominating Memorial Square where the roads meet and the market stalls gather on every side. The great ribbed column, 60 feet high, was set up in memory of the men who did not come back.

Sad Daughter of a Ducal House

COLD OVERTON. It stands high up near the borders of our smallest county, gathered about a little ancient church and one of the finest houses in Leicestershire.

The church, hallowed by seven centuries of prayer, has a pinnacled tower and spire and grotesque heads of animals carved about its base. A fine old yew shades the porch, and a lovely 13th century doorway with detached piers and sculptured roses leads into the south aisle whose walls still bear faint traces of figures painted six centuries ago.

Cold Overton Hall stands proudly overlooking the Vale of Rutland, noble trees bearing it company, in gardens with holly-edged walks sloping steeply down the hill. Built in the 17th century, it has a lofty porch and mullioned windows framed with creeper, while it has a beautiful oak staircase and a robust dog-gate designed to keep dogs from wandering upstairs.

Stately as its Jacobean ancestry has made it, its memories are statelier still. Here was one of the manors of the Mowbrays whose name was allied with the house of the Dukes of Norfolk. They held it till the fourth duke died in 1476, and it is through his little daughter Anne that this place is linked with one of the saddest chapters in English history. When she was only six Anne was formally married at Westminster to Richard, Duke of York, younger son of Edward the Fourth. It was five years after this ceremony of

57

marriage that the boy went to the Tower, there with his brother prince to be foully murdered by order of Richard the Third. Perhaps it was in this wild garden that the news of his death reached Anne; so is this corner of our fair countryside linked with

The most arch deed of piteous massacre
That ever yet this land was guilty of.

Memories of Poets and Painters

COLEORTON. Who could make the short pilgrimage from Ashby to Coleorton without enquiring for Coleorton Hall, where the Leicestershire Beaumonts, one of the few families of England with a family tree firmly rooted in the days of the Conqueror, have lived for so long? There were Beaumonts who were warriors, Beaumonts whose offshoots were judges or nobles, Beaumont poets who knew Shakespeare, and Beaumonts who knew Wordsworth, a Beaumont who figured in the Civil Wars, and a Beaumont who was the greatest of benefactors of the National Gallery. These and their guests all haunt the park and the big stone house hiding behind its trees.

It was odd, when we called, to hear that a baronet of this long family had lately surprised the village by selling his fruit and vegetables from door to door. When he found that local salesmen were asking 3d each for lettuces which he had let them have for 1d, he decided to do his own selling. He stood in the van and called his wares, while his gardener took the money. So eager were the people to buy that later he opened a shop in Coalville, taking his nine-year-old son, the present baronet, into partnership with him. A painting of Coleorton Hall decorated the shop, and the Beaumont flag flew over it.

The church, which stands prettily on its hilltop with a background of yews, has known many generations of Beaumonts, but does not enclose many of their monuments. The chief of them is the 17th century altar tomb of Sir Henry Beaumont. Sir Henry, less distinguished than many Beaumonts who have here no memorial, is shown as a bearded man in armour and ruff, long cloak and belted dress, with his wife in her bonnet beside him, and his son kneeling at a desk below.

In the tower window is some 15th century glass from Rouen, with saints and monks and priests, all richly coloured, and elaborate tabernacle work above them. The east window has graceful tracery and finely coloured modern glass with scenes from the Life of Jesus; another window with figures of Christ, apostles, and angels is a tribute to Francis Merewether, who was rector here for almost half of the 19th century.

At the front and side of the organ is some 17th century Flemish woodwork, less simply carved than the average English work. This also pictures scenes from the Life of Jesus as well as dignified figures typifying Temperance, Knowledge, Faith, and Courage.

Wordsworth and His Friends

IT may be questioned whether any private house in England has richer literary and artistic memories than Coleorton Hall, on the western side of Charnwood Forest in Leicestershire.

It has belonged for four centuries to the very ancient Leicestershire family of the Beaumonts, who came into it by marriage, its first Beaumont being a baronet, who also was a viscount in the Irish peerage, and a poet. Between 1762 and 1827 its owner was Sir George Howland Beaumont, the seventh baronet and a remarkable man. He was wealthy, travelled, artistic, generous, and had a fine capacity for friendships. Particularly he delighted in the society of poets and artists, and he had personal ambitions as a painter. The distinction of Coleorton Hall centres on him, so far as the Beaumonts are concerned.

As a young man he had known Dr Johnson, and Sir Joshua Reynolds was one of his closest friends; but it was when Beaumont had passed his fiftieth year that he came into contact with the great poet, 16 years younger than himself, who was to give him a lasting place in literary history.

In 1804 Wordsworth had married and settled in the Lake District, and Coleridge was hovering around with his headquarters there. Wordsworth was approaching the peak point of his genius and Coleridge had already benumbed his brain with opium. Sir George Beaumont, keenly feeling that here were "coming" men, had made the acquaintance of Coleridge at Keswick but not yet of Wordsworth. Apparently he felt that it would be better for Coleridge if Wordsworth were a nearer neighbour, and he bought ground at the foot of Skiddaw as a site for a suitable house for them. But Coleridge put an end to his scheme by going abroad for a couple of years, after the Wordsworths had patched him up physically and lent him £100.

Through this common interest in Coleridge Beaumont and Wordsworth met, and when Coleridge at last returned he found the whole Wordsworth family—the poet, his wife, his sister, the wife's sister Sarah, and two children had been living at Coleorton Hall Farm for nearly a year. Coleridge at once took his ten-year-old son Hartley with him and visited them there. By correspondence and by personal contact Wordsworth and Beaumont had cemented a firm and cordial friendship and Coleorton Hall had become like a second home to the poet. The hall, which had had a stormy history during the Civil War, was being rebuilt when Wordsworth first knew it, and the Beaumonts were occupying the hall farm. This house they lent to the Wordsworths from the autumn of 1806 to the autumn of 1807.

Wordsworth was now on the full tide of his power and charm as a poet. He had written many of the poems that gave him his distinctive place in literature. He was at home at Coleorton with congenial friends when he was with the Beaumonts, and though some of the poems he wrote there were written by request, for a special purpose, others were among his best, and preserve most haunting cadences. Repeatedly he was a guest of the Beaumonts after his long stay there, and his occasional writings at Coleorton continued at least till three years after his host's death in 1827.

There were many visitors to Coleorton—poets like Scott, who was there in what may be called Wordsworth's year, Byron, Southey, and Samuel Rogers; scientists like Sir Humphry Davy; artists like Constable, Wilkie, and Benjamin Haydon, the last, of course, gossiping about it in an ill-mannerly way afterwards. One cannot but feel, however, that Wordsworth was the nearest friend of Coleorton's urbane and generous host. Beaumont left him £100 a year for life as the cost of a yearly holiday.

When Wordsworth first went to Coleorton, in 1805, he was overshadowed by the tragic death at sea of his favourite brother John, and his grief first found expression, in Elegiac Stanzas on a picture Beaumont had painted of the "rugged pile" of Peele Castle on the Cumberland coast lashed by a stormy sea. Had he painted the picture as he last saw it, it would have been "the gentlest of all gentle things." He would have given it

LEICESTERSHIRE

The light that never was on sea or land,
The consecration, and the poet's dream.

. . . . . .
So would it once have been—tis so no more.

. . . . . .
O tis a passionate work ! Yet wise and well,
Well chosen is the spirit that is here;
That hulk which labours in the deadly swell,
This rueful sky, this pageantry of fear !

Painter and poet became friends over that picture and Beaumont gave it to Mrs Wordsworth.

During the long occupancy of the hall farm in 1807 Wordsworth wrote his fine sonnet on the conquest of Switzerland by Napoleon in which the Voices of the Sea and the Mountains typify Liberty. Then and there also Dorothy wrote the charming description of how the children welcomed their mother back after a month's absence in London, one of the sweetest of all studies of childhood.

The short poems made at Coleorton are all interesting, but best of all is the story of the Clifford of warlike race reared in secrecy as a shepherd boy, who comes into his own "to head the shock of war":

Love had he found in huts where poor men lie;
His daily teachers had been woods and rills,
The silence that is in the starry sky,
The sleep that is among the lonely hills.
To him the savage virtue of the Race,
Revenge, and all ferocious thoughts were dead ;
Nor did he change; but kept in lofty place
The wisdom which adversity had bred.

The inscriptions Wordsworth wrote for Coleorton's seats and trees prove here as elsewhere the transitoriness of such material devices. One on a stone, near a tree which Beaumont and Wordsworth jointly planted, has perished. It contained a tribute to Francis Beaumont, the dramatist colleague of Fletcher. Perished also has one on a seat looking towards Grace Dieu, the Charnwood home of the Beaumont family earlier than Coleorton Hall, and also the ruins of its Nunnery. The closing lines of this inscription tell the truth about such memorials.

Communities are lost and empires die,
And things of holy use unhallowed lie ;
They perish ; but the intellect can raise,
From airy words alone a pile that ne'er decays.

So the words of Francis Beaumont and of William Wordsworth live *in their books* after they have perished from where they are embossed.

Other written inscriptions, readable in the poet's works, relate to an urn in memory of Sir Joshua Reynolds, and a seat hollowed out of stone by the Wordsworths when they were living at the hall farm. In later years Wordsworth wrote elegies to Beaumont's sister-in-law, Mrs Fermor, with whom he and his family had lived "many weeks" at the hall, and who left him a legacy as a token of her esteem. Finally he wrote an Elegy on Sir George himself. Sir George's wall monument in the church in the grounds of Coleorton Hall has the meek appeal: "Enter not into judgment with thy servant, O Lord !"

Sir George Beaumont had all his life been a generous supporter of English artists, and a judicious purchaser of works of international fame. When he died he left 16 of his most valuable pictures to the nation including four Claude Lorrains, two Rembrandts, two Wilsons, and Wilkie's Blind Fiddler.

The most striking of the literary reminiscences of Coleorton was on the night of January 7, 1807. Coleridge, home from the Continent ill and miserable, went to the Wordsworths for Christmastide at the hall farm, and after his manner stayed on a while. On that January evening Wordsworth recited to the family circle the part of The Prelude that tells intimately of the growth of his own mind. Coleridge was deeply impressed. The contrast of the growth of Wordsworth's powers and the shrinkage of his own was poignant. He could not sleep but spent the night writing his poem to Wordsworth, beginning:

Friend of the Wise! and Teacher of the Good!

That, however, was not how he first wrote it. At first it was:

O Friend! O Teacher! God's great gift to me!

That night, under Wordsworth's influence, somewhat of his own lost genius returned. He saw his friend among the Immortals.

O Great Bard!
Ere yet that last strain dying awed the air,
With steadfast eye I viewed thee in the choir
Of ever-enduring men. The truly great
Have all one Age, and from one visible space
Shed influence! They, both in power and act,
Are permanent, and Time is not with them,
Save as it worketh for them, they in it.

That poem, struck out of him by impact with Wordsworth, was the last Coleridge ever wrote that has any claim to greatness.

A Forgotten Pepys

CROSBY. The stream runs down its street as it has done for centuries, crossed by little wooden bridges, but industry has marched this way, and only the church remains as of old, with its roots in the 13th century.

It has its roodloft stairs still, with a sculptured faun at the doorway, and ancient beams in the roof have carved bosses, one a grinning grotesque with protruding tongue, another gnashing his teeth. The 15th century screen is black with age, and there is a long dug-out chest bound with iron. The east window has fine modern figures of Our Lord in a rich red cloak, with archangels gorgeously arrayed in purple and green on either side and two angels kneeling above.

Among the names on the list of rectors is a forgotten Samuel Pepys of the famous Samuel's own century, and Thomas Rickards, who was here for 56 years in more recent times.

Lord Kitchener's Father

COSSINGTON. In this peaceful village, with its wealth of white thatched cottages, we came upon the chain of life which gave us our famous Lord Kitchener.

His father, Colonel Henry Horatio Kitchener, was born in the year of Nelson's death, spent some of his last years here, and here on a summer's day in 1894 passed away at the age of 90. In that year his famous son was Sirdar of the Egyptian Army and was consolidating the plans which culminated in the battle of Omdurman and the downfall of the tyrant Khalifa. On a summer's day 22 years later Lord Kitchener was to die tragically in the service of his country. His father rests here in the shadow of a fine 14th century church.

Time has effaced many of the traces of its six centuries, but in the nave is the stone figure of a medieval lady who worshipped here when the church was young, and in the chancel are the ancient sedilia, with ten battered heads grave and gay, that she must often have looked upon. Other relics of its early days include the panelled 16th century altar tomb with an engraved figure of Matthew Knightley, in fur-trimmed gown, many old bench-ends with linenfold pattern, and a few others with heads and beasts on their poppyheads.

The ancient oak screen after standing forlorn in the garden of the fine old rectory close by, was restored to the church and today seems little the worse for its fresh air treatment.

A Tragedy on the Stage

COSTON. Its red cottages, its barns, its haystacks, and its church, are gathered together in the valley of the Eye, where the rivulet begins to flow to the sea. The church has a small 13th century turret on which the 15th century set a spire. A stone frieze of foliage runs like a cornice on the south wall, inside and out, and there are corbels carved with men and angels and grotesques. One of the windows has a 14th century picture of Mary by the Cross, and another has attractive figures of James, John, Peter, and Paul.

A little-known tragedy of last century is recalled by a brass to Temple Crozier, a young actor of 24 who was accidentally stabbed to death in a play at the Novelty Theatre.

At the Death of King John

CROXTON KERRIAL. From its height on the Wolds it commands the wide Devon valley, with Belvoir Castle in its midst, and on a clear day Lincoln Cathedral like a shadow on the horizon 30 miles away.

It may have been on such a day in the year after Magna Carta that the simple peasants here looked on in wonder at a slow procession on its way to Croxton Abbey which had been built here a century before. King John was dead, and the Abbot of Croxton, who as physician and confessor had attended his last hours, was bringing back some part of the wretched king's body for burial in his abbey, the king's grave being at Worcester. That is the story, but whether it is true none can tell, and all that remains of the abbey are fragments of walls carefully preserved in Croxton Park.

The church, which was built a century after the king had gone to his account, and has long survived the abbey, stands happily in front of a grove of sycamores. Its 15th century tower and clerestory are well proportioned, and it has fine carving both old and new. There is a set of 42 splendid 15th century bench-ends with finials and traceried panels, carvings of birds and dragons, monks with shields, a hunter with his dogs, a man with two tongues, and a two-faced woman. They are believed to be the work of the old monks, but the tradition of fine carving did not perish with them, for the modern seats have similar subjects. The plain old font has a cover adorned with a lamb and birds and other designs; the pulpit has a figure of John the Baptist, who appears again in stone in a niche outside the porch. All these were carved by a local amateur, entirely self-taught, who used his talents to enrich the treasury of his church.

DESFORD. It has the king as lord of the manor by right of his Duchy of Lancaster, and two manor houses which, though not kingly, have their own charm. One with a whitewashed front and a thatched roof, stands in the cobbled street; the other is just outside the village, with gables of red brick and handsome chimneys. The ancient church, with battlemented tower and spire, has a font probably Norman and as plain as the village, but the modern pulpit has fine stone figures of Christ, St John, and St Martin.

In a corner of the churchyard are two touching memorials, marble figures of a little girl with a bunch of flowers in her hand and a book at her side, and a winged cherub at prayer.

Shakespear Minor

DISEWORTH. It lies among the hills, with wide roads and roomy houses, and a 700-year-old church with a slender tower and spire, ivied without and neat within. The church has a plain old font, an 18th century pulpit, and a 19th century monument to Ann Cheslyn with a graceful mourning figure.

Near the church is the old thatched cottage in which William Lilley was born in 1602. He was one of the most plausible astrologers of his time, predicting events with the assurance of the Fleet Street quacks of our own day, and he was clever enough to persuade Cromwell to grant him a pension of £100 a year. We come upon him again at Walton-on-Thames, where Elias Ashmole, another of his indulgent friends, set up a marble monument over his grave.

About a mile away is what is left of Langley Priory, an old house behind a lake in a hollow. It stands on the site of a nunnery built soon after the Conquest and still preserves some of the old walls. In the 19th century the house came into the possession of John Shakespear, son of a Leicestershire farmer, who had coveted it from his boyhood. There had seemed little prospect that it would belong to him, but his youthful talent attracted the notice of Lord Rawdon, who sent him to London to study Arabic. He became a professor of oriental languages and author of several standard books on them.

It was an undertaking unlikely to lead to great wealth, but John Shakespear, by the aid of prudent living, saved enough money to buy the home of his boyhood aspirations and lived there when he retired. Two years before his death, inspired by the thought that he might be a descendant of his immortal namesake, he gave £2500 toward preserving the poet's house at Stratford.

The Wizard of the Countryside

DISHLEY. Its monument is a farmyard with the old farmhouse and a pretty watermill by a bridge across a tiny stream.

It was the home of Robert Bakewell. Here he was born, here he bred his sheep and made them famous through the world. They laid him in the old church close by, standing in the shade of the yews he must have loved 200 years ago. Today it is a pathetic sight, for the church is in ruins in a farmyard, and open to the sky.

The new church is in the thatched village of Thorp Acre close by, hardly yet a centenarian but already a pretty picture with the church-yard limes and chestnuts, and a miniature avenue of clipped yews.

Here the Blackbrook, gathering other brooks on its way to the Soar, becomes a deepening stream, and those who love Leicester-shire may well make this hamlet a place of pilgrimage as the home of Robert Bakewell, the shepherd who would sit by the brook thinking and dreaming of his sheep. He lived all his 70 years here and, dying in 1795, waited until 1929 before the county erected a memorial in his honour. Yet he did as much for England as James Watt with his steam engine, and Richard Arkwright with his cotton machine.

The third of his name to farm here, he saw the rise of an industrial England with population concentrated in new towns where it was unable to feed itself, needing supplies of meat and milk which it could not obtain. Until Bakewell's day graziers had bred sheep for wool, and cattle for draught and leather; and poor scraggy animals they were, half-famished in winter for lack of roots and other essential crops.

Bakewell travelled far to find new and better stock, and practically invented new breeds of his own, powerful horses, cattle developing less bone and more flesh, and sheep providing abundant tender joints, the famous Leicestershires, which within his lifetime spread all over the kingdom, and to Europe and America.

To secure these results Bakewell set up a model farm, with a canal a mile long enabling him to irrigate his fields and mow grass four times in a year, to carry food to his stock, and to collect his crops by boat. His house, managed by an energetic sister, was the most famous agricultural home in the country, to which came Russian princes, French and German royal dukes, and British visitors of all degrees.

There was no inn, so he kept open house for all comers, proud to show them his rather terrifying hall, its sides surrounded with skeletons of sheep and cattle, the walls hung with carcasses, whole or in sections, preserved in brine, enabling him to show how he had evolved his stock, and increased the weight of cattle from 370 pounds to 800, of calves from 50 pounds to about 150, of sheep from 28 to 80 pounds, and of lambs from 18 to 50. Hiring out his stock for breeding purposes, he realised £3000 a year from his rams and proportionate sums for cattle and horses, and set a standard which, distinguishing him as the greatest agricultural pioneer in the world, so raised the level of stock-breeding in England that we became the stud farm of the world, with a revenue undreamed of by owners of the starved and stunted stock with which he began his revolution.

DUNTON BASSETT. It stands aloft, its church spire peeping above the elms. The nave beneath its 15th century roof, and the aisles with their clustered pillars, are seven centuries old, two heads over the arches probably representing their builders. The chancel is modern but has kept two windows and an arch of the 13th century, and on its walls an ancient head of Christ and four musical angels. A lovely arch, a window in the lady chapel, and a doorway in the vestry, are also 700 years old. The tower, with a grand and lofty arch, is 15th century, each belfry window being guarded by a pair of heads and the corners by a king and queen, a bishop and a saint. There is a piscina with a head of a careworn 13th century man carved on it, a coffin lid with a cross, a dozen 14th century benches, and a font with a medieval bowl.

The Night Before Bosworth

EARL SHILTON. Almost forgotten are those ancient days when Robert the Hunchback, first Earl of Leicester, built a castle here, or when the officers of another crookback, Richard the Third, slept in the church on the night before Bosworth. The village, more busy now than then, has long ceased to echo to the tramp of Norman retainers or Yorkist soldiery, and industry is here encamped.

The castle on the height from which the Norman baron laid levy is now a grassy mound, and the church among the trees has been made new, keeping only its medieval tower and spire. Inside its walls and chancel roof is gay decorative painting by a 19th century rector and the children of the village. In the wide street close by is a sculptured cenotaph to warriors of our own day, crowned by a figure of Peace.

EASTWELL. Its farms and cottages nestle among the hills of the Wolds where the River Devon has left its springs and become a rill. The church, with its massive pillars, belongs chiefly to the 13th and 15th centuries, but has a rare stone screen of the 14th like a wall with a central doorway and a traceried window on either side; it is one of about 60 medieval stone screens remaining in English churches. The figure of a priest who walked through this stone doorway 600 years ago lies under an arch in the chancel with a chalice sculptured on his breast. The only other relics of his day are the fragments of old stained glass with a golden-haired angel among them. The fine iron lectern, with grapes and roses, is modern.

Proud Smiths

EDMONDTHORPE. It lies near the border of Rutland, blessed by a tranquillity which is rarely disturbed. Its church, mostly 14th century but with a tower a century older, has a lofty 15th century screen with a fine band of foliage above its open tracery. In the south aisle are fashionable monuments to an aristocratic local family of Smiths, one, a great three-decker, covering the east wall. It shows the grave Sir Roger Smith, who died during the Commonwealth, handsome in marble with his two wives reclining on their elbows below him, busts of his son and grandson adorning the sides, and a long inscription tracing his descent from Henry the First.

The Eve of Bosworth Field

ELMESTHORPE. It stepped for a moment on to the stage of history, for King Richard Crookback arrived here one August night in 1485, his company of officers sleeping in the church. On the morrow they rode to Bosworth Field where the king and his cause alike were to perish (the day is done; the dog is dead) and the

Tudor dynasty began. The ivied tower, and the nave of the church where they assembled on that fateful day, have long been in ruins, and only in the chancel do the villagers still kneel.

The Squire of Enderby Hall

ENDERBY. It has lost its Past and grown up with the Age of Industry, developing its quarries, but veteran yews still shade the churchyard, and the church, though made new last century, has still its medieval tower and an arch 700 years old, carved with grotesque heads. The reredos with scenes from the life of Christ, the oak pulpit with figures of Our Lord and John the Baptist, and the font showing Moses in the bulrushes, are all modern.

The most notable memorial is a curious epitaph to Charles Lorraine Smith, the sporting squire of Enderby Hall, which still stands serene in its wooded park. He was a great rider to hounds, a friend of that wayward genius George Morland, and himself a painter of sporting scenes. We are told of him that

> *Here lies the tall Squire of Enderby Hall,*
> *With his bridles, boots, fiddle, brush, colours, and all.*
> *Some liked his scraping, though none of the best,*
> *And all liked the welcome he gave to a guest.*

EVINGTON. It is a pleasant two-mile walk from Leicester to the sycamore avenue shading the approach to the church. The chancel is modern, but the nave and tower have stood seven centuries and the aisles are but a century younger. The north aisle is notable for its lovely windows, one watched over by an old stone figure of St Denis and others with angels and heraldry in their original glass. The 13th century font and the old ironbound chest are still in service.

The churchyard is fringed with graceful limes, and opposite the tower is a grassy mound which may be a link with Roman Britain.

Weaver and Squire

FENNY DRAYTON. Its name alone should make it famous, for it was taken by the forefathers of that Michael Drayton whose place is secure in the temple of English poetry. But it claims more intimately another man whose power and influence are a part of that English faith which many waters cannot quench nor great floods drown, for George Fox the Quaker was born here.

Drayton-in-the-Clay the village was then called, it being hemmed in by marshlands. Christopher Fox the weaver was his father and Mary his mother "came of the stock of martyrs." Righteous Christer, as the villagers called the weaver, took his son to church for baptism and saw his name carefully entered in the records. The precious page, alas, has vanished from the register, but the simple font remains.

The first little church he knew is the chief link with the Quaker in the place of his birth, for his timber-framed cottage, so precious a piece of English history, has been pulled down, and the obelisk near to it, inscribed with his name, is an unsatisfying substitute. The church has been restored, and for the most part looks younger than the stately yews spreading their branches like a canopy over the churchyard wall; but it has a Norman doorway and two interesting monuments.

One is a 16th century altar tomb with engraved figures of Nicholas Purefoy and his wife, their five children, and two angels upholding the family shields. George Purefoy, one of their 17th century descendants and the village squire when Fox was born, has a finer monument showing him lying in his armour with two wives kneeling at a desk above him and six children below. One of his kinsmen was that William Purefoy who signed the death warrant of Charles Stuart.

George Fox's Quest for Peace

CHRISTOPHER FOX'S son George was a grave and thoughtful boy, early noted for his honesty. One day at a fair, on business for his employer, he was invited by two preachers he knew to drink with them, which he did, being thirsty. But when his friends had had one glass of beer each they began clamouring for more to drink healths, and the youth was so shocked that he left them and went home to spend the night thinking. As a result he left his work and family and travelled about the country seeking peace, and calling for help from men of various religious opinions.

One priest suggested that smoking and singing would cure his spiritual troubles; another would have bled him; and a third, who seemed likely to be helpful, was so enraged when George accidentally trod on his flower-bed that the young man gave up all priests in disgust, and presently came to see that he could find God for himself without recourse to church or minister.

In triumphant certainty that God was in every man, and spoke to every man direct, he began preaching, though at times a crowd would gather and he would sit in silence before them for an hour, not speaking until he felt he had a message to give. He became known far and wide as the Man in Leathern Breeches, and was welcomed by many seeking more than the parish church could offer; but his faith drove him to certain conclusions unacceptable to the authorities, civil and religious.

He was imprisoned at Nottingham when he was 24, after he had entered a church (a steeple-house, as he persisted in saying) and denounced the preacher's views. The next year at Derby he bade Justice Bennet tremble at the word of the Lord, and the magistrate retorted by calling Fox and his friends Quakers, a name which became popular for what was officially the Society of Friends. This time Fox's imprisonment was prolonged because he refused to serve in the army, but people came to him in gaol to dispute and to learn. He wrote letters to the judges telling them that it was not Christian to put men to death for stealing cattle or money, and to keep them so long in prison where they learned evil from each other.

After this Fox went north to Lancashire. At Swarthmoor Hall he was received gladly by the wife of Judge Fell, and after her husband's death Margaret Fell married the Quaker and worked and suffered with him. Swarthmoor Hall became a sanctuary for Quakers, and Margaret lived long enough to see an England where they were free to worship in their own way.

Fox won supporters among all classes, in spite of widespread persecution. He was opposed to established churches, to paid ministers, to military service, to capital punishment, and to the taking of oaths, holding that a man should always speak with the same regard for truth. This last principle was sufficient excuse for imprisoning him after the Restoration, when there seemed some hope of religious tolerance, for he could always be called upon by unfriendly magistrates to take the Oath of Allegiance. In all he was imprisoned eight times, and was frequently beaten and stoned by angry crowds, but while he was at liberty he continually travelled and preached, not only in England, but on the Continent and in North America.

He died in London in 1690, a hero who would not compromise with conscience, and whose life and writings are still an inspiration to a mighty host.

FOSTON. It is a secluded hamlet among the quiet fields, with a sprinkling of cottages, an old-world rectory, and an ancient church dwarfed by stately trees.

The church has kept a Norman arcade and a 13th century font, and from its tower arch peer two medieval heads. A coloured 17th century monument shows angels drawing curtains to reveal the figures of Henry Fawnt and his wife; at the back are two small cherubs who appear to represent much more than cherubs usually do, for one, like Atlas, is bearing a heavy globe on his shoulders, and the other, like Youth, has a globe at his feet.

The Saxon Cross

FOXTON. When John of Gaunt was lord of the manor it was Foxton Moor that he knew well, for there he hunted the stag of Charnwood Forest. Foxton Locks were one of the engineering triumphs of the 19th century which made the Grand Junction Canal.

The little hillside church, above the cottages and orchards, owes much to its hunting lord, but, though it bears the marks of our three great building centuries and the bowl of the font is Norman, there were worshippers here centuries earlier, for in the south aisle is a fragment of a Saxon cross at which the preacher stood before Harold fell at Hastings. In the north aisle is a brass engraved with horseshoe and anvil to one who for 27 years, like Longfellow's village blacksmith, rejoiced his heart by singing in the choir.

FRISBY-ON-THE-WREAK. Among its farms is at least one charming white thatched cottage, a medieval church, and an ancient stepped cross ten feet high.

In the base of the tower we see the work of the Norman builders. Eight grotesques look out from the 13th century arcades, and two merry masks grin at the choir. One of the windows has lovely flowing tracery of the 14th century; another has modern figures of the patron saint, Thomas of Canterbury, with those two Leicestershire heroes Wycliffe and Latimer. A window of Faith, Hope, and Charity is in memory of Henry Pearson, parish clerk for 46 years of last century. The choir stalls have some fanciful poppyheads, a pair of monkeys and a pelican among them.

LEICESTERSHIRE

John Smith

FROWLESWORTH. It has rich farms on the hills and green pastures below, a grey church tower rising above red houses, and a charming group of 18th century almshouses ranged with their little chapel round a quadrangle gay with flowers.

One of those John Smiths who have lived and died in thousands was born in this village in 1657, and left it to win fame and fortune as a judge. He never forgot the place from which he came, and he bequeathed this haven for the poor. Nor does his birthplace forget him, for over the porch is his name linked with this couplet by Pope:

Who built this Almshouse neat, but void of state,
Where Age and Want sit smiling at the gate.

The 15th century church has preserved the arcades from an earlier nave and a few fragments of ancient glass with four saints and two angels. The chancel screen is modern, but on either side of the altar are two fine Jacobean monuments, one probably sculptured by Nicholas Stone, with a figure of the handsome Francis Staresmore and 11 children below him, two in cradles. The other has the shrouded figure of his wife with her head on a cushion.

The Colonel on His Horse

GADDESBY. It is the proud possessor of one of the loveliest churches in the county, set up by the Knight Templars six or seven centuries ago, with a graceful 13th century spire soaring grandly above the rich stonework of its 600-year-old aisles, and with one of the surprises of the county indoors—an equestrian statue!

The 14th century chancel, strangely enough, is the least ornamented part of the church, but the aisles are lavishly adorned with lovely pinnacles, graceful flowing window tracery, and richly-moulded doorways. The south aisle has the added beauty of a sculptured frieze below the battlements, canopied niches, and a lovely window like a rounded triangle above its porch.

The interior of the church, though less ornate, has all the dignity that comes from good proportions. One of the clerestory windows has a few fragments of 14th century glass with leaves and flowers; there is a 14th century font with arches and foliage, a Jacobean pew, and some benches on which plain Leicestershire folk sat 500 years ago. On an altar tomb lies a 15th century knight in armour, his feet on a lion, and near him is a stone with graven figures of

73

William Darby in his 15th century armour and his wife in a long belted dress.

But the strangest monument here, also as large as life and dominating the church, is the equestrian statue of Colonel Cheney. Perhaps we may think him not unworthy of so extraordinary a monument, for he had five horses shot under him as he rode into battle at Waterloo. Brought here from the neighbouring hall it shows the gallant soldier with sword uplifted as his horse falls, a panel below showing him preventing a French officer from recapturing one of Napoleon's eagles.

The monument is one of a small group of equestrian statues we have come upon in churches. There are one or two in Westminster Abbey (where a rider is actually at prayer on his horse), and St Paul's has, of course, Wellington on horseback; but in small churches there are only four such monuments in all England—bronze ones in Cornwall and Somerset, a wooden one in Lakeland, and this marble.

Disraeli and the Hall

GARENDON. Here, lying serenely in a park below wooded heights, is an 18th century hall with its roots in Norman England.

Eight centuries ago Robert Crookback, Earl of Leicester, built an abbey here. For four centuries the abbots and their monks held sway, until with the Dissolution the abbey was acquired by the first Earl of Rutland. The estate passed through many other hands, and in 1683 Ambrose Phillips, King's Serjeant to Charles the Second, made this corner of England his own. A later Ambrose Phillips, following the 18th century fashion of copying classical architecture, set up in the grounds a round Temple of Venus and a copy of the Arch of Titus in Rome. They stand here still, imposing but somewhat incongruous monuments in our green countryside.

Another of the family built the fine house Disraeli so much admired. This is how he praised it in his preface to Coningsby:

In a valley not far from the margin of a beautiful river, raised on a lofty and artificial terrace at the base of a range of wooded heights, was a pile of modern building in the finest style of Christian architecture. It was of great extent and richly decorated. Built of a white and glittering stone, it sparkled with its pinnacles in the sunshine as it rose in strong relief against its verdant background.

GARTHORPE. It is a charming village spread out near the River Eye and watched over by a church 700 years old, with a 15th century clerestory and a handsome tower. On the walls are many stone faces that have kept their silent watches through the ages, and in the windows are two saintly figures in roundels of old glass, the work of 14th century craftsmen.

Witnesses of the Past

GLENFIELD. It has two witnesses to the Past, one to the very long ago and one to the days when the great world we know was coming into being.

The modern witness is the entrance to a tunnel, a historic mile of underground England, for it is the tunnel built by George Stephenson for carrying coal from Swannington to Leicester. It was the longest railway tunnel in the land, and from then till now trains have been passing through it unceasingly.

The witness to the long ago is the ruin of the little church which shares the churchyard and the shade of graceful limes with the new-comer of last century. There are two relics of the old in the new, the side of an ancient altar tomb preserved with three figures in a wooden frame, and the figure of a lady of the 15th century in a long-waisted dress; she is leaning wearily against the wall.

The Saxon Princess and the Soldier

GLEN PARVA. It has nothing for us to see, but the traveller passing this way may remember that here a thousand years ago they buried a Saxon princess with all her ornaments. After the thousand years had passed they found her still with her string of beads, three brooches, and two rings.

We do not know who the princess was, but near her was found a rare tumbler made of glass (called a tumbler because it could not stand upright), and not far away was found a soldier with his sword at his side and his spear-head on his shoulder, as he may have stood sentinel at the door of the lady's hall.

Edmund Cartwright and George Crabbe

GOADBY MARWOOD. It stands serene among its shaded ways, high up on the Wolds, with a medieval church by a Jacobean hall where George Villiers, Duke of Buckingham, spent some of his early years preparing for a courtier's life.

The church has a traceried 14th century font, and ancient glass with figures of Christ, the Madonna, John the Baptist, and a bishop. In the south aisle, notable for its window tracery, is an arch carved with foliage in memory of lords of the manor from 1300 to 1680. In the chancel are four ancient seats with carved ends and an old chair with leaves, roses, and a crown.

One of the 19th century rectors of this small church was Edmund Cartwright, the inventor of the first power loom which altered the whole industrial life of Leicestershire, the Midlands, and the North generally. Though he ministered here for six years there is no monument to him, but perhaps it matters little, for Cartwright belonged not to Goadby but to England and to the world. Here he cultivated the rectory glebe, his inquiring mind making farming an experimental calling. It was not profitable, but neither was it expensive, and these were perhaps the happiest years of his life.

Before he left this place, George Crabbe, whose poetic genius unfolded the story of the countryside, came to live close by, and the two men began a friendship which lasted nearly 40 years. In 1785, when Cartwright was leaving Goadby to experiment with his power loom at Doncaster, Crabbe wrote to him from Belvoir Castle:

I am not a little surprised at what you tell me of your enterprise. I have a thousand good wishes for your success, without one idea of your contrivance. Mrs Crabbe has a better conception of your plan, and no less desire that you may accomplish it. I am about my contrivances too, but mine is spinning—spinning flimsy verses.

Though Goadby Marwood little dreamed it, the days of Edmund Cartwright's ministry were its most historic days.

The Painted Wall

GREAT BOWDEN. Market Harborough has almost engulfed it, but the spacious green, with the medieval church looking on, stamps it as a village yet.

The finest antiquity of the church is a wall painting of the Last Judgment. It shows Our Lord seated on a rainbow, with the sun on His right, the moon on His left, and the celestial city below, the Madonna standing near and St Peter pointing the way to the risen dead. Below the saints are fiery jaws into which demons are dragging poor chained souls.

There is an ancient font with a Jacobean cover, and a 14th century brass with two sides engraved, one with a figure of a bearded man and a dog at his feet, the other with an inscription to a 14th century rector, William Wolstanton.

One of the modern windows has a pleasing imitation of 14th century colouring and an unusual subject. It shows Jonathan following David to bid him his last farewell, with a lad carrying the arrows he has shot. In the background a man sowing a ploughed field, two little shepherds and a sheepfold, a squirrel on rocks, and a herd of deer, all help to make up a delightful pastoral scene.

GREAT DALBY. On its patch of green stands the simple cross with the names of its heroes, and round it are the thatched and red roofs of cottages and a lovely old thatched inn. Over the roofs peep the church tower and spire, fitting the grey stones like a nightcap. An odd little church, it has between its medieval tower and its medieval chancel a curious nave of the 17th century. Perhaps we may think ourselves in the hall of a Jacobean manor house as we come into this square chamber, with mullioned windows reaching almost to the roof and old shields set between.

The Boy Astride the Weathercock

GREAT EASTON. It looks across the Welland into Northamptonshire, a tranquil place with some old stone cottages and a cross of memory on its green.

For seven centuries the church has watched over it, though its windows are 200 years younger, and its tower and spire have been made new in living memory. When we called we found a sexton with a special pride in it, for he had rung its bells for 50 years and remembered how as a lad the village blacksmith had set him astride the weathercock when it was being repaired.

There are six small heads of women above the nave arcade, the battered figure of a 14th century priest in the chancel, a richly-panelled Jacobean pulpit, and a moving 18th century inscription to Mary Ireton who " never gave her parents grief but when she died."

The Eve of Naseby

GREAT GLEN. It may have played its tiny part in the Civil War, for an old historian tells of an ancient dwelling here in which Prince Rupert slept the night before Naseby. All that remains of it is a tradition of the dashing prince coming here to rest and riding off in the early morning to share the bitterness of the defeat.

In a churchyard like a garden stands a little granite church into which we come by the Norman doorway, with rare carvings of horses on its capitals. In it is the font at which the village children have been baptised for centuries.

Friend of the Black Prince

GREAT STRETTON. Great in name, it is in itself remote and tiny, yet with a Norman doorway to a little church made new. It has been restored for occasional service, and has kept the traceried font at which Robert de Stretton was baptised many years before he went from here to become chaplain to the Black Prince. He was not a great scholar, but the prince thought little of learning and much of his chaplain, whom he made Bishop of Lichfield. Nor did he forget his birthplace, for before he died he founded a chantry here. Perhaps we may think of him as the only really Great Stretton.

Groby Pool

GROBY. Who wants a quiet picnic on a sunny day, let him come to Groby Pool and have it with the water fowl. It is a pleasant place. One of Leicestershire's ways of saying a thing is impossible has long been to say that you might as well thatch Groby Pool with pancakes. Those who come here to rest and to pray will find a modern church with a slender spire and a chancel with a window making a curious patchwork of rich colour.

It is for those who seek romance and history that Groby holds the richest store. Its story begins with Hugh of Grantmesnil, who came over with the Conqueror and received exceedingly rich favours. Governor of Leicester and Sheriff of the Shire he was made, and of 67 manors he was lord, his Norman castle overawing the county. Groby Castle walls were thrown down in 1176 and nothing remains now but a mound. The manor passed to the Ferrers and then to the Greys, and here Sir John Grey brought his bride Elizabeth Woodville. Sir John was slain at St Albans fighting for the Lancastrians in 1461, and Edward the Fourth made the widowed Elizabeth his queen. It was a tragic union, which brought little happiness to either and much strife to England.

The Literary Squire

GUMLEY. It is perhaps the prettiest village in the county, set amid steep hills and dales, with a footpath leading through a wood to its church and hall.

The church has its roots in the 13th century, but much of it has been made new. Its modern chancel has a finely-carved oak screen, and an angel on each side of the east window. Another window with coloured figures of the Madonna and St George and St Michael in shining armour is in memory of two brothers who sleep in foreign soil that is for ever England. They were Arthur and Geoffrey Smith, grandsons of George Smith, founder of our famous Dictionary of National Biography.

Next to the church is Gumley Hall, a fine 18th century house with a lake and trim lawns where rabbits play. It was built by Joseph Cradock, who was unusual among the Leicestershire squires of his day in having no taste for hunting but a great love for the company of literary men and wits. One of his greatest friends was David Garrick, who during a visit to some private theatricals here playfully offered to play the Ghost to Cradock's Hamlet. Cradock himself had a brief but memorable stage triumph, for he wrote a tragedy which was successfully staged at Covent Garden. It was based on a work by Voltaire, who in acknowledging it wrote:

> *Thanks to your muse, a foreign copper shines,*
> *Turned into gold, and coined in sterling lines.*

Cradock, who had spared no expense on his house and grounds, was finally compelled to sell his lovely home and live more modestly in London, dying in the Strand when he was 84 years old.

HALLATON. It has streets winding up and down the hillside, displaying many charming thatched cottages, and a little green with an old market cross like a cone on steps.

Its church, with a 13th century spire among the best in the county, stands in dignified splendour among fine chestnut trees and cypresses. Its clock enlivens the passing day by playing a tune every third hour, but this is only one of the surprises it holds in store. Built into the wall of its timbered 14th century porch is a Norman tympanum showing St Michael slaying the dragon, with three small figures sheltering behind his shield, and three others with hands uplifted begging him to rescue them. In this porch are two Saxon coffin lids, and the 14th century north aisle, remarkable for its elaborate sculptured stonework, its small turreted spire, and its little vaulted crypt, has another. Within the church are two Norman arches with sculptured capitals, and a font with Norman carvings of heads and evil beings. The 700-year-old chancel has a modern stone screen.

Hallaton Castle, half a mile away, is the name of a well-preserved grassy earthwork whose dry moat was in fact the ditch with which the Ancient Britons reinforced their ramparts. Who were its first defenders it is hard to say, for coins of Tasciovanus, the father of Cunobelin whom Shakespeare presents to us as Cymbeline, have been found here, as well as Roman ones. The Saxons also found the defences valuable, but when origins are sought at Hallaton the choice is bewildering, for even now it has strange yearly festivals, sometimes waxing uncouth—the hare pie scrambling and the bottle-kicking which suggest forgotten pagan customs.

He Would Not be Rich

HARBY. Under a clump of trees on the edge of the village is an old windmill, with a white wooden cap and sails still turning. On the green stands a fragment of the old cross built up anew as a memorial to those "unreturning brave" who went out from these farms and cottages. Through a living screen of trees in the churchyard can be seen a magnificent panorama of the Vale of Belvoir, the green and fertile vale that was their own fair corner of our land.

The ancient church still keeps its traceried 14th century font, but the pulpit and the screen, both with fine carving, are modern.

Here, it is thought, was born that Geoffrey Hardeby who became privy councillor and confessor to Edward the Third, and of whom it was written:

> *He would not let this world his soul bewitch,*
> *Nor be a bishop, lest he should be rich.*

HARSTON. Between the sycamores in its churchyard are seen many distant hills and valleys, and from another vantage point Belvoir Castle appears boldly against the sky.

In the chancel wall of the church is one of those Saxon sculptures of which the county has such a treasury at Breedon Hill, a stone decorated with knotwork, perhaps part of a tomb. The panelled font, with tracery and roses, is almost the only other relic of an ancient past. Among the figures shining in modern glass are the Madonna, two saints, and three archangels.

Groby   The Beautiful Pool

Hallaton   Market Cross   **Sutton Cheney**   Richard's Well

Market Bosworth   Park Street

LEICESTERSHIRE

No Honour in his own Country

HATHERN. It still has its ancient village cross and a 14th century church made new, but keeping its ancient arcaded font as an honoured pensioner. In the clerestory is some beautiful window tracery, and on the wall is a tablet to a 19th century rector who ministered here for 51 years.

From one of its thatched timbered dwellings more than a century ago came the lace-making machine which was to revolutionise the industry and confer new wealth on the Midlands. It was the idea of John Heathcoat, a clever youth of 20 who constructed a machine described by Brunel as one of the most complete mechanical inventions. So complete and so labour-saving was it that when Heathcoat took his machine and his Hathern bride and set up in Loughborough, the Luddites smashed 55 of his frames and threatened also to smash him. He shook Loughborough's dust from his feet, took his frames, his wife, and his determination to Tiverton, and there prospered and died a wealthy man.

The Belcher Dynasty

HEATHER. Its 14th century church stands pleasantly in the shady churchyard looking down on the valley below. It has a fine 17th century monument with kneeling figures of Stephen Everard in cloak and tunic, with his four sons in tunics behind him and his wife and daughters facing him in tight-waisted dresses with ruffs about their necks.

The east window, with its bright figures, pays tribute to a family of rectors who ministered here for more than a century. Paul Belcher was the first, beginning in 1775, when war was breaking out between America and the Mother Country, and serving for 48 years. The Paul Belcher who followed him served a few years till the dawn of the Victorian Era, and then came George Belcher to minister for another 48 years. Evans Belcher kept the family flag flying for 14 years more, and when he passed away in 1898 it was the end of a dynasty that had held sway here for 123 years.

The Trenches of the Civil War

HEMINGTON. It has something we have come upon in Huntingdonshire, the trenches of the Civil War. They are on the slopes above the trees and lanes with the earthwork raised for the attack on Hemington Hall.

It stands with the ivy creeping over its stone walls, its great yews shading its green lawns, its porch covered with roses, and the old stone doorway still here as in the days when the manor house depended on its own fishponds.

The trenches, the fishponds, and the hall have survived the centuries, and with them Time has saved for us one of the loveliest lanes in the county, with cottages set in bowers of trees and roses.

But the old church is no more, for its stone tower, crowned with a spire, looks down on a roofless ruin. After 600 years the little shrine has gone.

The Great Book of Melancholy

HIGHAM-ON-THE-HILL. It stands on a hill near Watling Street, with a Norman tower rising up among much that is new.

In the churchyard sleep three rectors, Fishers by name and fishers of men, who ministered here for over a century, from the days of our wars with Napoleon to the dark days of 1915.

A mile away is the site of Lindley Hall, where two of Leicestershire's great men were born, William Burton the county's historian, and his brother Robert, famous as the author of the Anatomy of Melancholy, which was named by Dr Johnson as the only book that ever took him out of his bed two hours before he meant to get up.

The Burtons were an old family; one of them carried the standard of Henry the Sixth in France. Robert, who was born in 1577, passed to Oxford by way of the free school at Sutton Coldfield and Nuneaton grammar school. He held a vicarage at Oxford, and at Seagrave, but little is known of him outside his university. There his life was passed. "I never travelled but in map or card," he says. But he had a world of his own, peopled by other men's thoughts and sayings, from which he gathered such a collection from all literate peoples and languages, as no man before or since had made.

He was a blend of humour and melancholy, and to ward off his dreaded malady, he wrote a colossal work on the subject: What it is, with all the Kinds, Causes, Symptoms, Prognostics, and Several Cures of it, in Three Partitions, with their Several Sections, Members, Philosophically, Medicinally, Historically Opened and Cut Up.

In no other language is there anything comparable to this vast body of matter, packed with quotations from ancient authors, classical and obscure; sighs and laughter, philosophy and philology, rare vigour, and boisterous beauty.

It first appeared in 1621, and edition followed edition, making a fortune for the publisher. The author's fame was established. The Anatomy is a quarry in which a host of authors have worked. Some of the finest things in Sterne are taken bodily from it. The rhyming introduction to the book inspired Milton's L'Allegro. The book influenced the wits of our Augustan Age, and was beloved of Lamb, Byron, Coleridge, and Dr Johnson. It did not cure Burton's own melancholy, but it has made countless readers happy.

A Town That Shakespeare Knew

HINCKLEY. Shakespeare touched the old marketplace with immortality. "And, Sir, do you mean to stop any of William's wages, about the sack he lost the other day at Hinckley Fair?" asks Davy of Mr Justice Shallow in Henry the Fourth. So we may easily imagine the poet walking along the narrow streets that since have grown so wide and busy, and noting with his perceptive eye the passing throng of drovers, farmers, and serving men. He may have sauntered along Church Walk, where the old timbered houses still lean forward under the bent brows of their thatch as if to listen. We can fancy his sober figure in one of the yards that still hide behind busy commercial streets, and have the same muddle of tiled and gabled roofs that were there in his Elizabethan day.

If it were possible for all the modern growth of railway station, post-office, municipal buildings, hospital, and public library to melt away in dissolving views through the centuries, how should we see Hinckley with Shakespeare's eyes? The Garden of Remembrance of those who went from here to a greater war than Shakespeare knew would vanish, but Castle Hill would remain, though no more then than now would any castle be set upon it. Perhaps, in spite of the legends of a Norman stronghold set there by the Grantesmils and held by John of Gaunt, the only foundation ever there was that of the earthworks raised as a Roman outpost.

The church would not have its tapering spire, for that is not more than a century old, and it would be smaller than the spreading group of transepts, and chapels, porch, and aisles which now make it one of the biggest churches in the county. But the core would be there, the church already old, for its tower and nave were raised three centuries before Shakespeare was born. He would have seen the fine carved roof, and the wooden figures of angels that uplift it. He might have seen the rich old glass of which only fragments now remain, with the head of Henry the Fourth and the meagre company of two monks among them.

He could have gazed upon the fine brass of some unknown 15th century lady in her long dress, and perhaps the ironbound oak chest. But the church has gathered unto itself many new possessions since Shakespeare's day. One is the coloured wall monument with portraits of John Oneby and his wife and five children in their 17th century costumes. More recent acquisitions are the wooden reredos with its figures of Christ and the Twelve, and the elaborate oak screen with St John and Mary, beautifully carved.

Looking down on the pulpit is a painting (by Giordano) of Simeon in the temple with the infant Jesus, the interest of which is less in its painter than in the man who gave it to the church. He was John Nichols, the famous printer and friend of Dr Johnson, who found a wife at Hinckley in 1778, and wrote eight massive volumes of the history of Leicestershire. He founded a printing business which gave a great number of important books to the world, and was carried on by his son and his grandson. His History of Leicestershire, which he regarded as his monument, lost him £5000, but he completed it for his honour's sake. No adversity could overcome him. His works were burned down and his stock of books destroyed, but he went ahead, and his shop in Red Lion Court drew a great literary circle round him. His 17 volumes of literary anecdotes and biographies of the 18th century have become a standard work.

Among the buildings of Hinckley now growing venerable is St Peter's Priory, which was built in 1824 as a college for Dominican students. In its chapel is the ancient font from the parish church, and a number of fine paintings. On its walls it has also some fine wood carvings, illustrating the last hours of Our Lord.

HOBY. It is set on a twisting lane close to the River Wreak, with a church bearing in its tower and spire and window tracery the honest workmanship of the 13th and 14th centuries.

It has some ancient benches with old carved ends and new ones to match, and some linenfold panelling from its medieval screen. At the base of the modern screen are paintings of the Disciples, while on the other side six angels look towards the east. Angels indeed seem to be everywhere about its chancel. Eight little ones are painted on the panels of the altar, and three wooden angels with red and white wings guard the east window. The wooden reredos has painted panels showing Our Lord in Majesty with another company of angels and our four patron saints at the sides.

Marble tablets record the faithful service of two men, each of whom ministered here for over half a century. The first was Henry Browne, rector for 55 years from 1783, the second Gilbert Beresford, rector for 54 years in the 19th century. A yew in the churchyard has for company the stump of an ancient cross.

The Grumbling Vicar

HORNINGHOLD. It is sheltered in a valley with sycamores, chestnuts, and holly gathered about its 13th century church, a slender spire rising among them graceful as a poplar. A Norman doorway with a lamb, a dove, a lion, and demons on its capitals leads into the church, where the oldest relics are a plain 13th century font, bench-ends carved by medieval craftsmen, and grand oak beams in the roof.

Humphrey Michel, one of the strangest men who ever took holy orders, was vicar here for nearly half a century. As late as 1702 he was still crying out against "the murderers of King Charles the martyr," and he kept a diary full of quaint grumbles. On January 22, 1709, he noted that "It was such a cold freezing winter that I was forced to preach but once a fortnight, sometimes for fear I should starve myself and my hearers." In September, when the weather was right, his servant was wrong: "Mary Ellis I would not hire again because she is a heathen in point of knowledge. Very idle in her way of work, has spoiled several vessels of wood, pewter, and brass, and lost my door key."

To the last day of his life the vicar was grumbling about Horninghold, and when he died in 1722 he elected to be buried at Blaston, a mile or two away.

HOSE. It lies with its red and white cottages in the Vale of Belvoir. Its church, with a lofty clerestory built in Shakespeare's century, has an ancient font resting on roughly carved birds with outspread wings, and an oak reredos with four scenes of the last days of Christ painted in the panels.

HOUGHTON-ON-THE-HILL. It has a matchless situation on the great escarpment of the county, above the Plain of England. The medieval church, with a great spire visible for miles, has an ancient font with curious faces on the bowl. The east window is a memorial to James Colman who ministered here for nearly half of last century. The peace memorial is an oak reredos with the Saviour of mankind standing with arms outstretched, a crown in either hand, a soldier and a sailor kneeling at His feet.

HUGGLESCOTE. It lies in the shadow of the wooded slopes of Bardon Hill, with the River Sence running by. Its fine modern church has a central tower and a richly coloured east window with Christ in Majesty. In the hamlet of Donington-le-Heath close by there is, behind a wall at the top of the street, a small house which has been almost as it is for about 700 years, oblong with two storeys and small projecting wings. It is William de See's house, now a farm, and has a cottage with it that has kept it company through the centuries. There is a fine old oak at the cross-roads.

Three Generations

HUMBERSTONE. The buses from Leicester come past its church and almost to the high ridge where lies the block of granite called the Humber Stone. So does the new come out to meet the old. The stone, which has survived many other legendary names and superstitions, was probably left by the glaciers in our Ice Age.

Most of the church was made new last century, and only its tower and spire are medieval. Below the battlements on one side are rough sculptures of Peter and Paul, and above some of the windows are symbols of the Evangelists. The chancel is adorned with modern carving in wood and stone, and there is an alabaster altar tomb with the graven figure of Richard Hotoft in armour, with sword and dagger at his side and a dog at his feet, on guard since 1451. John Dudley, one of the 19th century vicars of this church, was here 62 years, succeeding his father, John Dudley, who was here 35 years, and his grandfather, Paul Dudley, whose service spanned 54 years, so that three generations of this one family attended to the spiritual welfare of this village for 151 years.

Honest George Ashby

HUNGERTON. Three fine old houses and a medieval church give it the distinction and dignity that go hand in hand with antiquity. The church, coming chiefly from the 13th and 14th centuries, has a Norman font with a roughly carved figure of the holy lamb, some 15th century woodwork in its screen, and chancel panelling fashioned from cedars planted here in the 17th century. In a niche on the porch is a small figure of Christ.

On a hill about a mile away is Quenby Hall, 120 feet long and finely proportioned. Three rows of stone mullioned windows are set in the red brick, and its beautiful doorway, with six-sided tower rising like a gatehouse above it, and its beautifully spaced windows make it one of the finest examples of Jacobean architecture in the county. Its iron gates are in Leicester Museum. For 400 years it was the home of the Ashbys, one of whom, Honest George Ashby, a planter, was a friend of John Evelyn the diarist. It was he who planted the nine fine cedars in front of the house whose timber was later to enrich the church.

In the neighbourhood are two other halls, Ingarsby and Baggrave, with older histories and interest. Ingarsby Hall, partly Gothic, has stables which were a chapel before the Reformation, and preserves a copy of the bed on which Cardinal Wolsey died. In its grounds and those of Baggrave (home of the Burnaby family from Tudor days) have been found not only the spears and shields of Saxon warriors, but burial places and fortified earthworks of those who dwelt in Leicestershire long before Saxons set foot here.

Silver-Tongued Smith

HUSBANDS BOSWORTH. On the churchyard wall in the shadow of a 14th century tower stands a Cross of Memory; in the rebuilt church two swords lie buried, and one of them we may devoutly hope was a sword which helped to bring everlasting peace.

One is that of John Shenton, Captain of Cavalry in the Royalist Army, who fought at Naseby; the other belonged to Austin Shenton, captain in His Majesty's Corps of Engineers, who fought in Flanders and died in the last months of the Great War. John Shenton was buried a few miles away at Barwell, his descendant Austin Shenton at Amiens, but both their names are here inscribed on a monument, on which hangs the younger soldier's Military Cross.

There are other names which make this village memorable. In the year 1588 when the Armada was on its way to England and defeat, the most popular preacher in the land was a Husbands Bosworth man. His name was Henry Smith, known throughout the land as Silver-tongued Smith. When he became lecturer at St Clement Danes, all London was drawn by his reputation and flocked to hear him, fluent, eloquent, and of prodigious memory. He was the fashionable preacher of his day, but at the height of his fame his health failed and he returned here to die and here he was buried.

Another man of perhaps more enduring fame was its rector John Duport, who as one of the makers of the Authorised Version of the Bible shared in the loveliest translation in our literature.

It is sad to reflect that while the piety and eloquence of these two men was still vividly remembered the village surrendered itself to a stupid belief in witchcraft which produced a cruel act of injustice. One morning in 1616 no fewer than nine women were executed as witches because some poor epileptic boy had become subject to fits. The boy's affliction continued after this massacre and six more unhappy women were accused of provoking the fits, sentenced to death, but fortunately reprieved. It is a chapter of hideous cruelty in the tragic story of witchcraft.

IBSTOCK. It is a mining village with a dignified 14th century church finely reflected in the passing stream, an avenue of beeches marching in leafy procession to its porch.

Archbishop Laud was rector of this church for nine years, but it is doubtful if he was ever here, for it was one of many preferments showered upon him. But if he ever held Communion here he must have passed through the fine 14th century doorway with its scroll of foliage and have seen the plain font which is sometimes believed to have been his gift. An ironbound oak chest has been here since 1699, half a century after the archbishop, like his king, had fallen a victim to the executioner's axe.

ILLSTON-ON-THE-HILL. It is a pleasant climb from the shady avenue of sycamores to its cottages and hilltop church. Most of its antiquity is lost, but the church still keeps its plain old font, and hidden by its modern organ are two interesting 17th century monuments. One shows John Needham kneeling with his wife, three sons and three daughters with them, all labelled; the other shows Edward Needham and his wife stationed on either side of a Death's head.

LEICESTERSHIRE

Tom Moore's Happy Days

KEGWORTH. Industry has laid a heavy hand on it, and its houses are huddled together. But in more leisured days 600 years ago it found time to set up a most graceful church and adorn it with works of beauty. The nave roof has a medieval choir of 14 men and women, all carved in wood, playing musical instruments or bearing shields, and the chancel roof is supported by ten angels of stone. There is a panelled 14th century font, and some fragments of beautiful glass with figures full of life and vigour, though just as old. In one fragment is Christ's betrayal; in another the descent from the Cross; others have golden-haired angels and figures of Sebastian and Augustine.

A tale told of the church is that the spire was once repaired by a steeplejack named Wootton, who celebrated the end of his labours by sitting on the top and playing a tune on a horn, while the villagers gazed up in awe at the music-maker on his perilous perch.

In the days before the factories came to make Kegworth busy, Thomas Moore lived here with his young wife Bessie, and in those two happy years he wrote some of his Irish Melodies. His house, the Cedars, with its bay window and red wooden porch, still stands in the Loughborough road. This was the small place where the poet worked so contentedly with his muse while Bessie ran wild about the garden, and it was here that their daughter Anastasia was born. She was Tom Moore's favourite, and her death from consumption when she was only 16 was a blow from which he hardly recovered. "Such is the end of so many years of fondness and hope," he wrote. "Nothing is now left but the dream that we shall see our pure child again in a world more worthy of her."

More than a generation after Thomas Moore left Kegworth there was born here, in a tinker's house which still stands facing the church, a man who gave his life to the poor. He was Sir John Kirk, who joined with Lord Shaftesbury in building up the great work of the Ragged Schools, which had been started early last century and are now the charge of the Shaftesbury Society. The name of John Kirk became known all over England wherever people were interested in the welfare of poor children.

For more than fifty years he spent himself for poor children. He saved thousands of boys and girls from miserable lives and made them good citizens. He helped Lord Shaftesbury in the days when

THE KING'S ENGLAND

that great man was pleading in a callous Parliament for ragged
children in the street, and he carried on Lord Shaftesbury's work.
He was associated with fifty movements for social welfare. A
newspaper once wrote of him by a slip as St John Kirk, and it was
not far wrong, for those who knew him best, the staff he worked
with, put on his grave a wreath with the words "There was a man
sent from God whose name was John" and Harold Begbie wrote
of him at his jubilee:

What's kept your heart so lightsome? What kept you young, John Kirk?
Faith in the one Great Father, and good clean slogging work.

A Village Roll of Fame

KIBWORTH. It bestrides the main road between Leicester and
Market Harborough with a dignity of ancient standing, for here
the manors of Kibworth Beauchamp and Kibworth Harcourt unite.

Kibworth Beauchamp was longed owned by the Beauchamps, Earls
of Warwick, and the Harcourt family held the other manor until 1270
when it passed to Walter de Merton, and thence to the college he had
founded at Oxford. These were the great names of Kibworth long ago,
but names of not so proud a lineage have added since to its renown.

One of Kibworth's handsome veterans is a windmill with four
sails almost sweeping the ground, another is the big church standing
boldly on the hill amid a clump of trees, an avenue of limes leading
through the churchyard to its south porch, where the patron saint
Wilfred sits in a niche. Save for its modern pinnacled tower, the
church belongs chiefly to the 14th century; the nave with its lofty
arches on either side being impressive in its medieval simplicity.
There is a beautifully carved old screen finely restored, and close to
it a modern pulpit with canopied figures of the Four Evangelists.

The plain old font recalls a fighting parson, for it is the successor
of one thrown out by John Yaxley, who became parson here after
serving in Cromwell's army. A strong man for the Puritans was
John, but he suffered for his opinions after the Restoration, when in
one of his sermons he was indiscreet enough to suggest that "hell
was broke loose" in the land. Not long afterwards some of the
new soldiery came and threw him out of his rectory, dragged his
wife from her bed, shot at her when she would have returned to save
a grandchild from its cradle, and blinded her for the rest of her life.
John Yaxley never entered rectory or church again and he died a
prisoner in Smithfield.

90

On the wall of the church is a tablet to Louis Powell Williams, a surgeon who died in 1771. It proclaims him "the first that introduced into practice inoculation without preparation in this kingdom," but it can only be that he was some daring practitioner who adopted against smallpox the measures advocated by Lady Mary Wortley Montagu before Jenner superseded inoculation by vaccination.

Other names less obscure shine in the annals of Kibworth. There was John Jennings, who succeeded his father as independent minister and founded a Nonconformist academy here early in the 18th century. There was the hymn-writer Philip Doddridge, who came to this academy as a pupil when he was 17 and was afterwards a teacher there. That this was one of the happiest periods of his life is proved by one of his letters. "One day passeth away after another," he wrote, "and I only know that it passeth pleasantly for me. As for the world about me, I have very little concern with it. I live almost like a tortoise shut up in a shell, almost always in the same town, the same house, the same chamber, yet I live the life of a prince, not indeed in the pomp of greatness but the pride of liberty."

He preached to a small congregation in the chapel here, but all the world was one day to hear of him, for his book, The Rise and Progress of Religion in the Soul, was circulated in ten languages, and his hymns have had a longer life than his book and are still sung in church and chapel.

The first of Dr Doddridge's pupils at Kibworth was a young Scot named John Aikin who afterwards became his assistant and whose son John and daughter Letitia were both born here. The younger John Aikin was a prominent physician, a writer of genius, and a friend of many famous people, but his sister Letitia, better known as Mrs Barbauld, has a firmer claim to immortality. Some of the lines she wrote are as haunting a requiem as could be inscribed on any memorial:

> *Life ! We've been long together,*
> *Through pleasant and through cloudy weather.*
> *Tis hard to part when friends are dear,*
> *Perhaps twill cost a sigh, a tear.*
> *Then steal away, give little warning;*
> *Choose thine own time ;*
> *Say not Good-Night, but in some brighter clime*
> *Bid me Good-Morning.*

Her first book of poems, which she reluctantly published when she was 30, at once gave her a literary reputation. A year later she married a Nonconformist minister, Rochmont Barbauld, and went with him to Palgrave, Suffolk, where, in addition to his pastorate they conducted a brilliant little school. After a year of continental travel they settled in London, where the husband died insane in 1808, leaving her grief-stricken but unbroken.

Admired and loved by the literary spirits of the age, she edited a fine series of English Novelists, and wrote a poem, Eighteen Hundred and Eleven, which, in a mood of deep despondency over affairs in Europe, contained a prophecy that on some future day a traveller from the Antipodes will, from a broken arch of Blackfriars Bridge, contemplate the ruins of St Paul's. This and her familiar lines on Life have served to keep her name alive, for it was this phrase that inspired Macaulay's famous picture of a New Zealander viewing a ruined St Paul's from a broken arch of London Bridge.

KILBY. Its church standing aloof in a field is screened by tall lime trees. Its east window of three narrow lancets has small panels of the Nativity, Crucifixion, and Ascension, paying a tribute to a 19th century rector, Henry Kebble, during whose ministry of 54 years the church was rebuilt.

KIRBY BELLARS. It is for the most part a tranquil place, gathered about a lane that turns from the Melton Mowbray highway and soon becomes a shaded grassy track leading to the church. A spire with heads sculptured about its base rises in splendid dignity above a vaulted tower, combining with the wide chancel arch, the graceful nave arcade of the 13th century, and the 14th century windows, in presenting a picture of fine proportions and impressive harmony.

From its early days the church has preserved a few fragments of 14th century glass, a traceried 15th century screen, and a canopied monument of Roger Beler, a 14th century lord of the manor. He rests under a canopy in the aisle, a lion sculptured on his armour and another at his feet, and his wife is with him wearing a veiled headdress and long mantle, and with two playful dogs at her feet.

In the churchyard is the stump of an ancient cross about which the men of the village would gather to talk over the news and rumours of the day.

LEICESTERSHIRE
The Ruined Castle

KIRBY MUXLOE. It has a 700-year-old church, beautifully
kept but with little to show save the fine churchyard view
across wooded hill and dale. It is to seek the 15th century castle
that the traveller turns his steps across a field.

The castle was built by Lord Hastings when, as Grand Chamberlain of Edward the Fourth, he stood at the summit of his prosperity
and power and the Norman castle at Donington did not suffice
him, nor the one he raised at Ashby-de-la-Zouch. This, at Kirby
Muxloe, has survived the others, and now belongs to all who visit
it, for it was given to the nation in 1912 and is cared for by the
Office of Works. The wide moat, with its flotillas of moorhens and
ducks, is fed by a stream of the Soar. The way across it is by a new
bridge raised on the supports of the old oak bridge.

It leads to the stone doorway of the gatehouse in the noble front
of red brick which centuries have mellowed, though they have taken
toll of the upper storeys. At the four corners of the gatehouse are
ruins of the turrets which were its bastions, their basement floors
below the level of the water in the moat. On the right is the great
square west tower, the best preserved of all the castle buildings.
Behind the great façade little remains save the ruined walls of the
quadrangle, with daisies growing on the lawn.

In this ruin may be discerned the symbol of the fate of him who
owned it. When his royal master died, the power of Lord Hastings
fell from him like a garment. He was summoned to a council in the
Tower by Richard Crookback, wading through blood to the throne,
who fiercely denounced him as a traitor, and with no more than that
had him thrust out of the room and beheaded. In Richard the Third
Shakespeare puts the scene into these words—Richard crying out:

Off with his head ! Now by St Paul I swear
I will not dine until I see the same.

Lord Byron's Wife

KIRKBY MALLORY. About the grave old church, with a battlemented tower rather the worse for wear, and the hall of white
stone built in Queen Anne's reign but scarcely looking it, dwells the
shadow of a melancholy story.

To this hall in January 1816 (barely 12 months after her marriage)
came the unhappy wife of Lord Byron, on a visit to her father who

had inherited the estate. Here she wrote the letter to the poet declaring that she would never return to him, and here, many years later, almost within sight of the hall, she raised a monument to her only child, Ada Augusta. The monument is a decorated arch enclosing in its recess an inscription from which we learn that the child of a tragic union was Countess of Lovelace. She does not lie here, but with her father at Hucknall Torkard, in Notts.

Her mother, Anne Milbanke, was Baroness Wentworth in her own right and something of the family history is reflected in the monuments of the 14th century church. After the Mallorys had gone, bequeathing only their name to Kirkby, the Noels came in Queen Elizabeth's day, and Anne was the granddaughter of the Edward Noel who became Viscount Wentworth. There is a wall monument to him with a tree sculptured between two urns. An 18th century monument of the generation before him has two heads of Sir Clobery Noel and his wife.

On the north of the chancel is an elaborate monument with the figure of Sir William Noel who died in 1675; he is wearing plate armour with a wig flowing above it, and holding a helmet. A later monument was to Thomas Noel, who is buried at Gibraltar; above the inscription to his memory an anchor, gun, pistol, sword, and dagger are carved in stone. Earlier than any of the Noels was Richard Dilke, who died in 1594, and on whose engraved stone we see him as a bearded man in a long coat, standing between his two wives with their 13 children. Still farther back is the 15th century priest whose portrait is engraved in stone by the tower wall. The old font has disappeared and is replaced by a modern one on which a charming angel holds a small scalloped bowl. It is one of the beautiful fonts made in our own time.

There are finely carved Jacobean choir-stalls and an ancient ironbound chest.

On the Desford road is an enclosure in a wood with trenches and what passes for a dry moat, bearing the name of Kirby Moats, and by tradition Saxon.

The Prophets

KNAPTOFT. Amid its fields and pastures, spreading away on every hand, is part of the central watershed of England. Within the parish boundaries three streams rise, one flowing into the Welland and so Eastward to the Wash, the second to the Soar, a tributary of the Midland Trent which winds Northward to the Humber, and the third to the Swift, a tributary of the Avon, and so joining the Western seas.

The country all about the sources of these waters was once more prosperous, its people more numerous, and the church here a valuable living. John Moore, one of the rectors in Queen Elizabeth's time, a reformer with less honour in his country than he merited, wrote a pamphlet protesting against the Enclosure movement and foretelling the depopulation of the countryside if tillage should be turned into pasture. His son, another John Moore, who also became rector of Knaptoft, felt as strongly about it as his worthy father and published a pamphlet wherein enclosure "such as doth unpeople towns and uncorn fields, is arraigned, convicted, and condemned."

Both father and son might see the fulfilment of their prophecies could they return and gaze on the remains of the church where once they preached, for nothing is left but broken walls dwarfed by haystacks. Yet amid these forlorn fragments of the past services are sometimes held, prayer still rises, and hymns of praise resound.

In William Cobbett's Day

KNIGHTON. Perhaps we may remember what a traveller wrote of it as he went round England long ago:

"Standing on the hill at Knighton, you see the three ancient and lofty and beautiful spires rising up at Leicester; you see the river winding down through a broad bed of the most beautiful meadows that man ever set his eyes on; you see the bright verdure covering all the land, even to the tops of the hills with here and there a little wood, as if made by God to give variety to the beauty of the scene, for the river brings the coal in abundance for fuel, and the earth gives the brick and the tile in abundance."

Thus wrote William Cobbett when he came here on his Midland tour a hundred years ago, but since his day Leicester has come nearer and nearer until the modest village has grown into the town.

The church, chiefly of the 13th and 15th centuries, has been well cared for. The tower enshrines a statue of Mary Magdalene, and above it soars a handsome spire. The plain font is centuries old, the fine oak pulpit is modern, and above them is the richest treasure of the church, a grand 14th century roof beautifully carved.

Knighton has a modern church of St John the Baptist, its great roof crowned by a dainty lead spirelet adorned with quaint winged gargoyles. The striking interior has walls of yellow brick and stone pillars with rich capitals. Round tie-beams support the fine simple roof, the altar front has kings and bishops in niches, and the elaborate reredos has a carved and coloured Crucifixion scene, gleaming with gold. The unusual feature here is the arched gallery round three sides, carried on a double row of pillars and arches which lend a cloister-like effect to the aisles.

KNIPTON. It is a smiling village, set in the valley where the River Devon sparkles and the waters of the Knipton reservoir run for a mile among the wooded hills.

Its houses and thatched cottages are gathered in ordered neatness about the green, with its Cross of Memory designed by the Duchess of Rutland. The massive tower of the 700-year-old church stands like a guardian close at hand.

In the wall of the porch is a 16th century stone with the raised figure of a child, John Eyre, wearing a stole over his swaddling clothes. Here also is a curious alabaster panel which was perhaps once part of a reredos, showing a man on horseback, with some sunflowers in the background. Inside are two old carved choir-stalls. The east window has the Nativity, the Baptism, the Crucifixion, and the Ascension, in memory of an 18th century rector, George Turner. Matthew William Peters, who was rector here for a brief spell a few years later, was also a Royal Academician. He was for some time curator of the paintings of Belvoir Castle, and there is treasured one of his own, showing Lady Elizabeth Manners and her brother with a bird in a cage, the girl in the same frock she wore when Reynolds painted her portrait.

Colonel Cole Was a Brave Old Soul

LAUGHTON. It is a pretty hamlet seemingly remote from all the world, with a little church hallowed by seven centuries. One of its memorials is to a 17th century lord of the manor who went from this peaceful spot to take a fuller share in his country's affairs. It is a monument of slate to Colonel William Cole, who served four kings. He was in the losing army of Charles the First, aided the return of Charles the Second, served James the Second till he ran away, and at the last joined the forces of William of Orange. At the time of his death in 1698 when he was 85 he was (we may be sure) a soldier still.

Ibstock   The 14th Century Church

Kirby Muxloe   The 15th Century Castle

Loughborough   **The Carillon Tower**

A Dull Cromwell

LAUNDE ABBEY. Launde is said to signify a green level space between two woods, and there could be no better description for the secluded valley through which the River Chater runs near the Rutland border, and on which the Elizabethan house of gables and mullioned windows has sunned itself for more than 300 years. It is a simple manor house, deriving its name from a Norman priory founded here in 1125.

All that remains of the ancient abbey are two arches (Norman and 13th century) leading to the chapel. It was a place of wealthy revenues, and when Henry the Eighth set Thomas Cromwell to the congenial task of dissolving the monasteries the ruthless destroyer cast covetous eyes on it. "Item to remember," he wrote in his diary before the Suppression, "myself for Launde." But it did not long remain with him, for his master, even more ruthless than he, sent him to the block, but by a curious twist of fortune his son Gregory, dull without ambition, was allowed to enjoy the property his father had usurped. Perhaps his dullness saved him, or probably it was his wife, sister to Jane Seymour, Henry's third queen.

The manor house was built partly from the stones of the priory, and its 15th century chapel is attached to it. Here is a stone wall monument to Gregory Cromwell, who must be deemed fortunate in being allowed to die here in bed. It has his arms with two unicorns holding up a shield, small boys above and cherubs below. The chapel roof is of oak borne up by stone figures of the Evangelists and men, women, and angels, but the great treasure here is the 15th century glass, with three big figures and 24 small ones, the Madonna, a queen, and angels and saints among them.

The Wonderful Town of Yesterday and Today

LEICESTER. It stands in the middle of our great Midland county, and it would be hard to think of a city more truly English.

In these difficult days of the world its people are as prosperous as any community in the British Empire, busy at a thousand trades and making boots and shoes for all over the world, a hundred thousand pairs for every full working day. There is not an article of clothing from head to foot which is not made in Leicester. Its factories hum from morning till night. Its municipality is as pro-

H   97

gressive as any in the land. Its great roads go everywhere like spokes on a wheel. It is easily accessible to all our waterways. It has one of the best airports, with a run of a thousand yards in any direction and a beacon seen for nearly fifty miles. It is building up one of the finest health centres in the kingdom. It has given its people a thousand acres of open spaces, has made a lovely park from a swamp round the grave of Cardinal Wolsey, has over a hundred cricket pitches, over a hundred hockey and tennis grounds, and over sixty football grounds. Its cleansing department sweeps 200 miles of streets a week and calls at 70,000 houses, and its own municipal works make paving stones by the thousands from the rubbish they collect. This marvellous municipality has 2000 acres of land on which it produces fine stock and keeps 8000 fowls, supplying 6000 eggs a week to the hospitals and institutions.

Leicester has not been content to put all its eggs in one basket. With nearly a hundred industries of its own it claims to engage in a thousand, though two (footwear and hosiery) are by far the most important, for in these it is the biggest centre in the world. Its work-rate is well above the average and its death-rate well below the average for our industrial towns. Leicester, with all its trades, is free from the smoke pall of industry. It owns its public services, and was wise enough to tackle its housing problems before they became acute. It adopted electricity in the first year of this century, and the service has never been a liability on the rates. Over a hundred million units are sold a year at very cheap rates.

The city has grown in just over a century from a population of 25,000, and has now 17,000 acres and 260 miles of streets. Too many big cities are handicapped by narrow streets, but Leicester has boldly pulled down a whole frontage in the heart of the city, and made a roadway 85 feet wide for over half a mile, sweeping away hundreds of houses and lining the road with fine new buildings, one notable block being the police headquarters. Charles Street has cost a million pounds, but has given dignity and spaciousness to the route from London to the North; it is a piece of national public service. The city, in fact, is a good transport centre with seven great roads radiating from it, three big railway stations at its hub, and the Grand Union Canal linking it with the Trent and the Thames. It was from Leicester that Thomas Cook organised his first excursion (to Loughborough!) and it is right therefore that the city should set a good example to the world in the business of getting about.

It will be seen that Leicester is carrying on in the spirit that has made it so long one of England's great towns, for a great town it has surely been. Chaucer is said to have lived here and to have been married here. Here was born an idea that has transformed the life of the world, the idea of Parliament. Here walked out of history and out of life that bloodstained king whose death made way for the Tudor Age with all its glory. Here is a Roman spectacle as fine as any that can be found in the heart of a city. Leicester is guarding this Roman heritage as nobly as can be; there is no industrial city in England with a finer appreciation of the past than this.

Everywhere its benefactors are remembered, in stone and glass, in pictures and in fine schools. Four of them stand round the richly decorated Clock Tower in the hub of the city. Simon de Montfort, the Frenchman who became the Father of our English Freedom, was a very good friend to Leicester and is here in armour. William Wyggeston, on the Clock Tower in gown and ruff, was the 15th century wool merchant who founded a hospital for the aged poor, now housed in fine new buildings on the Fosse Road, while some of the city's finest new schools are also proud to bear the name of Wyggeston. Alderman Gabriel Newton, with curled hair and lace cuffs, was the 18th century innkeeper whose Green Coat School for poor boys has become another important education centre. Sir Thomas White, whom we see fingering his jewelled chain, was a kindly 16th century merchant who left a fund for helping young men in business. In Walford Place is the marble statue of John Biggs wearing his frock coat; he was three times mayor, and three times M P for Leicester before he died in 1871. Robert Hall, standing in the green De Montfort Square, wearing a cut-away coat and a cape with a fur collar, was the famous preacher of the Harvey Lane Baptist Chapel from soon after Trafalgar till long after Waterloo. In pretty gardens by the river, looking down a short street to the site of the Roman Forum, is the fine bronze statue of the Duke of Rutland, brought here from the marketplace where it was set up in 1852 to mark his jubilee as lord-lieutenant of the county.

Leicester's municipal buildings are attractive, built of brick and stone and draped with flowers. Its factories and warehouses, flaunting names known the world over, have a pleasant dress; one near a bridge across the river is crowned by a statue of Liberty. But factories and shops and public buildings are not by any means all there is to see in this great and busy city, though we may pass through it in our cars a thousand times without realising how much lies hidden. It has few spectacular sights, but a step this way or that will bring us to thrilling peeps of the interest of the past or the beauty of the present. The roads to the suburbs stretch out like arms holding trees, charming houses, and gardens; but we have to find the wide green spaces, the park made from a swamp where stood that religious house in which Cardinal Wolsey said a long farewell to all his greatness. Here is a little medieval Guildhall, there are the remains of the great baronial hall from which Simon de Montfort ruled over England. One of the string of old churches has something left of Roman and Saxon days.

So long is it since Leicester began its march through history; its oldest story is even now unfolding in an open space in the heart of the town, which will tell for all time the date of its birth. On this historic spot is being revealed as we write something of the grandeur that was Rome.

The City Fathers have decided in their great wisdom that here, where the Roman Forum stood, no other building shall come. The Forum itself is a recent discovery, though it has long been known that the Romans were here, for the Jewry Wall has never been lost to sight. Two sides of the Forum have already been uncovered, and in the course of the digging the Jewry Wall, one of the most massive fragments our Roman builders left behind them, was revealed as part of the west wall of the basilica of the Forum. Here the Governor administered justice. Here Roman laws were passed on to the British people. Here public meetings were held and business was transacted, for this was the town hall, and, we may believe, the first Corn Exchange. Here the races and customs of two people were mingled, and conquered and conquerors all but merged into one. Whatever the rigour of the Roman rule, the people were far better off under it than in the rude village above the marshes of the Soar. Traces of this prehistoric village have been found by the excavators of the Forum. The ancient village was the first step in Leicester's history.

Before the Romans went another great change came to Leicester, for three bishoprics were founded, and in the third century the

Lutterworth
Unknown 15 c. man

Bottesford : Henry de Codington

Lutterworth
Unknown 15 c. Lady

Lutterworth
John Fielding

Stapleford
Geoffrey and Joyce Sherard

Lutterworth
Joan Fielding

LEICESTERSHIRE PEOPLE ENGRAVED ON BRASS

Roman town hall was probably used for Christian worship. Then, in the Dark Ages, the walls of Roman Ratae (as they called the city) fell into ruin, though the Jewry Wall, still 75 feet long and 20 feet high, remained. The Saxons came, renaming the place Leircestre, the fortress of what was then the River Leire, and the Forum for a second time regained its old faith. The Jewry Wall may then have become the west end of a new church, and centuries later the Saxon church of St Nicholas, a few feet away from the wall, was built largely of the Roman stones and tiles lying about in the ruins of the Forum.

When the Normans came to take possession of Leicester, bringing their law and customs with them, they set up a system of 24 jurors to settle disputes. It is thought these jurors may have held court by the ancient place of justice, the Wall by the buried Forum, and if so it may be that the Jewry Wall should be Jury Wall. It is a pleasanter explanation than that the wall marked the boundary of the Jewish ghetto. However this may be, this new open space, between a modern railway and a road of great antiquity, is for ever now a place as sacred as the Roman hearth. Here history has set its mark; here is the birthplace of the prosperity of the empire's most prosperous city, its government, its religion.

The pick and spade of the excavator have been used to good purpose, and very early in the digging Miss Kathleen Kenyon, directing operations, was able to prove that a mass of Roman masonry long believed to be part of a gateway is actually part of a basilica of noble proportions. Not only has the basilica been placed on the map, but the Forum too, with its courtyard surrounded by shops and other characteristic features of a rich Roman town. This prosperous British town of our own time was clearly prosperous in the days of Caesar.

It has long been known that Leicester was an important place in Roman times. It stands on the junction of the Fosse Way and the Via Devana, and was the Ratae Coritanorum which was captured and fortified in the year 52. It grew to be one of the richest towns in Roman Britain, as its mosaic pavements prove.

The noble Jewry Wall by the church of St Nicholas is, however, the chief witness of its prosperity. Its alternate courses of stone and brick extend for 70 feet. Until now the deep arched recesses, edged with tiles, on the east face of the wall could not be definitely explained, though many believed they were openings in the western gateway of the city. The clearing away of a next-door factory has given the opportunity of solving this mystery, and the wall is found to go down much deeper than was suspected. The openings were windows of a basilica, not doorways. The wall has now been exposed ten feet below the street level, and it reminds the beholder of that great fragment of a basilica standing in a field at Wroxeter. Behind the wall a courtyard 175 feet wide has been opened up, and round it are revealed porticoes opening into shops. The fragments of columns which are a feature of the church of St Nicholas are a mystery no longer, for they are evidently part of a colonnade. A lofty arch which stood at the head of a flight of steps from the Forum into the basilica is here in the wall for us to see. Just outside the Forum part of a cobbled street has been uncovered, showing the deep ruts made by chariot wheels. Deep trenching has proved that buildings older than the Forum stood on the site, coins and pottery of the first century having been found. Among the discoveries are Roman tiles showing the clear impress of a dog's feet, but most remarkable of all is the discovery, in the open space in the centre of the Forum, of a Roman bath. It is odd that the bath (one of the biggest remaining in the country) should have been found, for it was while preparing for a public bath that these great discoveries were made. For a time it seemed as if the ruins must be sacrificed for a bath, but the wisdom of the Corporation overcame all difficulties and now Leicester, losing a modern bath on this great site, has in its place the biggest ancient bath in England.

Only a step or two from the Forum, in the cellar of a shop in St Nicholas Street, is a beautiful tessellated pavement like a coloured carpet, its leafy border enclosing nine medallions patterned with roses, cubes, and a peacock. Here, too, is a smaller and simpler pavement, with quite a modern touch in its formal design of two colours. Another charming pavement remains where it was found over a century ago, now under the Great Central Railway. About eight yards square, this also has a leafy border and nine medallions, divided by bands of plaiting and patterned with flowers and intricate formal designs. The entrance to it is in Blackfriars Street. For threepence anyone can see these relics of bygone days, and there are other fragments of pavements in the City Museum.

A small museum with no great age in it, but with a human story, is hidden away in Harvey Lane, a stone's throw from the Forum.

It is the simple brick house where William Carey lived, where there came to him the great vision of Christian India. Nottingham has unhappily destroyed the little chapel in which he preached the famous sermon from which foreign missions sprang into being, but Leicester keeps his home. Here is his chair by the fire, his precious bookcase, the work-table with the cobbler's tools he used while teaching his pupils, and the bedroom where he rose early in those hard years before he sailed for India in 1793. His favourite motto is on the wall:

Expect great things—Attempt great things.

This cobbler from Northants did both. Rich in memories of one of the noblest spirits of the Motherland is this little house, facing the graveyard of the chapel where Carey used to preach.

In a house which stood hereabouts two other immortal spirits used to stay when they came preaching here, John Wesley and John Bunyan. As a lad Bunyan took part in the Siege of Leicester, and tradition says it was the death of a sentinel who had taken his place that brought about his conversion. It was a short siege, and a successful one for the king, though the victory was shortlived. It began on May 28, 1645, when Sir Marmaduke Langdale, with a force of Royalist cavalry, invested the town on the east side; it ended by the morning of the last day in May, after the townsfolk had begged for quarter and the garrison at the Newarke had been forced to surrender when threatened with attack on all sides.

It was an uneven struggle, for though months earlier an embankment had been built as a line of defence outside the walls, and the fortifications of the Newarke had been strengthened, the forces in the town were only 2000. The Prince attacked the town from the Raw Dykes (the ancient line of earthworks on the meadowland) which were conveniently ready for his cannon. On the morning of the 30th Rupert offered pardon for immediate surrender, but the Council of War in the Mayor's Parlour of the Guildhall delayed too long with their reply, and in the afternoon a breach was made in the wall of the Newarke and at midnight the town was stormed on all sides. Fierce fighting took place by the High Cross before the people finally gave in and the garrison had surrendered.

The thousand acres of green spaces in which we may rest and find tranquillity in Leicester are sometimes small oases in the city streets and sometimes vast stretches of parkland; but one of them

Leicester   **Arch of Remembrance**

Leicester   **Cardinal Wolsey's Memorial**

Leicester   The Old Guildhall

Leicester   Scenes in Abbey Park

Leicester   Foundations of the Abbey

Leicester   Cavendish House Ruins on the Abbey Site

is unique among the rural ways of cities. It was a walk for the Romans, but it is called New Walk today, and in it no wheels may run. It is only nine paces wide and is shaded by trees, and it leads us from the heart of the city to the 70 acres of Victoria Park. It brings us, that is to say, from the very hub of the stress and strain of Leicester's life to the garden of rest where are remembered Leicester's 12,000 men who gave their lives for freedom. Here in Victoria Park is the De Montfort Hall, with a colonnaded front and gardens that are a riot of colour; the hall seats 3500 and is much used for conferences, having a splendid organ and being famed among musicians for its acoustics.

But the impressive monument here is Leicestershire's Arch of Remembrance. Designed by Sir Edwin Lutyens (who also designed the beautiful iron gates opening to the park, the gift of Sir Jonathan North in memory of his wife), this magnificent arch is Leicester's most impressive sight, standing out boldly against the sky as it rises from a lawn at the end of an avenue of flowers and trees. There are few of our peace memorials more finely conceived or more nobly placed; it is superb. For the best view of it we must come to the gates on University Road, within reach of which is a group of fine things to see.

Past the park and the shady Mayor's Walk are the grey buildings of University College, and the Wyggeston Boys School of brick and stone, very striking with its wide flight of steps. The Memorial Arch looks down on the Wyggeston Girls School, one of the finest schools of the century, set in a green belt of playing fields and gardens. Opposite the school is what we think must be the most magnificent fire station in the land, showing what can be done to make a necessary institution a beautiful place. An air of peace and quiet pervades these lawns and gardens, with their trim hedges. The houses of the firemen are gathered in pleasing fashion round the central station, where all can see the shining engines, and high above all rises a tall grey watchtower looking over the city. It crowns this admirable colony of firemen and their homes, a witness to the good government and the fine imagination of this industrial capital of the Midlands.

In the lowly haunts north of the city Leicester has done another beautiful thing which many other towns might copy with great advantage to themselves and to the nation. Here, by the Abbey grounds and the River Soar, a swamp has been turned into a glorious park through which we may either walk or ride. There are lawns and flower beds, rockeries and glasshouses, a boating lake winding in and out, and a shady avenue by the river, which is spanned by a charming new bridge of five arches. By the bridge is a tree-shaded island where the river makes a weir. There are flowering shrubs and many trees, and only the chimney-tops peeping over them here and there remind us of the workaday world.

Joining the Abbey Park is the great space known as the Abbey grounds, a place of fame to which all travellers come, for here is the memory of one of the haunting figures of our Tudor Age and one of the pathetic scenes in Shakespeare. Here came the fallen Wolsey who did not shed a tear in all his misery; here he lies.

Founded and richly endowed by Robert Bossu 800 years ago, the Abbey of St Mary de Pratis was one of the wealthiest in the land. Kings and princes were sumptuously entertained in its hall, and the grandeur of its church was famous even then. Now there is only its plan for us to see, outlined in walling, which has been built a foot high. We walk the length of the church in 120 strides, its width in half as many, and as we picture the long nave with its avenue of arches (added by Petronilla, wife of the third Earl of Leicester) we recall the story of how she made a rope of her hair for hanging the holy lamp. It is on the site of the lady chapel that Wolsey is believed to have been laid. If anything more than memory were needed to stir the heart in this poignant place, the simple but beautiful stone is enough; it is adorned with his arms, his name, the date of his death, and the infinitely pathetic words which Shakespeare has made to live:

Give him a little earth for charity.

All his life he had loved pomp and power. He had been arrogant, proud, and overbearing, but he had done great things for England, and at the end, broken, disgraced, and sick at heart, he came slowly to the door of Leicester Abbey, so weak that he was nearly falling from his mule. In his heart was fear of the axe on Tower Hill, for he was on his way to answer a charge of treason, and as the monks came out with torches blazing in the darkness he raised his hand to bless them. "Father Abbot," said he in a low voice, "I am come to leave my bones with you."

History has few pictures more tragic than this. Stripped of his pageantry and shorn of his power, he came to this place as a tired old man, and here in not many days he died among the quiet meadows. It is significant that when his spirit fled they found that this proud man was wearing a hair shirt next to his skin.

As the cardinal passed into the shadows the abbey's day was nearly done. The gateway through which he passed is gone. All that is left of the abbey itself is some of the old stone walling round the grounds, and part of the fine red brick wall built in those great days by Abbot John Penny, the letters of his name still recognisable here and there in the patterning of dark brick. The ruined house (built by one of the Cavendish family from the stones of the abbey) stands serene and impressive in the garden, reached by a later stone gateway flanked by low towers. After the town's surrender in the siege of 1645, Charles Stuart stayed at the house for two days, when he levied the sum of £2000 on the inhabitants as punishment for their rebellion. It was after he left that his royalist soldiers set fire to the house, leaving it the ruin we see today.

A lovely spot for the heart of a city is the Municipal Square, with lawns and flowers, and a stone fountain where water comes from the lion's mouth. Here is the memorial to the soldiers of the South African War, with bronze statuary, symbolising Grief and War and the Angel of Peace. Here, too, are the seemingly countless names of Leicestershire's heroes of the Great War, whose lasting memorial is the Arch of Remembrance in Victoria Park.

Looking on to the garden is the City Hall, an attractive 19th century building of brick and stone with a clock tower, its window boxes gay with flowers. Portraits of mayors adorn the walls, and in the windows of the hall are men whom Leicester delights to honour. There is Sir Thomas White who founded a loan for young men "of fair name and fame"; Bishop Latimer (who was born near Leicester) with a background of the Corn Exchange and the Guildhall; Henry the Third (in chain armour) who extended the charters and privileges of the town; William Wyggeston, in red cap and blue hose, carrying a model of the hospital he founded; and Gabriel Newton with a long curly wig, one hand on the head of a Green Coat boy. In the strong room of this City Hall is a collection of old charters and documents going back to the time of Henry the First, and including rolls with a quaint reference to the battles of Crecy and Agincourt, a licence giving permission to John Bunyan to preach here in 1672, and a letter from Prince Rupert demanding £2000 from the mayor.

Another fine block of brick and stone, now the Municipal Reference Library, is by the City Hall. Among the pictures and engravings on the staircase is one of remarkable Mary Linwood, who copied pictures in needlework. Here, too, is Lady Jane Grey, seen in an interview with Roger Ascham. Not far away are the County Assembly Rooms, their fine classical exterior enriched with reliefs and figures of the Comic and Lyric Muses, the work of John Rossi R A. The stone building was designed by a native of Leicester who became a noted London architect, John Johnson, and, though originally meant for an hotel, it has long been used for social functions. The fine cream and gold ballroom has a moulded ceiling painted with allegorical figures, and among the portraits here is that of Sir Henry St John Halford, a famous rifleman and first chairman of Leicestershire County Council; it is by John Collier. The rooms are largely used by the Council, and here the Assize Judge stays. Near the County Rooms is Leicester's oldest theatre, the Theatre Royal built in 1836, proud to remember on its stage such actors as Charles Kean, Barry Sullivan, Henry Irving, J. L. Toole, Sir John Hare, and Kate Vaughan.

Right in the city, yet just withdrawn from the rushing traffic, is the open market covering about four acres, with room for 600 stalls. Some of the stalls creep into the ground floor of a fine building crowned by a clock tower, which began as a market hall in 1850, and was given a new storey to serve as the Corn Exchange. There is a Venetian touch in the pallisaded bridge of steps leading to this floor, but the attractiveness of the building is spoiled by the stalls.

Set in the seclusion of the New Walk through the city is the museum and art gallery, housed in an imposing classical building with a colonnaded front designed by Joseph Hansom (famous for his hansom cab) as a school for Nonconformists. An ornate clustered column near the entrance is in memory of James Francis Hollings, master of the school and mayor of the town. In the middle of last century the school was bought by the Corporation to house the collection presented to the town by the Literary and Philosophical Society, which became the nucleus of the town museum. Here we may now read the story of Leicester from Celtic to modern days. We can study its geology, its natural history, and its botany in this bright place, which has space enough for us to walk about it with delight, and is not overpowering with useless possessions.

There are examples of Stone and Bronze Age weapons, parts of columns and capitals and carved stones from Roman Leicester, a Roman lead coffin and a Roman milestone with its inscription still plain, discovered by Dr Percy (of the famous Reliques) in time to save it from being used as a garden roller. There are Roman ornaments, shoes, and bone pins; and fragments of Roman pavements showing a woman with a stag and Cupid shooting his arrow. Near the skeleton of a Saxon lady are the brooches and necklace found with her. With his chair and his cudgel are the clothes of Daniel Lambert, England's heaviest man, who was born in 1773 and went on growing till he wore the biggest waistcoat in the world and weighed over 50 stones. Here also are iron gates that were once the glory of Quenby Hall.

A very fine giraffe looks down from the head of the staircase leading to the collection of birds, butterflies, and insects. In the aquarium are live snakes, lizards, and chameleons; fishes swimming; and living flowers of field and hedgerow. Among the paintings is one of Orlando pursuing the Fata Morgana, given by the artist, G. F. Watts, and among the pieces of sculpture are works by Epstein. Down among the mummies from ancient Egypt is a charming lily pool, and here are the old hand-frames and the knitting machinery that have helped Leicester to grow rich. We see them as their workers saw them, admirably staged. At one end are reproductions of two old cottages with the hand-frame knitter at work with his pattern strips, his winding wheel, and his cops; and the cobbler surrounded by old boots and shoes, his fiddle on the wall, his canary at the window. The knitter and the cobbler are startlingly lifelike as we come upon their cottages with the cobbled pavement in front and the boot-scrapers at the door. At the other end of this downstairs room is another great surprise, a hansom cab, and we remember that it was this that made Joseph Hansom famous, and not his architecture, though he built the building we are in, now housing his cab as a curiosity of his inventive age.

One of the grim and curious things we came upon in this museum was the shrunken head of a Red Indian, the features perfectly preserved and in perfect proportion, though the whole is no bigger than a small clenched hand. It is one of the most remarkable exhibits we have seen among the millions in our collections. Used as trophies by victors in battle, the heads of their victims were shrunk by the insertion of hot stones into the skull, the skull being removed after the head had been boiled in a decoction of herbs, with the result that the head and the features are reduced to a perfect miniature.

One of the most interesting possessions here is a collection of pictures in worsted embroidery, the work of Mary Linwood, who sleeps in St Margaret's church. Of exquisite stitchery, and remarkable in their resemblance to paintings, they hold us astonished as we stand before them. One shows a ferocious lion emerging from a cave. Lightning is flashing in a picture of a woodman and his dog in a storm. There is a lovely Pieta and a charming Nativity with cherubs.

A rare treasure of the museum is a collection of painted glass, believed to be early 16th century, which for over 300 years enriched the window of a house in Highcross Street, perhaps belonging to a wealthy merchant. In the 28 pieces of glass (most of them roundels, all black and gold) are over a hundred small figures—the rose and dragon of Leicester, figures of saints, Christ in Glory, and delightful scenes telling the story of Mary from her birth, with two angels rocking her cradle at the foot of a four-poster bed. A quaint roundel in this group is a Resurrection, with three soldiers asleep and the fourth looking dozily on. The Seven Sacraments and six of the Works of Mercy complete a collection of glass which is perhaps unique as a set of religious pictures for the window of a house.

In all Leicester, with its great variety of historic appeal, is nothing more charming than the Guildhall, now a museum where we are free to come and go. It is only a step from the street to its peaceful courtyard, where we breathe the atmosphere of bygone days whose story is writ in the buildings enclosing it on three sides. Delightful it is when the quiet is broken by the deep tones of the organ of the neighbouring cathedral church, the only thing to disturb the old-world picture of timbered walls and many gables being the house on the south side of the courtyard. This was built last century when the police headquarters were established in the Guildhall. In the cells of that time, lit up by the pressing of a button so that we can see the wooden beds and pillows, are old village stocks and the formidable gibbet irons.

LEICESTERSHIRE

The Great Hall on the north side of the quadrangle is divided by timber arches into five bays. The three eastern bays were the original hall, built late in the 14th century as a meeting place for the members of the Corpus Christi Guild; the other two bays were added in the 15th century, when the hall was used by the mayor and his brethren. The gallery belonged to the old Exchange, and was set up a century ago. After being acquired by the Corporation in 1563, the hall was used as town hall till the new municipal buildings of 1876. In this historic little place a great feast was held to celebrate the defeat of the Armada. Remains of a boar's head (a relic of this or some other feast) are under a floor-stone in the hall, on the spot where they were discovered some time ago; we may raise a stone and look at it. Travelling players used the hall in Elizabethan days, and it is thrilling to think that, as many people believe, Shakespeare himself may have acted here.

The mayor's parlour, adjoining the great hall, was built early in the reign of Henry the Seventh, a lofty room turned into a three-storeyed building in the time of Elizabeth. Its sumptuous chimney-piece, its fine oak panelling, and the mayor's chair (in which Prince Rupert sat after the capture of Leicester by the Royalists) are all 300 years old. Set in the leaded panes is old painted glass of black and gold, showing the Tudor rose, the Prince of Wales feathers, a chalice, and some of the seasons.

Over the Parlour is the Grand Jury Room used now by the Leicestershire Archaeological Society. Here are fine old carved and inlaid chairs (one a charming high arm-chair for a child), a cedar-wood chest of 1621 delicately chased, and a little medieval oak chest with delicate ironwork in scrolls, and two rings for lifting. Here too is the portrait of Robert Herrick, a mayor of Elizabeth's day, one of the family to which the poet Herrick belonged. He wears a black gown and a skull cap, white beard and ruffs, and in a corner of the picture are faintly seen the curious lines:

> *His picture whom you here see*
> *When he is dead and rotten*
> *By this shall he remembered be*
> *When he should be forgotten.*

Reached by a modern staircase are the Recorder's bedroom and the Library, the Library a big room much altered since it was built. After being for a time in the belfry of St Martin's church, the collection of books was brought here in 1632. Now there are about 900, including the Codex Leicestriensis, a Treacle Bible, and a Latin Grammar with Ben Jonson's autograph.

A fine relic seen outside is a lead cistern of 1773 in the courtyard, embossed with griffins, mermaids, a sea-horse, and a bird with a woman's head.

If Leicester Castle were still in existence it would be one of England's most historic places, but in spite of its charming setting, with the riverside gardens on one hand and its spacious green on the other, the castle is at first sight Leicester's most disappointing thing. Anything less like a castle than its 18th century brick exterior would be difficult to imagine.

The earliest stone castle here is believed to have been that built by Robert de Beaumont, who became the first Earl of Leicester in 1107, though from Saxon times there is said to have been a castle of sorts close by, on the mound which was levelled in the 18th century for a bowling green. The chief feature of de Beaumont's new castle was its great hall; the rest of it was enlarged in the 14th century by the Dukes of Lancaster, who made the castle a home; but of their range of buildings nothing is left save some stones in old houses near by.

The outline, and some of the original walling of the Norman hall, is incorporated in the building we see, the interior of which is sadly spoiled by its adaptation for Assize Courts, for this Castle Hall became a Hall of Justice in 1274, and has continued to be so used. There are two Norman windows with zigzag round their splay at one end of the hall, and a slightly pointed arch with zigzag in a room upstairs. The finest relic of the past is the original roof of braced beams, still spanning the whole length of the building, though it was repaired some years ago. A Norman capital of one of the oak pillars supporting the roof in the old days is still to be seen. A great gate-leg table and a high-backed armchair are 17th century.

An outside flight of steps leads down to what may have been cellars or a dungeon, with original stone walls, and a stone roof repaired in the time of Charles the Second. As we think of it as a dungeon, we are reminded that the lovely Castle Green was once a place of execution, where a score of skulls have been dug up.

Momentous scenes this place has witnessed, for here has been written Leicester's medieval story, with something of England's

Leicester   Norman Castle and St Mary de Castro

Leicester   City Hall and Municipal Square

Leicester   Museum and Art Gallery

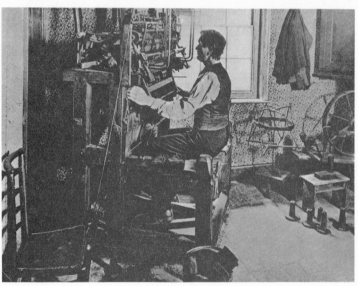

Leicester   Old Stocking-Frame in the Museum

struggle to be free. Here in 1201 was held a meeting of the barons, the first of many which had their climax in Magna Carta. Strange and of widely varied natures were the hosts and guests who gathered under its roof, and none played a greater part in national affairs than Simon de Montfort, the last Norman Earl of Leicester, French champion of English liberty. In 1264 he entertained here Henry the Third and his son, with a great company of nobles. Before long the king and the prince were his captives, taken in battle at Lewes, and Simon was summoning our first regular Parliament. Parliament met at the castle in 1349.

Restless as he was, the powerful John of Gaunt, spent much of his time at the castle, where he is said to have had Wycliffe and Chaucer as his guests. It was when his son Henry of Bolingbroke came to the throne that the castle began to decay. So much was it dilapidated by 1485 that it is said to have been unfit to house the most sinister figure in the pageant of Leicester's great men, Richard Crookback, whose passing ended one of the shameful chapters in England's story. It is said that he came hurriedly to the town one evening in August, and stayed at an inn, dreaming strange dreams. It was the fine old Blue Boar Inn in Highcross Street, demolished a century ago; over the shops is a tablet telling of the king's visit. After a night or two here he rode out at sunrise on a white horse, his crown on his head, and with him an army believed to have been the biggest ever seen in England. Splendidly he went forth, and proudly he crossed the old Bow Bridge, but on Bosworth Field he would have given his kingdom for a horse. There he lost his crown and his life, and his dead body, head downward and with a halter round the neck, was brought back over the bridge. So came true the story which tells how, as he rode forth in the morning, his spur struck a stone on the bridge, and a wise woman foretold how before long his head should be dashed against the same stone. After being exposed for two days, his body was buried in the church of the Grey Friars, but on the dissolution of the church in the following century his coffin was unearthed by the mob and his bones flung into the river. Later they were recovered, and buried near Bow Bridge, which was newly-built last century and bears a tablet telling us that here was Richard's resting-place.

During the Siege of Leicester, when Prince Rupert successfully attacked the town, the castle is said to have been used by both sides. On the south wall of the churchyard of St Mary de Castro is part of the old wall which bounded the castle defences, and in it are holes said to have been pierced for cannon. The 18th century made the castle largely what it is today, and now that it belongs to the city everyone hopes that before long it may be restored more nearly to its old self. Its companions across the green are the old church of the castle and the charming timbered and gabled Castle House and Tudor gateway through which we come and go. The gatehouse was built as a guard room to protect the castle then disused, and of the more imposing building it replaced there are still remains in the stone base.

A few yards away is a ruined stone gateway which once had a turreted house above it. It comes from late in the 14th century, and was the fortified southern gateway leading from the precincts of the castle to what was called the Newarke, whose site is preserved in that name today. This New Work was a walled enclosure of about four acres, outside the castle boundaries, in which stood the beautiful collegiate church of St Mary, and its almshouses and infirmary, Trinity Hospital. These were founded by Henry, Earl of Lancaster and Leicester, who recovered the family wealth and honour after they had been forfeited on the attainder of his brother. After an eventful career, the earl spent his last years at Leicester Castle, which he greatly improved, and in his day the great hall was the scene of much splendour and rejoicing. He built a church in the Newarke as a private chapel and mausoleum, and there he was laid to rest in 1345. The fame of the church grew till it brought pilgrims from afar, but it fell under the heavy hand of Henry the Eighth and was finally destroyed.

Like his father, the first Duke of Lancaster was a great benefactor to the town, where he was known as the Good Duke. He enriched his father's church and doubled the foundation of Trinity Hospital, which still stands as a monument to father and son. Rebuilt in the time of George the Third and again in 1901, it is now a spacious place, half brick and half stone, with the arches of an old corridor blocked in an outside wall. Wide corridors run from the central hall, where there is still a bay and a half of an old stone arcade, and here are treasured an enormous cauldron in which porridge is said to have been cooked as far back as 1331, and an Elizabethan nutmeg-grater ten inches long. The charming little chapel for the

40 old folk is chiefly original and carefully restored. The trussed roof is part of the old woodwork, some of which came from the chapel of Wyggeston's Hospital by St Martin's church. There is traceried stallwork, and linenfold panelling on the sanctuary walls and in the pulpit. The altar rails and some patterned tiles are old. Lovely glass from Christopher Whall's workshops, in the four lancets of the east window, shows angels with outspread wings in purple and red. On a tomb in the chancel lies the figure of a woman with praying hands, wearing a graceful gown and flowing headdress, two angels at her head. It is thought that she may be Mary Bohun, mother of Henry of Agincourt, who was buried in the church of the Newarke in 1394.

The other original relic of the Newarke is the lofty stone gateway at its eastern side, with three arches, a vaulted roof, and square-headed windows adorned with faces. Its use as a storehouse for arms has given it the name of the Magazine Gateway.

At the corner leading from the Newarke to the Turret Gateway of the castle stands the three-storeyed stone house built in 1512 by William Wyggeston for the two priests who served the chantry he founded in the church of St Mary, where he was laid to rest. Over the doorway are his arms. Next to it is an old gabled and embattled house, now a school, its fine iron gates enriched with scrolls. Opposite Trinity Hospital stands another old chantry house. An impressive modern block in the Newarke houses are the Colleges of Art and Technology, standing on the site of the lost church, of which there were till recently two arches still seen in the basement. Owing to alterations they have been removed, but are to be set up again as near as possible to their original place.

Leicester has become a cathedral city in our time, and has a fine group of churches, one of which, St Martin's, is believed to be on the site of a Saxon church mentioned in Domesday Book. It has nothing to show of Saxon days, but evidence of a still older building is given by portions of two Roman pillars now in the City Museum, discovered in the original foundations.

The Norman church had the shape of a cross, but all that is left of it is a fragment of moulding and some of the walling in the majestic 19th century central tower, with a graceful spire soaring to 200 feet. The 13th and 14th centuries gave it aisles; the 15th saw the chancel made new; the restorations of last century and this have made it worthy of its high place, for St Martin's was hallowed as the cathedral church ten years ago.

A path where the churchyard has been transformed into a lovely garden, gay with roses and sheltered by rows of trees, leads to the splendid south porch with floral bosses in its vaulted roof. Its gabled front is flanked by pinnacled buttresses enriched with saints in niches, two of them Dunstan with pincers and Katharine with her wheel. Among the figures in the fine row of niches over the entrance arch are Guthlac, Hugh with a swan, and Wycliffe. The porch is in memory of the Vaughans, father and three sons, who were vicars here for nearly 80 years. One was headmaster of Harrow School and Master of the Temple; one was Master of Wyggeston's Hospital and a great friend to what is now named the Vaughan Working Men's College, a brick building with a stone portico in the place called Holy Bones, with the words over the doorway, *Sirs, Ye are Brethren.*

In the south doorway, with its five shafts on each side, hangs a beautiful door enriched with tracery, vines, and a band of roses and lions. There is an old west door, and another, framed by a medieval doorway, is in the fine north porch, which has a rare 15th century oak vaulted roof with fan tracery. The porch itself is new, built of brick and richly carved timber, its plaster-work ornamented with sprays of roses.

Graceful old arches and rich woodwork (most of it modern) make the interior charming. The nave arcades are 13th century. Carved heads and beautiful angels with wings outspread adorn the old roof of the chancel; the modern hammerbeam roof of the nave has angels with Passion symbols. The arches between the chancel and the chapels are 15th century. The splendid chancel screen has linenfold panels, arches enriched with vine and grape, and a traceried loft. Rich screenwork encloses the chapels. In pleasing contrast are the plainer stalls, bearing the names of men famous in the town and church, among them Archbishop Laud, Bishop Latimer (who preached in St Martin's), William Carey, John Wycliffe, Simon de Montfort, and Handel.

The Bishop's Throne is splendid. About 16 feet high, it reaches almost to the roof, its diminishing tiers adorned with tracery and pinnacles. It has carvings of St Martin and the Good Shepherd, both under canopies, and on the desk in front are poppyheads of birds pecking berries, and an angel with keys between two lizard-like creatures with beaked heads. One of two old carved chairs in the sanctuary has a vigorous scene of a horse falling over a fence, the huntsman in the ditch with only his legs showing, hounds rushing, and pigs scattering in alarm.

Four golden angels guard the altar. The sanctuary panelling and the reredos, and the lovely Whall glass in the east window, are all in memory of those who fell in the Great War. Shining in red, blue, green, and gold, the window shows Christ in Glory, St George and St Michael, Joan of Arc with a banner and a child, and the Descent from the Cross, Mary having with her children orphaned by the war. Two gilded candlesticks are in memory of Betty Stevenson, who won the Croix de Guerre and died for England while serving as an ambulance driver. The names of 11,000 of the fallen of city and county are in a book on a cabinet round which are kneeling golden figures of a soldier, a sailor, a nurse, an airman, and a smith with his hammer.

Some of the panelling in the north aisle chapel is to Charles Hancock, who was organist here for 52 years till 1927; the organ case is another memorial to him. A painting of the Resurrection by Vanni (about 1563) hangs on a wall, and in a south chapel are lovely sedilia and a piscina. St Martin's fine peal of 13 bells rang out for the first time on Coronation Day in 1937, ten of them recast, three of them new. A fine medieval chest about nine feet long has iron bands, three locks, and an iron ring.

The Four Evangelists with St Martin and St Dunstan stand as a row of golden figures (all with symbols under their feet) in niches in the modern reredos of St Dunstan's chapel. A richly gilded Crucifixion is the reredos in St Katharine's chapel, and above it is beautiful glass from the Powell workshops. It shows in delicate colours Katharine with wheel and sword, Francis preaching to the birds (there are two ducks peeping behind a stork), and Robert Herrick, the poet, sitting among the flowers by an old church, a book on his knee and a pen in his hand. This has long been known as the Herrick Chapel, and has been charmingly restored by Sir Charles Nicholson at the cost of a Herrick family in the United States. Lining the walls of the chapel is a striking collection of slate memorial stones of 17th century Herricks, with a fine display of their armorial bearings in colour. An alabaster stone has an inscription to John Herrick of 1589.

The Herricks came to Leicester in the 16th century, having acquired the grounds of the Grey Friars Priory founded by Simon de Montfort. It stood south of St Martin's, and after the dissolution of the monasteries some of the material of the priory church was used to repair St Martin's, to which the Herricks were always good friends. Nicholas Herrick was the father of the poet. Sir William, who lies in this church, was a London goldsmith and banker to Queen Elizabeth; it was his son Henry who migrated to America. In the old Guildhall hangs the portrait of Robert Herrick (mayor of Leicester and M P in Elizabeth's day). Dean Swift's mother, Abigail, who sleeps in St Martin's, was one of the Leicester Herricks. An elaborate wall monument in the north aisle has busts of John Whatton and his two wives, one of whom was a Herrick. John was esquire to the body of Charles Stuart and High Sheriff of Leicestershire. He died in 1656.

A bronze plaque in St Katharine's chapel has the bust of Frank Theodore Woods, Bishop of Peterborough and Winchester, founder and first Dean of this cathedral. His inscription describes him as Pastor, Prophet, and Pilgrim.

Of great interest to Leicester folk is a monument in the chancel with busts of the two wives of Gabriel Newton and his only son George who died at 18. But for this early death Alderman Newton might never have founded his Green Coat School.

At the west end of the south aisle is the beautiful screened chapel of St George, restored and dedicated to the men of the Leicester Regiment who gave their lives for peace. Their names are in a book of memory. There are also memorials of men who died in the South African, Burmese, and Afghan wars, and flags of the regiment hang round the walls. In the old days the chapel was connected with the Guild of St George, founded in the 15th century in honour of the saint, of whom a lifesize figure on horseback stood near the altar. This took a prominent part on the feast day of the Guild, when, in the event known as the Riding of St George, the figure was carried through the streets, complete with the dragon.

The children are not forgotten in this church of many interests. In their delightful corner are tiny arm-chairs and a table, and an oak statue of the Good Shepherd. Alice in Wonderland was among their collection of books when we called.

LEICESTERSHIRE

Neighbours old and new, associations with famous folk and great events, has St Martin's. There is only a passage-way between it and the Guildhall. The Wyggeston Hospital which stood close by was pulled down to make way for the Wyggeston Boys School (now used for that of Gabriel Newton's foundation). A tablet marks the spot at the corner of the churchyard, where the hospital's little chapel stood.

Standing where the Saxons built their church on the site of the Roman Basilica, of which the west wall (the Jewry Wall) is only a few feet away, St Nicholas bears striking witness to the story of the years. The early church was built with material from the Roman ruins, and in the walls of the church we see are stones from Roman, Saxon, Norman, and medieval England. One of the fragments of Roman pillars in the churchyard is about seven feet high. Courses of herringbone masonry formed by Roman tiles are round the massive central tower, which the Normans built and enriched with arcading, some of this showing the pointed arch which ushered in a new era of building. There is Saxon masonry in the west wall of the church, and over a Norman arcade of two bays are two small deeply-splayed Saxon windows, their round heads formed by double rows of Roman tiles.

The Normans adorned the south doorway with zigzag and nail-head. The timber framework of its sheltering porch is 13th century, and there is a fine wooden head on a roof beam. The spacious interior is spoiled by a great brick arch which replaced a Norman arcade over a century ago. The tower rests on four Norman arches. Between the chancel and the south chapel is a 13th century arcade, its two arches resting on a charming middle pillar with detached and banded shafts.

Old relics are three sedilia and a piscina, fragments of the medieval roof of the nave, a lancet window west of the porch, and a big 15th century stone niche in the north aisle, brought here from the lost chapel of William Wyggeston's Hospital. The medieval clerestory is restored. The best window picture shows Simeon with the Holy Child. Of our own day is a Flanders cross from the grave of one of two brothers who died for peace within a week of each other.

The neat little street east of the church (Holy Bones) keeps green another memory of the past, for here long ago were found many bones of sacrificed animals.

Standing proudly on a little rise, its splendid spire soaring above the historic spot where some of our first parliaments were held, is the church of St Mary de Castro, the church of the castle and of the Earls of Leicester. St Mary's long story is one of much change and some disaster. After Hugh de Grantmesnil had been given the greater part of Leicester by the Conqueror, he rebuilt the Saxon church, and of his simple place of nave and sanctuary there are still some remains. It was Robert de Beaumont (Earl of Leicester in 1107) who rebuilt church and castle on a grander scale. During the time John of Gaunt was Earl of Leicester Wycliffe may often have preached in this church, and story says that Chaucer was married here, he, like Wycliffe, being under the duke's patronage. It was here that a five-year-old king was knighted in 1426, afterwards riding on horseback down the church and into the castle yard, scattering money among the people.

The church fell into neglect as the centuries passed away, but today, though its much-needed restoration is by no means completed, it is a fine place eloquent with age. The slender crocketed spire comes from the end of the 14th century, but has been much repaired. The tower with its leafy pinnacles and a belfry adorned with lancet arcading was begun in the 13th century, when it stood apart from the rest of the church. Now its fine old arches (resting on clustered shafts with faces peeping between the capitals) are enclosed at the west end of a great south aisle like another nave. The story of this aisle reminds us of a curious arrangement in the church in days gone by, for St Mary's is two churches in one. The aisle was built 700 years ago to serve as the parish church, and the two were divided by screens between the piers. Till 1400 it was a usual thing for services to be conducted simultaneously at the two altars.

The two western bays of the south arcade are 13th century, with a charming sculptured figure between them. Over them is a row of round-headed Norman arcading, seen only from the aisle except for two open bays. Higher still is the 13th century lancet arcading of the clerestory. The three eastern bays of this arcade are 19th century.

The much-worn Norman west doorway, adorned with zigzag, opened into the castle yard ; the restored Norman doorway with its rich zigzag was rebuilt when the north aisle was refashioned in the 15th century. It frames a beautiful modern door with tracery, a

Leicester   St Martin's Cathedral

Leicester   Wyggeston Girls School

Leicester   University College

Leicester   De Montfort Hall and Gardens

Leicester   Police Headquarters

Leicester   Tower of St Nicholas Church

Leicester   Chancel of St Mary de Castro Church

border of vine and grapes, and a band of dainty roses and lion faces. A lovely old door leading to the vestry has a great wooden lock, a fine iron plate and ring, and a rare panel of plaited bands.

Here and there in the walls are traces of Norman windows. Of the arcading with scalloped capitals in the west wall of the nave, part is Norman and part new. There is a blocked Norman arch in the fine chancel, which has five Norman windows on the north side and one on the south. It is here that we find St Mary's arresting relic—three magnificent Norman seats for priests, their round arches a mass of zigzag resting on double pillars whose capitals are carved with varied foliage. It is a Norman masterpiece, worth coming far to see.

Three lovely but battered 13th century sedilia in the south aisle have double shafts. The beautiful 700-year-old font has a deep round bowl enriched with small faces and shields under arches, and a band of figures representing the Four Evangelists, an angel, a lion, a bull, and an eagle. In the floor near the font are 14th century tiles, and part of a coffin-lid that may be 12th century. A broken stone coffin has a shattered lid. The chancel screen has tracery in 14th century style, and slender pillars differently carved. There is a richly carved old chest. The roofs are chiefly old; the nave roof has floral bosses and heads, and tracery in the gables; the roof of the south aisle has a remarkable span of 36 feet. It was an 18th century vicar of St Mary's who founded Leicester's first parochial school across the way. On the new building are delightful statues of a charity boy and girl in their 18th century dress.

Everyone knows All Saints in Highcross Street, taking its name from an ancient cross replaced in Elizabethan days by a charming eight-sided building with an open arcade and a domed canopy. This was taken down when the street was widened in the 18th century, and one of its pillars was set up on steps. A hundred years ago this also was removed, and is now on a lawn in King Street. Stones forming a cross in the roadway mark the spot where the ancient High Cross stood.

Near the site of the old cross is the Free Grammar School founded in 1572 under the patronage of the queen. It was the town's chief school till the beginning of last century, now it is forlorn, used as a warehouse, but still with the arms of Elizabeth. The memory of a sadder queen clings to a building in High Street near by, where an inscription tells that Mary Queen of Scots rested there a day and a night.

The last of three ancient churches in its neighbourhood, All Saints was made new in the 14th century and has since been much restored. It has three things to make it familiar to the passer-by. One is the unusual position of the embattled tower projecting at the north-west corner of an aisle. Another is the fine west doorway only a yard from the pavement, which the Normans enriched with zigzag and scalloped capitals, framing an old traceried door with a wavy border of leaves. The third is a fine canopied clock of the days of James the First, with a painting of Father Time sitting with hourglass and sphere, and two carved and gilded men holding slender hammers, with which they strike the quarters on gongs. Restored at the close of last century, the clock is now over the lofty south doorway which saw the dawn of the 13th century. This too frames an old carved door.

The pleasing interior, airy and light, has lofty medieval arcades, a 13th century arch leading to the brick chancel, and a fine narrow archway of the same time opening to the tower, its short arch on very tall shafts. Five old bells stand in a row in the nave, a 14th century one recast in the 19th. Other relics are traceried panels of screenwork, a tapering stone coffin, a little glass in a tower lancet, a 15th century oak pulpit with tracery, and a mayor's chair looking none too comfortable. Fine old beams and quaint wooden faces remain in the aisle roofs, that of the north aisle resting on grotesque stone heads. The 13th century font is a treasure, its great round bowl elaborately carved with deeply-cut foliage and worn faces.

Alderman Gabriel Newton, who was mayor in 1736 and sleeps in All Saints churchyard, has a memorial in the chancel. One of the four benefactors we see on the Clock Tower, he lost his only son who was still in his teens, and bequeathed much of his money to found a school for poor boys which has become an important centre of education, housed now in a modern building by St Martin's. It was originally known as the Green Coat School from the old dress of the scholars, a green coat with scarlet facings, and brass buttons, grey stockings, and a round cap with a red button. One of the best windows in the church was given in the alderman's memory by Old Green Coat Boys. Glowing red, blue, green, and gold, it shows St Nicholas in the middle light, with a scholar in his green coat on one side and a choirboy on the other, reminding us that one of the terms of the alderman's foundation was that the boys should be carefully instructed in "toning and psalmody." The other good window is a memorial of the centenary of All Saints School and of its scholars who fell in the Great War.

A fine peal of ten bells rings out from St Margaret's 15th century tower, which rises magnificently above some of Leicester's lowly streets, and was built (it is said) from the proceeds of the Smoke Farthing, a tax levied on every hearth or fireplace in the parish. With its panelled belfry, its buttresses, its crown of battlements and pinnacles 108 feet from the ground, and its grand view of the city and away to Charnwood Forest, this tower is only one of the good things the imposing church has to show.

It comes from the three medieval centuries, with a little left of the 12th, when it is said to have been begun (perhaps on a Saxon site) by Robert le Bossu, Earl of Leicester. Of his day there remain only the eastern bays of the stately arcades, coming from about 1170. The rest of the arcades are 13th century. Like the tower (which stands within the church on three fine arches resting on great clusters of shafts), the chancel, the clerestory, and the south porch are 15th century. The chancel, light with big windows, has traceried sedilia, and a string course on which are quaint stone faces. By the east window are two beautiful niches, resting on an odd little man and a lion. The unusual group of a round and two three-sided windows over the entrance to the chancel were found and renewed when the arch was rebuilt last century.

Arresting in its beauty is the two-storeyed porch, with two peep-holes in its upper room. On the tip of the entrance arch is a pelican on her nest, and among the bosses of the vaulted roof with fan tracery is a grotesque head. The recessed inner doorway, with 14 columns, is 13th century. The 500-year-old font is enriched with quatrefoils and trefoils; there is lovely 14th century ironwork on the north door; four misereres of the modern stalls have carved and painted shields. A great treasure is the ancient dug-out chest, studded with nails and rivets, and bound with three iron bands. It has slots for coins in the lid.

The charming reredos in the south chapel is a carved and coloured Nativity. Mary is in the shelter, the richly-robed Magi are offering their gifts, their servants and horses in rich trappings are standing by (a monkey perched on one horse), and children with censers are hastening from the woods. In this chapel is a tablet to Mary Linwood who has been sleeping in the church since 1845. Though not a native, she lived for most of her life in Leicester, and won wide fame as an artist in needlework, using coloured worsteds which she had dyed in the town, or dyed them herself if special tints were required. She copied famous pictures, old and new, and we read that when a collection of her work was on exhibition in Leicester Square early last century, it was considered one of the sights of London. For her Salvator Mundi, copied from the Burleigh Collection, she was offered £3000, but she preferred to give it to Queen Victoria. It is amazing that one woman could accomplish so much with her hands, even in a life of all but ninety years. The only help she had in her art was in the threading of her countless needles, and for a long time she carried on the school her mother had begun. There is an engraving of her in the Reference Library, and in the City Museum are wonderful examples of her work.

On a tomb in the chancel lies the finely preserved alabaster figure of John Penny, who built the wall round the abbey grounds and put his name in it in darker bricks. We see him here as a bishop in robes and mitre, with his staff under his arm. His head rests on a double cushion, and he has rings on his fingers.

There are three curious things to see outside. Among the heads on a buttress west of the porch is the jovial whiskered face of a verger who posed for the 19th century mason. Many grooves on the tower walls and buttresses are said to be due to soldiers sharpening their weapons in the Civil War, when the churchyard was used by the troops. A stone in the north-west corner of the churchyard tells of Joe Robert Phipps who died in "the 121 year of his age," which we may believe or not as we choose.

Leicester has a group of modern churches, spacious and cared-for. St Mark's on Belgrave Road has a high tower and a striking spire crowning the stone exterior. Inside is a peace memorial window, where, for the first time in our church windows, we came upon the League of Nations. In the middle light Christ in His crown of thorns is with a soldier in the Somme Valley; the rest of the glass symbolises the righteous hopes of man and his struggle to be free. A Kaffir, a priest, a Free Church minister, a girl with arms full of flowers, and a statesman holding the Covenant of the League, are grouped on one side; on the other are a boy and a girl symbolising higher education for the poor, and a woman with her arms freed from chains. The impressive thing here is the setting of the altar, reached by flights of steps. The seven great panels of the apse are filled with oil paintings of special interest to this church, for St Mark's stands in the midst of many homes of Leicester's workers. The theme of the pictures is the redemption of the poor and oppressed through fellowship, leadership, and love, and the final dedication of all labour to Christ. We see the workers bowed down and fallen under the weight of their burden: Mammon with his money-bags and indifferent Society looking on untouched, and there is only the Angel of Sorrow to pity. The man who can find no work, the young worker who should be still at school, hopeless old age—all are here. Then the spirit of Society begins to change. The sceptic begins to believe, man is out to help his fellow, the conditions of toil are improved, and even the factories take on a kindlier shape. In the middle panels comes the gift of service to Christ, source of light and love, standing with arms uplifted, the marks of suffering in His hands, the symbol of the Cross behind Him; while on each side the Twelve Apostles are sharing His glory. The sculptor offers his model, the architect his church, the woman her daily tasks and motherhood, the king his government, the teacher his training of the young, the Arts their music and painting. The artist of this fine scheme was Eadie Reid, who designed the glass of the peace memorial window.

Not far from St Mark's Church is that of St Matthew in Chester Street, treasuring a 13th century font, with a bowl on a cluster of shafts. The attraction of St Saviour's Church, near Spinney Hill Park, is some fine modern glass showing Doubting Thomas, Samuel kneeling by Eli's bed, Jesus with His father in the carpenter's shop with Mary passing by the window, David with his sheep playing the harp, and the boy Jesus in the Temple with the doctors. A stone spire crowns St Saviour's great brick tower.

On the London Road, not far from Brookfield, the Bishop's fine house (of which we get a peep beyond its lawn and flower beds), is the church of St James the Greater, looking on to Victoria Park. Its arresting front is flanked by two domed towers, and the patron saint stands in a niche on the gabled tower. Its stately arch inside is crowned by an angel, and cherubs playing instruments adorn the font cover below it. Arches, like a lofty avenue lead to the aisles, where angels guard the oval windows, two of which have golden frames for lovely glass showing a winged knight kneeling with his sword (a peace memorial) and David with the harp. A striking window has three mothers with their sons, Mary with Jesus, Elizabeth with John, Hannah with Samuel.

A frieze of angels in porcelain enriches the low stone chancel screen, and on the walls of the domed sanctuary, below the star-spangled roof, are porcelain figures of saints and their symbols. When we came to the church the lower walls of the sanctuary were unfolding the story of the patron saint in the clever hands of a young lady artist—Christ calling James and John from their boat where Zebedee is mending the nets, and James before Agrippa, the man who offered to die with him being at his side, the executioner standing by, and two Jews looking on. The striking figures we saw in outline gave promise of fine wall-painting when complete.

On the hill, where the London Road climbs from the city, is the Victoria Road Baptist Church, with a spire soaring high enough to be seen from Charnwood Forest. As we look down Prebend Street near by there faces us the gabled end of a building adorned with canopied statues of two of the county's great Englishmen, Wycliffe and Latimer. Since 1872 it has been the Wycliffe Congregational Church, but for 30 years from its building in 1836 it was a school for boys. One of the masters was Alfred Russel Wallace, who while in Leicester made the acquaintance of Henry Bates, and here these two great naturalists talked of that adventure into the heart of Brazil which gave us two imperishable books about the Amazon.

On the north side of the city, not far from St Margaret's Church, is the Great Meeting Chapel of 1708, a square red-brick building with a stone pillared portico, and some interesting associations. It was Leicester's first brick building of any note. It claims to have had the first Sunday School in the town, established in 1783. In its old churchyard, now a green lawn, some of the townsfolk met for drill during the rising of the Young Pretender.

Sandwiched between shops in Belvoir Street is the Baptist chapel designed by Joseph Hansom, its squat round shape having won for it the local name of Pork Pie Chapel. A stone's throw from it is one of Leicester's most pleasing new buildings, the stone, timbered, and gabled offices of an insurance company at a corner of Wellington Street. Here too is the City Lending Library.

Neighbours at the cross-roads where the Aylestone and Welford roads meet, are Leicester's great institutions for healing and correction. The County Gaol, over a century old, is an extraordinary building with a stone front like a baronial hall with battlements, flanking towers, imitation portcullis, and formidable surrounding brick walls. The other is the Infirmary, grown from a simple place of 1771 with accommodation for 70 patients to a fine block of buildings where 7000 in-patients and 150,000 out-patients are dealt with every year. Most of its income is derived from the weekly contributions of Leicester's workers.

Leicester grows, and into the city bounds has now been gathered the old village of Belgrave. Near where the River Soar is spanned by a fine old bridge adapted to modern traffic there is a quiet corner where we step into days gone by. Here an ancient elm stands guard at one end of the little Church Road, on what was once the village green; at the other is the old church with four splendid chestnuts in the churchyard and a fine sycamore just outside. As we walk to the church there is a fine old house on each hand.

One of them is Belgrave Hall, built early in the 18th century by Edward Cradock, whose arms are seen on the leadwork, with the dates 1709 and 1713. The fine old iron gates are open now for all who will to enter the house, for it belongs to Leicester and is being used as a Period museum. Fresh from the bustle of the highway, it is a rare experience to slip back in a moment into Queen Anne's day, crossing the threshold of this gentleman's home of her time as easily as if it were ours. We sat on a 17th century settle in an entrance hall panelled with pine from a Baltic port, and here are several old carved chests. There are Chippendale chairs and a Regency table among the mahogany furniture in the dining-room, a charming bureau with the walnut pieces in the drawing-room, and Persian rugs in both. On the red-tiled floor of the kitchen were a pair of wooden pattens, and the wooden device used for pulling off jack boots. Queen Anne and George Prince of Denmark looked down from a wall as we climbed the staircase to a spacious landing with three lovely 17th century carved chests and a 15th century relief showing St George fighting the dragon. The big bedroom was inviting with a four-poster bed and red hangings, and a charming hooded cradle. Among the treasures shown under glass in a small bedroom are a tea-caddy and a card case in tortoiseshell, a chatelaine of cut steel, a pair of silver and crystal slides worn on a lady's curls, and (daintiest of all) a filigree patch-box. A harp and a piano of early last century are in the elegant music room. The grounds are pleasant with herbaceous borders, glasshouses, and a botanic garden in the making.

St Peter, the patron saint, stands in his niche on the north porch of Belgrave's church, whose walls outside are here and there a crazy patchwork of tinted stones. Though most of it is medieval and restored, the new south porch shelters a wonderful Norman doorway, with mouldings of dainty and unusual carving. It is a striking display of interlacing work. The arch has bands resembling chevron, and festoons ending in fleurs-de-lys; while the capitals of the shafts have double rows of interlaced loops.

The sturdy tower, with great buttresses, is 13th and 14th century. Its arch, coming from the close of the 12th, rests on slender shafts with graceful capitals of leaves and stems, and there are lovely modern corbels carved with vine, and three heads with ivy leaves coming from their mouths. The Good Shepherd shines in the tiny lancet in the tower. Three capitals on the clustered pillars of the old arcades are adorned with delicate leaves. There are two quaint faces on the old chancel arch, and holding up the nave roof are ten wooden shield-bearers resting on stone heads. Two more fine heads watch over the priest's doorway in the chancel, which keeps its fine old piscina and canopied sedilia under leafy arches. A pleasing touch here is a low window with two pictures of a golden ship, one driven in the storm, the other coming into the harbour. The rich panelling of the chancel is new, and the round bowl of the font may be medieval.

It is good that Belgrave should come within the watchful guardianship of Leicester, a city throbbing with the spirit of our age yet not unmindful of the past and of its own great place in history.

Stilton

LITTLE DALBY. It lies in a wooded valley bordering our smallest county, its church like a sentinel on the hill above with a spire peeping over the tree-tops.

Though much of it is modern, the church still has its 13th century arcades and a lofty 15th century clerestory with 12 new angels

The Wycliffe Memorial by Westmacott

Wycliffe's Chair   Wycliffe's Pulpit

IN LUTTERWORTH'S OLD CHURCH

The 15th Century Nave Roof   The Wycliffe Obelisk

The Bridge Across the River Swift
IN JOHN WYCLIFFE'S VILLAGE OF LUTTERWORTH

between the windows. The capitals at the door are finely carved and two ancient benches have fierce dragons.

In the beautiful park by the church stands Dalby Hall, an Elizabethan manor house changed with the centuries.

Little Dalby has one outstanding claim to fame; it was the birthplace of Stilton cheese. It was called Stilton cheese because it first became known through an innkeeper of Stilton in Huntingdonshire buying it in quantities and retailing it to travellers, but John Nichols, the historian of Leicestershire, has recorded that actually the cheese was first made here by Mrs Orton about 1730. "At first," says Nichols, "it was supposed that it could be made only from the milk of those cows which fed in one close, now called Orton's Close; but this was afterwards found to be an error. In 1756 it was made only by three persons, and that in small quantities; but it is now made, not only from one, but from almost every close in this parish, and in many of the adjoining ones." Now, of course, it is made in many parts of Leicestershire and Rutland, but to Little Dalby and Mrs Orton must belong the praise due to the pioneers.

The Peerless Pair

LOCKINGTON. It is tucked away in a remote northern corner of Leicestershire, and here, as in the Middle Ages, curfew rings out on every winter's eve.

Although the church is chiefly 14th century it has a Norman doorway retained as a legacy from an earlier building, and a massive 15th century tower standing out against a background of lofty elms. Many old treasures are in its safe keeping. There is a Norman font decorated with interlaced arches, some worn old benches with carved ends, and some fragments of 14th century glass with heraldry and golden-headed angels. The 15th century gave the church its richly panelled roof, and the chancel screen generously adorned with Tudor roses and surmounted by the Commandments and the royal arms of Queen Anne. The two-decker pulpit, another screen with finely carved foliage, and some of the pews are Jacobean.

The oldest monument is the 15th century altar tomb of Elizabeth Ferrers, whose husband, Lord Ferrers of Chartley, was slain on Bosworth Field. She is sculptured in graceful flowing robes, rich necklace and coronet, with angels, and six arcaded figures of monks in cowls.

THE KING'S ENGLAND

Other memorials pay a last tribute to the Bainbrigges, who lived at Lockington Hall in the 17th and 18th centuries. A Jacobean monument has coloured figures of William Bainbrigge in cap and gown with his wife and 13 children, the couple shown reverently with hands as big as their heads, raised in prayer, and their epitaph telling how:

> *A peerless payr lies here beneath*
> *Linkt long in love and now in death.*
> *Foure times ten years and somewhat more*
> *One soul in bodies twain they bore,*
> *Which multiplied its own perfection*
> *To thirteen payres of chaste affection.*

Philip Bainbrigge, who died in 1759, is remembered by an inscription supported by cherubic infants, one weeping and one smiling; and a later 18th century monument has a figure mourning Mary and Elizabeth Bainbrigge, Lady Bountifuls long beloved in the village.

LODDINGTON. It is set in delightful seclusion on a hill amid the enchanting countryside near the Rutland border. Its finely proportioned church has a Norman doorway, a grand tower arch, one particularly beautiful window of the 13th century, and a rare low-pitched 14th century roof. The arcaded font is 13th century, and the oak pulpit, said to have come from Launde Abbey, is Elizabethan. One of the chancel windows has fragments of 15th century glass, a mitred bishop among them.

LONG CLAWSON. Where the River Smite flows at the foot of the Wolds, the 13th century men raised its church, dedicating it to St Remigius, who baptised Clovis and some of his army when much of England was still pagan.

Some massive pillars in the transept belonged to its Norman forerunner, but the sturdy tower, one of the few in the county which rises in the middle of the church, was added in the 14th century. There is an ancient font, but the only hint of those who first worshipped here is the stone figure of a 13th century knight in chain armour, cross-legged with a dog at his feet.

Near the church is an old house, comely and stately among its trees, with creepers climbing to the stone mullioned windows, and on a hillock not far off the smock windmill stands forlorn, without its sails.

5

Tale of a Bible

LONG WHATTON. Among the shadows in its long wide street are many charming old houses, but none more attractive than the thatched and ivied cottage at the churchyard gate. Beyond it the gables of the 14th century church and its Norman tower rise boldly above a hedge of yews.

Although much of the church is new, it has kept a number of relics left by the passing centuries. The finely-carved old screen and pulpit came from the ruined church of Colston Bassett in Notts. The 13th century font, with its star and cable ornament, has a modern cover adorned with four angels, and the chancel has a 17th century chair and a modern reredos with lovely stone figures of the Madonna and St Peter.

There is, too, a Bible with a curious history, for it was once stolen by a villager, who threw it into a brook and was condemned to death for his offence, all little more than a century ago ! The poor man was reprieved, and after his release atoned for his offence by helping to build the churchyard wall.

Second Town in the County

LOUGHBOROUGH. We may call it the town of the bells, for they ring out across the world. Here is one of the finest carillons in the land, and here the biggest bell in all England was made.

This town so musical is a bright well-ordered place not unworthy of its high repute, and the traveller who is drawn to the little park in the heart of its streets is not disappointed, for here among the flowers and trees rises the great carillon set up in memory of the men who never came back from the war. Loughborough was the first town to set up a carillon after the war, and this was the first grand carillon in the country. From it was made the first effective broadcast of bell music.

Wherever it had come from, this carillon would be famous for its sight and sound, but Loughborough is proud of it because it stands in its own birthplace, fashioned in the famous foundry started by John Taylor a hundred years ago, when he came from Oxford to recast the bells of the parish church and liked the place so much that he set up the foundry which ever since has been sending its bells to ring all round the earth. They are famous, and much of the sweetness of our English bells we owe to the experimental work and the inventive genius of the men of Taylor's foundry. A bell sound has at least five tones contributing to it, and all five must be precisely tuned. Such precision depends upon exactness in the contour of the bell and upon its shape and thickness and on infinite carefulness and skill. These things have been so perfected at Loughborough that the five tones are tuned to the accuracy of a single vibration. Big Ben is not more accurate than a Taylor bell. In this fine foundry where any traveller is welcome to look round was cast great Paul of St Paul's Cathedral, the biggest bell that rings in England. It stands nine feet high and weighs almost 17 tons, and its voice can be heard above streaming London's central roar. The metal poured into its mould took six days to cool, and the bell was carried from Loughborough to London by road because there was no railway truck to hold it.

The Grand Carillon in Queen's Park rang out for the first time in the summer of 1923, its tower from the ground to the top of the cross is 151 feet high, and its total weight with the bells is 1300 tons. It rests on a deep concrete foundation in the middle of a wide stone platform, the base of the tower inside its neat stone balustrade being 28 feet square. The main part of the tower is built of small red bricks all made at home. It rises 87 feet from the ground beyond which is a gallery of wood encased in copper projecting beyond the red brick walls. The projection is over three feet, and is very effective, 16 square pillars supporting its roof. Above this roof rises a smaller octagonal gallery and above this again is a turret with a cupola roof ending in a golden ball and crowned with a cross. The climb to the top is by 138 steps, past a little museum room in which are kept a few relics of the war, and we come into the chamber where hang the 47 bells arranged in a steel frame in four tiers. The heaviest bell weighs over four tons and is over 20 feet round and five feet high. The smallest bell weighs over 20 pounds, and is just over 20 inches round and just over seven inches high. All the bells together weigh 21 tons. The bells are played on regular days each week, and the town, on Armistice Day and other special occasions, has its official carilloneur. It is never forgotten that the bells *toll for the brave, the brave that are no more*. This famous line from Thomas Campbell is at the head of all the recital programmes, and this is the tribute that is always paid by the solemn tolling of the great bell.

The bell tower, so fine a spectacle in itself, gives the traveller a spectacle of the countryside across which the bells ring out. From its gallery we see over the town with its two steeples, the drill hall, and the town hall, and beyond the valley of the River Soar rise the Wolds, with Stanford Hall near the front horizon. (It was this hall's grounds where Percy Pilcher crashed in a glider, before he could finish the small horse-power engine with which he would have doubtless become the first man to fly.) Passing round from the front to the left we look in the direction of Derby 17 miles away, and on our left is the church of Breedon-on-the-Hill. Still going left we see the country of Charnwood Forest, beginning with Bradgate, the home of Lady Jane Grey. Then comes Windmill Hill near Woodhouse Eaves, and the Hanging Stone Rocks at the foot of a rise which leads to Beacon Hill, 800 feet above the sea. The range of wooded hills ends with the cone-shaped Ives Head; just below it stands Burleigh Hall. Farther round, looking south-east, we face Leicester 11 miles away, and in the far distance is seen Billesdon Coplow, and nearer to us is Quorn, the centre of the hunting country.

The bells are all inscribed with the names of those who gave them, and those in whose names they are given; they are all the gifts of individuals for their families, or schools for their teachers and pupils, or firms for their workpeople. The big bell has on it the proud name of Taylor, John William and Arnold Bradley Taylor who fell in 1916, and Gerard Bardsley Taylor who fell in 1918.

Loughborough's Church of All Saints has a bell tower 500 years older than the tower of the Carillon, and in it still ring some of the bells John Taylor recast when he came to Loughborough and liked it so much that he set up a foundry here. The noble tower is nearly 100 feet high and richly decorated, and it is remembered that a great feat of bellringing took place within it on Easter morning in 1909, when ten picked ringers, starting at eight in the morning and not stopping for food, rang a peal of 18,027 Stedman Caters in just over 12 hours. No other achievement of bellringing has ever equalled this, and even those unacquainted with its technicalities will realise its magnitude on learning that one mistake would have spoilt the record.

The rest of this church, with its lofty pinnacled clerestory and its magnificent arches, is worthy of the impressive tower. There are battered brasses with figures of a 15th century fishmonger, Giles Jordan, and his wife Margaret, another woman and two groups of children all mounted with other fragments on a wall. More decorative is the organ case, with a pattern of leaves and acorns carved by a grateful Belgian refugee. There is a wall tablet to the town's most notable benefactor, Thomas Burton, who died in 1496. He was a prosperous wool merchant, and, as his monument tells, was mindful of the poor. Long after his death the money he had left to the church was applied to the foundation of a grammar school. The old school has vanished, but a finer school has taken its place, handsome with many gables and a central tower, and in its setting of splendid avenues one of the proudest possessions of the town.

The school is Thomas Burton's monument, but he has yet another in the church, for the Burton chapel, where he lies, has been lined with oak and has the names of the school's governors on the panels and the ancient deed of the school's foundation behind two folding doors. In this chapel also is a curious altar table of iron and alabaster.

Loughborough is the second biggest town in the county, grown prosperous through the hosiery trade and more lately by its electrical works, and it remains a monument to the irrepressible growth and vitality of the Machine. In the early days of the stocking loom it was the scene of more than one riot by the Luddites, and John Heathcote, who set up his lace-making machines here early in the 19th century, was driven from the town after an affray in which 55 of the machines were destroyed.

Another name writ large in the annals of Loughborough is that of John Chapman, who was born here in 1801, and became secretary of a Peace Society and one of the foremost radicals of his day. In 1834 his lace business was ruined and he set off for London, there, after finding employment where he could, to become editor of the Mechanics Magazine and to achieve some small fame for his work in the improvement of the hansom cab. His best memorial is the Great Indian Peninsular Railway, of which he was a pioneer.

A Best-Seller of His Day

JOHN CLEVELAND, the Cavalier poet, was the son of a Loughborough schoolmaster. He was for a little while the popular poet of his day, but his popularity soon passed, for it was won by writing mostly of events and people of the day, and interest in them is now small, or dead. He was devoted to the Stuarts, and died almost on the eve of the Restoration. As he had satirised the people of the Civil War and the Commonwealth he was read with avidity for the next twenty years or more. At least 23 editions of his poems were published and sold. His name would sell almost anything. He was dead and the booksellers announced discoveries of more Cleveland poems that were not his, until in the volumes of his verse the true and false were ridiculously mixed. Now he is read only by the studious and the curious.

He was born at Loughborough, the son of a curate who became vicar of Hinckley. Father and son were both consistent royalists. The boy, scholarly, clever, and witty, went to Cambridge, became a fellow of St John's, and stayed there nine years. He was at Cambridge when Milton was there, and Cleveland wrote a memorial poem when their fellow student Edward King was drowned, as Milton wrote Lycidas. The two poems appeared together, with those of other men, in a memorial volume.

When the Civil War broke out Cleveland was too good a loyalist to keep quiet, though Cambridge was Parliamentarian, and when Oliver Cromwell was put forward as member of Parliament for Cambridge he opposed him vigorously. Cromwell won, and Cleveland's opposition drew so much attention to what was called his malignancy that he was glad to slip away to Oxford and join the king in his capital there. Charles welcomed him, for he knew the power of his pen. From Oxford Cleveland went to Newark, where he was appointed legal officer to the besieged garrison in the castle. He was there at the surrender of Charles to the Scots, and bitterly resented that action, in a satire on the Scots that is hard to forgive.

For the rest of his life, after a Scottish general had told him he had no use for a ballad monger, Cleveland seems to have had a wandering existence, satirising his political foes, doing some teaching, and being welcomed to the houses of his fellow royalists, now under the cloud of the Commonwealth. In 1655 he was arrested at Norwich and tried as a vagabond with no visible means of support. It was also mentioned against him that he being a person of great ability "was able to do the greater disservice" to the State. For three months he was imprisoned at Yarmouth, and then, in answer to a direct appeal from Cleveland, Cromwell personally released him. In the three years that followed before Cleveland's death, in 1658, he seems to have lived chiefly in London.

Cleveland was not a considerable poet. His subjects did not allow him scope. As a satirist he was forceful and clever. When he ceased to be forceful he became too clever, and tortured his thought into obscurity. He was admired because it became a fashion to admire his writing. The fashion passed, and the poverty of his subject matter and the contortion of his style left him neglected.

Colonel Hutchinson's Trees

LOWESBY. Here in a lovely park studded with noble trees and graced by a rustic bridge stands Lowesby Hall, with all the charm of Georgian architecture and fragrant with memories. Its red brick is mellowed by two centuries of sunshine, its surface broken by long rows of windows perfectly spaced, with a bold cornice overhanging their even lines, while in front is a broad terrace with a flight of stone steps leading down to a lawn where a sundial tells the hours.

Colonel Hutchinson, Parliamentary Governor of Nottingham Castle, lived for some time in the earlier manor house, which he had bought during the Commonwealth after his house at Calthorpe had been battered in the Civil War. It was he who planted many of these trees and made the fishponds, and it was here that Lucy Hutchinson wrote the greatest tribute that ever a wife paid to her husband, the memoir in which Colonel Hutchinson's figure stands out with the tenderness of a Van Dyck portrait.

But the manor's history and its legends go back long before the Civil War. From the Conquest to the 15th century it belonged to the Burdetts, one of whom, returning from a crusade, slew his innocent wife in a fit of jealousy and founded a priory near Tamworth to expiate his crime. Many an owner has the manor had since those days, but none more gallant or romantic than Colonel Hutchinson.

The church, built in the 13th and 14th centuries, sits in the friendly shade of beeches and chestnuts, with a frieze of finely carved animals adorning the outside walls of its chancel. Within it is protected by a grand oak roof decorated with fruits and flowers, animals and heads, and a simple font stands as the only witness of its very early days.

The Hall of the Huguenots

LUBENHAM. It has some pretty thatched cottages, a pond on the green, and the River Welland flowing by, bordering Northamptonshire.

The humble church, with a 15th century tower scarcely higher than the clerestory, is almost as its medieval builders left it. One of the nave pillars has a 13th century capital with carved heads and foliage, and in the chancel is a 14th century Easter sepulchre with four heads looking down from the canopy. There are two much-worn 15th century seats and with them a great assemblage of high box pews, one of them almost filling the small south aisle. The carved wooden reredos has adorned the church for about 300 years, and a Flemish chest with traceried panels is perhaps as old.

The old manor house that once stood proudly here was pulled down in the 18th century, and is remembered only because it sheltered Charles Stuart for three days before the fateful Battle of Naseby. A mile away is the many gabled Papillon Hall, made new last century, but bearing still the marks of its 17th century architect, David Papillon.

The Papillons were a Huguenot family and when the religious wars grew dangerous for them David sailed for England with his mother and two sisters, only his father, valet to King Henry the Fourth, remaining in France. Their ship was wrecked off Hythe and only the children were saved, to be brought up by kinsmen already settled in London. David made good as an architect, bought an estate here, and built Papillon Hall, where he lived in peace and comfort to the end of his days.

John Wycliffe's Village

LUTTERWORTH. It is one of the immortal places of the world. Its High Street climbs steeply from the bridge across the shallow River Swift, and leads the way to its famous church, with a tower rising boldly against the sky. It is not the tower John Wycliffe knew, but it is the church in which was heard the voice which was to resound through the world.

It was the place from which his utterance reached to Rome, and it was here that he spent his last years in work on the translation of the Bible. From this place he sent forth his Poor Priests to bring the Word to humble homes throughout the land. Here he died and here he was buried.

Though Lutterworth has now an obelisk in its streets to the Morning Star of the Reformation, it was here that hate pursued him after death, for 43 years later his poor bones were unearthed and burnt, and the ashes thrown into the stream at the foot of the hill:

Then this brook hath conveyed his ashes into Avon, Avon into Severn, Severn into the Narrow Seas, they into the Main Ocean; and thus the ashes of Wycliffe are the emblem of his doctrine, which has dispersed all the world over.

The Swift at Lutterworth is unromantic now, a narrow stream into which much rubbish has been thrown, but its waters go on into the green countryside and it is thrilling to stand here and imagine the scene when Wycliffe's brook carried his ashes away, for this place he made famous for all time.

The church was ancient when Wycliffe came to it under the protection of John of Gaunt, for it had been founded in the 12th century by Norman de Verdun. Although the antiquarian may discern traces of 13th century work in the chancel and the tower, most of the earlier church has vanished and the building we see is a strange mixture of later centuries. The chancel, the clerestory, and the nave roof with its gold bosses and little coloured figures of shield-bearers, are all 500 years old, and the top part of the tower, with its massive pinnacles, was built up again in the 18th century after it had crashed with the spire in a terrible storm. One of the stones that fell in the storm is kept in the church. The restoring hand of the 18th century wrought its changes, but the aisles and the lower part of the tower and the nave belong to the 14th century, and are the stones on which Wycliffe's eyes so often rested.

The medieval craftsmen have bequeathed two paintings to this famous village. There is a fresco in the north aisle he may often have seen; it shows three crowned figures, two kings and a queen, engaged in hawking. It has been suggested that they may be Richard the Second with his queen and John of Gaunt, but comparison with more complete wall-paintings of the same kind points to the belief that the fresco was part of a favourite 14th century subject of the Three Living Kings and the Three Dead Kings, in which a royal hunting party comes suddenly face to face with three crowned skeletons who urge them to repentance. The other painting is over the chancel arch, the familiar 15th century scene of Judgment

Day, showing Christ seated on a rainbow which rests on the sun and the moon, with angels blowing trumpets to summon the dead, and in the foreground the dead clambering from the graves and away from the consuming fires.

It was natural that in the centuries which followed Wycliffe's death, when the love for him and the pride in his greatness was steadily growing, any possession of the church which could be associated with him should be preserved, and venerated as a saintly relic. The pulpit with six panelled sides is said to be his, although much of its seems to be of Tudor craftsmanship. But the topmost part is at any rate of very ancient workmanship, and may well be the 14th century woodwork on which his arms would rest as he spoke to his small congregations.

In the chancel is a chair which by long tradition is known as Wycliffe's Chair, and the refectory table now used as an altar in the side chapel may have been used by Wycliffe when, quill in hand he bent over his work, writing and translating. In a glass case is an embroidered vestment said to have been worn by Wycliffe, and near it, in another glass case, is a copy of his translation of the Bible and a chained copy of Foxe's Book of Martyrs. Other Wycliffe associations are a battered font attributed to his day and covered by a curious wooden copy of the ill-fated 14th century spire he so often beheld; an 18th century painting of him; and a marble relief showing him with hand upraised, addressing student and priest, learned and simple, gathered about his altar. The group is by one of the Westmacotts and is of great dignity, showing Wycliffe standing by the altar with an open Bible, preaching to a little group: a merchant, a scholar, a soldier with his son holding his cap, a mother with a child in her arms, while behind Wycliffe stand two priests listening in tense attitude as if fearful of his bold words. He also appears in the east window among the sacred scenes, the angels, and the saints portrayed in rich modern glass.

But the finest monument in the church is not of its immortal man, but of Sir John Fielding, with a sculptured figure of a 15th century knight wearing a fur-bordered gown over his armour, his wife in a veiled headdress and gown beside him, and three angels below, under delicately carved canopies, carrying their shields. He has a short dagger, broken. There are two 15th century brasses with another John Fielding and his wife, and an unknown civilian with

his wife in butterfly headdress and a dagger at his girdle. Some
fragments of the 15th century screen are worked into the screen of
the organ chamber; others were added to the pulpit, and among the
many precious antiquities must be counted the brass candlesticks
of Archbishop Laud's day. There is also a marble tablet with a
portrait of Henry Ryder, who was rector here before he became a
bishop, and a wall monument with a fine bronze head of another
rector, Frederick Alderson, chaplain to Queen Victoria and Edward
the Seventh.

The church has a wooden model of Sir Gilbert Scott's suggested
design for the complete restoration of the church, with the addition
of a new spire. The work of a Lutterworth schoolmaster, it is about
a foot long with every detail correct in proportion, even to the
window tracery, and below the tower is a baptismal scene, with the
clergyman in white robes and the family gathered round the font.
Nothing else in this pleasant market town can compare with the
interest of its church, but where the roads to Coventry and Hinckley
meet stands a granite obelisk 30 feet high in memory of the man
who made the name of Lutterworth known everywhere and laid
the great foundation stones of our common English speech.

A Founder of English Freedom

ONE of the greatest of all Englishmen, who boldly introduced
freedom of thought into the sphere of religion, Wycliffe was born
about 1320 near Richmond in Yorkshire. He was educated at
Balliol and remained in intimate relations with Oxford nearly all
his life, being there a student, tutor, lecturer, and for a short time
Master of Balliol itself. He held livings at Fillingham in north
Lincolnshire, Ludgershall in Bucks, and Lutterworth in Leicestershire, but it was really around Oxford that his life revolved, and
sustained a lasting influence over the thought of teachers and those
whom they taught.

His period was one of confusion and corruption in the Church.
Rival Popes, in France and Italy, each claimed to be supreme on
earth. Heavy demands for money were made on England by Popes
who claimed the right to bestow the best English benefices on their
foreign friends. The English ruling classes resented this unfairness
fiercely, and those who felt deeply were convinced that there could
be no defence of such an intrusion from abroad.

LEICESTERSHIRE

Two men stand out prominently as representing the English types of opposition. One of them, John of Gaunt, was a bluff stand-no-nonsense sort of man, intent on keeping power in the hands of the nobility, who now felt themselves English, and he resented papal or any other clerical domination. The other was Wycliffe, a scholar of distinction and a clear and fearless thinker about religion in its truer and its falser forms.

The blunt soldier and the thoughtful reformer were thrown together by having some aims in common, but otherwise they had little sympathy. Wycliffe was essentially spiritual, and Gaunt was not. Gaunt saw the Church gathering too many spoils and meant to check it; Wycliffe wished to purify the Church of its manifest faults, its superstitions, and its craze for wealth and power, which made it appear the successor of the conquering Roman Empire rather than the inheritor of the gospel of Christ. Both were against the extension of papal power in England, Gaunt because he felt it to be grasping, and Wycliffe because it had become in some respects corrupt. He boldly proclaimed the belief that no Authority which did bad things could come from God.

Undoubtedly Wycliffe swayed Oxford. His ideas were widely accepted. He was both the most influential academic lecturer and the most popular preacher. His personality dissolved opposition and his reasoning commanded respect. A large band of itinerant preachers, after the manner of the friars, spread his ideas far and wide. Though at first Wycliffe did not challenge any doctrines of the Church, he did not spare some of its practices, and those who were hit called the attention of the amiable Archbishop of Canterbury to his uncomfortable stirring up of thought. A scrutiny of Wycliffe's writings led the Archbishop to order him to appear at St Paul's before the Bishop of London, and to answer certain charges. Wycliffe attended, but so also did John of Gaunt, and Percy, the Earl Marshal of England, with a strong following of armed men; and so roundly did they abuse the bishop that the meeting broke up in confusion.

This was a rough-and-ready announcement that Wycliffe had friends who would not see him ill-used. Then his clerical enemies did a foolish thing. They appealed to the Pope, who at once sent out bulls to the Archbishop of Canterbury, the Bishop of London, the King, and the University of Oxford, ordering the University to arrest Wycliffe and send him to the Pope. These were just the kind of papal encroachments which all concerned resented. The King had died, and Richard the Second, a ten-year-old boy, had come to the throne, and his new Council was actually at the moment asking Wycliffe to advise them whether they might prohibit treasure being sent out of the country at the demand of the Pope. The University did not admit the right of the Pope to send them a bull, much less to imprison one of their members, and the bishops knew better than to ask the University to send Wycliffe to them. Wycliffe himself answered the Pope's bull and defended his views, which the University endorsed, and when he appeared before the bishops at Lambeth Palace the King's mother (wife of the Black Prince) sent a warning to them not to give judgment against Wycliffe. They confined themselves to requesting him not to discuss troublesome questions in the future.

Pope Gregory died and the state of the Church became more chaotic. Wycliffe did not follow the advice given him by the bishops. His questioning of the methods of the Church was extended, and included some of its doctrines. He began to write his thoughts in English and to urge on the translation of Jerome's Latin Bible into English, much of it being done by his followers. At this time the Peasants War (Wat Tyler's rebellion) broke out. Wycliffe stood aloof from it, but it is possible that the freedom of opinion he was using may have had indirect effects in adding to the excitement.

He did not in any way abate his efforts to present to the populace a Christianity shorn of what he regarded as its errors. The crisis came when he denounced the central Romanist doctrine of transubstantiation, the mystic change of the bread and wine into the actual body and blood of Christ. That could not be ignored by the Church authorities, and the Archbishop grappled with the difficulty by holding a Council and securing a condemnation of no fewer than 24 opinions enunciated by Wycliffe. All the Wycliffites were now silenced or expelled from Oxford.

Wycliffe himself was never brought up for formal condemnation. He had withdrawn to his rectory at Lutterworth, where he quietly continued his work to the end, which came from a stroke while he was at a service in his own church at Lutterworth on December 28, 1384, followed by another stroke on New Year's Eve. He was buried at Lutterworth. Thirty years later he was condemned as a heretic by the Council of Constance, and it was ordered that his bones should be dug up and burned. After another 13 years this order was carried out by Richard Fleming, Bishop of Lincoln, who finished his hideous duty by casting the ashes into the waters of the River Swift.

Wycliffe's influence lasted in England, notwithstanding the terrible persecution of his followers known as the Lollards, till the Reformation came in Tudor times. His translation of the Bible was widely circulated, and the influence of his writings was felt abroad. The goal of all his work was to lead men back to the simple Gospel.

Dr Johnson at School

MARKET BOSWORTH. No longer do the shadows of old wars fall on this placid town as it slumbers about its ancient marketplace, hedges bordering its streets and cottages. Four and a half centuries ago the Wars of the Roses ended on the stricken Field of Bosworth, two miles away, but it seems almost as if, having once been in the glare of history, Market Bosworth had resolved to step back happily into obscurity.

In the emptied marketplace, where the greatest of all wars has set its cross of remembrance, is the grey stone Grammar School, very square, with stone-framed windows, handsome and rather stern. Originally founded in early Tudor times, it was in 1601 given a new lease of life by Sir Wolstan Dixie, who had inherited the fortune of his namesake, a Lord Mayor of London in Queen Elizabeth's day. To this old Grammar School came Dr Samuel Johnson as a poor usher who taught the boys grammar. Long afterwards, in one of his few references to this unhappy time, he said that his life here was as unvaried as a cuckoo's note, and he did not know whether it was more disagreeable for him to teach the boys or for them to learn. His duties appear to have included acting as a sort of private chaplain to the latest of the Dixies, another Sir Wolstan, and it was the humiliation he suffered at the hands of this tyrannous man, as much as his drudgery at the school, which caused him to leave it after a few months.

Henry Salt, who was a pupil of the school generations after Samuel Johnson had left it and, like him, came from Lichfield, was Consul-General in Egypt early in the 19th century and one of the earliest to encourage Egyptian excavation. The colossal Rameses the Second

in the British Museum was partly his gift, and the sarcophagus of
Seti the First, now in the Soane Museum in Lincoln's Inn Fields,
was another of his treasures.

Those who cross the marketplace to walk to the old hall may in
fancy follow Samuel Johnson's slow footsteps on the way. He was
not then the sage whose portrait Reynolds has painted for us, but
a young and rather uncouth man, shabbily dressed, with small hint
in his demeanour of the greatness within him. The fine house with
its portico and cornice, and its handsome Georgian windows spaced
above the terrace, was built by the Dixies about 1700. In the deer
park is a group of trees on a hillock said to be the spot where Richard
of York raised his standard for the last time. The spot is only
traditional, but at any rate the trees have for long been known as
King Dick's or Richard's Clump.

The prettiest of streets leads to the 15th century church, rising
finely among its trees, its pinnacled tower crowned by a spire.
Modern figures of Peter and Paul stand in the old niches by the east
window, and among the old treasures are a 14th century font with
shields on its six sides, and a medieval ironbound chest. One of
many memorials to the Dixie family is an 18th century wall monument with a figure of a woman mourning John Dixie. The newer
possessions, all of oak, include a reredos with lovely figures of
angels, a lectern with the Four Evangelists, a screen with a quaintly-
carved eagle and an owl, and a pulpit with Moses, Elijah, John the
Baptist, and St Peter.

In the churchyard are a number of slate tombstones, one by the
north door having a medallion with a graceful figure of a woman.

A Letter from Oliver

MARKET HARBOROUGH. We can hardly stand in its market
square, widening out of the main street, without feeling what
a pleasant place it is. There is the great church with the spire rising
magnificently 164 feet above its tower, the quaint grammar school
beside it, and the sturdy old houses which are none the worse for
having fitted themselves with shop-fronts. They are pleasant to look
on, and are a symbol of that steadfast, steady, Midland spirit which
patiently pursues its way and stands immovable against aggression.
During the Civil War that same spirit showed itself indomitable in
Market Harborough.

Newtown Linford   **The Ruins of Bradgate House**

Market Harborough   The 17th Century Grammar School

The Tower and the Magnificent Clerestory

The Clustered Pillars of the Nave
MELTON MOWBRAY'S CHURCH OF GREAT BEAUTY

LEICESTERSHIRE

In three days of 1642 the balance between King and Common-wealth swung here. It was the eve of the Battle of Naseby, and the streets and square were filled with Royalist soldiers. At the end of the three days the church was filled with the Royalist prisoners. The first act of that drama took place when Charles Stuart, sleeping at Lubenham a few miles away, was roused at two in the morning with the news that Fairfax had marched from Northampton to Naseby. He came riding down this street in the darkness to his headquarters, to hold a Council of War. The rashness of the Cavalier leader, Prince Rupert, prevailed, the Royalist army marched from its entrenched position to give battle to the New Model Army and at mid-day the fight began. By nightfall the king was a fugitive, his army destroyed, his throne lost. While he fled to Leicester, the church here was being packed with the wounded prisoners, and Oliver Cromwell sat down to write that trenchant letter to the Speaker of the House in which he described the destruction of the King's army:

Sir, this is none other but the hand of God and to Him alone belongs the glory, wherein none are to share with Him.

The general served you in all faithfulness and honour. Honest men served you faithfully in this act. Sir, they are trusty; I beseech you in the name of God not to discourage them. He that ventures his life for the liberty of his country, I wish he trust God for the liberty of his conscience and you for the liberty he fights for.

Charles Stuart was here again twice, first in disguise on his way to join the Scots, and then again when these had failed him, as a prisoner on his way south. Sad must have been his reflections as he passed through the old town.

The church stands as it stood in his day, almost on the pavement of the square, splendid and strong in its proportions. Tradition makes John of Gaunt its founder, and it was certainly begun in the 14th century. It keeps in the roofs of chancel and nave a number of old grotesque figures, but most of the ancient treasures have vanished. There is a great company of angels and sacred scenes in the modern glass of the east window, and the alabaster pulpit with its carving of the Sermon on the Mount is interesting because it was given by four brothers of the vicar in 1860 as a thank-offering for having passed through the Indian Mutiny unharmed.

Robert Smyth, a Harborough man who made his fortune in London, founded the Grammar School in 1613. The space below the schoolroom was once a butter market, but although, alas! both schoolboys and market women have vanished from the scene, the old building remains Market Harborough's little gem. It has half-timbered walls and gables with ornamental bargeboards all supported on round wooden arches with pillars resting on stone piers.

On a hillside near the station is the humble church of St Mary in Arden which is no more than a nave and porch. It was built in 1693 out of the ruins of an old church, blown down in a winter gale. Out of its ancient heritage it has preserved a Norman doorway with beak head ornament and a battered figure of a woman who worshipped here 600 years ago.

Although Market Harborough has taken it under its wing, the neighbouring hamlet of Little Bowden has preserved its thatched cottages and its flower-decked churchyard. In its little medieval church is a tablet to Thomas Reynolds who ministered here for 53 years before they laid him to rest in 1829, and somewhere within the shadows of its walls sleeps Jane West whose novels, plays, and poems, were best-sellers 150 years ago, but now are forgotten.

MEASHAM. It is a workaday place of brickmaking and coal-mining, with the Ashby Canal flowing darkly past its houses and the River Mease as a companion at no great distance. From its coal-beds a number of stone hammer-heads have been excavated as well as solid wooden wheels and wedges of flint bound in hazel which owing to the nature of their burial had survived decay.

The medieval church with its 15th century nave roof and clerestory has a striking vaulted porch with rounded stone ribs and a massive, nail-studded, 17th century door. There is also an old panelled font and a few fragments of ancient heraldic glass worked in with the new. There is a marble tablet to Joseph Pickard, who was for nearly half a century master of the school and organist of the church, and an oak peace memorial with St Michael and St George by the Cross.

Treasure on the Rubbish Heap

MEDBOURNE. It has thrown a great treasure on to a rubbish heap, a beautiful Roman pavement dug up in 1721, but we may see a picture of it in the church. It was found at the foot of the hill where the brook runs by the churchyard wall and under a medieval packhorse bridge.

LEICESTERSHIRE

Sycamore, oak, and beech surround the 13th century church, which is notable for the great beauty of an aisle in the south transept, a window 20 feet high flooding it with light. In the tower arch the huge pendulum of the tower clock is seen swinging. There is a 13th century font, a recessed tomb with a poor battered figure of an unknown man, and an 18th century wall monument to John Goodman with three winged cherubs, little studies in expression.

Near the church is the T-shaped manor house first built in the 13th century. During its restoration some curious 17th century wall paintings were found, one of a man in doublet and trunk hose, another of a lady with a feathered hat.

The Church of Very Great Beauty

MELTON MOWBRAY. Where the huntsman rides to hounds down the smooth vale the Bronze Age hunter rode along his trackways, the Romans made a road and raised a tumulus, the Saxons left a burial ground. Then the Norman Mowbrays set their proud name here. Such is the past of Melton Mowbray famous for its hunting and its pies.

Today it is a pleasant country town with streets ever echoing with the patter of hoofs, but quiet for the most part, except on market days when crowds assemble with their usual noise and bustle. A fine stone bridge bestrides the River Eye as it flows to join the Wreak, and close by is a park with yew-fringed pathways and noble cedars shading the lawns that run to the water's edge.

Among the old houses two are notable. One is the graceful low stone building which Robert Hudson built in 1640 as a Bede House. Here 12 old people spend their last years in blissful peace, and here also is housed one of those country museums filled with odds and ends. The relics which belong to it by right are Saxon spearheads found in the neighbouring burial ground, but these alone do not make a museum, and so a strange medley of stuffed birds, shells, butterflies and books, coins and beetles, bear them company. Snowshoes and a cat-of-nine-tails, a statue of Richard Lionheart, and Chinese mandarins, all are in good neighbourhood here.

The other notable house is by the church, and is old enough to justify the reputation of having sheltered Anne of Cleves after she had escaped the misfortune of being married to Henry the Eighth. Another story that Elizabeth stayed here for a time when she

147

was princess completes its slender and somewhat legendary regal history.

Melton Mowbray church, standing in beauty in its bright church-yard, is known to Leicestershire men as the most perfect of all their shrines, and is indeed acclaimed by them as the most beautiful parish church in England. Certainly it ranks high in that noble company. It was begun in the 13th century and the shape of the cross on which it was planned was faithfully followed by every generation adding to its splendour. Its transepts have aisles on both sides, a feature rarely found in churches of less than cathedral scale. In the 16th century the lower storey of the tower was enriched with ornament, and its upper one added and adorned with battlements and pinnacles, in noble fashion. The upper storey, like the magnificent clerestory which crowns both nave and transepts, was built by Sir John Digby, one of seven brothers who fought at Bosworth, and in these splendours he left an abiding monument. Below the west window is the superb Galilee porch 600 years old, its doorway graced with ballflower ornament and six sculptured niches with foliage and heads of men and beasts.

Over the north door is a worn head of Peter that has looked down on many generations of worshippers. Inside pillars cluster magnificently to support the tower, groves of pillars uplift the lofty arcades of nave and transept, while above their graceful lines 56 carved angels are bearing shields and 48 clerestory windows bring in the light.

The 14th century chancel has fine modern oak panelling, a reredos adorned with figures of angels, carved stalls, and a canopied screen, all in keeping with its ancient dignity. One of the south aisle windows is filled with old stained glass, collected about 1800 by Parson Ford, its hundreds of fragments skilfully arranged, coats-of-arms with lions and griffins, heads of saints, canopies and foliage, and other innumerable details in rainbow hues. One of the best of the modern windows has richly canopied figures of Boaz, Ruth, Naomi, and David. In the south aisle is the 13th century cross-legged figure of a warrior with sword and shield and a dog under his feet. An iron helmet of later date hangs above him and a small slate tablet tells that "This is the Lord Hamon Belers, Brother to the Lord Mowbray." A Purbeck tomb from which the brasses have vanished covers the body of Sir John Digby, builder of the tower and clerestory, and hero of Bosworth Field.

In the south transept, on a 14th century tomb, lies an unknown lady with angels at her jewelled head and dogs playing at her feet. Under a table in the children's corner is a 17th century monument with engraved figures of Sir John Pate, his wife, and 11 children.

Such are the ancient memorials of Melton Mowbray church, but it has a memory which transcends them all. In October 1553 the sum of twopence was paid "for ringing the great bell for master Latimer's Sermon." He was an old man then, white-haired and feeble, and it was only two years later that he was to go to the stake with those words on his lips which are the noblest ever spoken in the hour of death—Be of good comfort, Master Ridley. . . In this town where he was revered the people would crane their heads from the windows of houses to see him pass along the marketplace, his frail hand grasping his staff, his Bible hanging from his girdle, and the church was crowded to hear every word he spoke.

The Queer Parsons of Melton Mowbray

MELTON MOWBRAY has had two queer parsons who are well remembered, the scholar-buffoon John Henley of the 18th century, and the eccentric vicar Dr Ford, who was here all through the exciting days of Napoleon.

Son of one vicar of Melton and great-grandson of another, John Henley went from the vicarage to enter Orders at Cambridge, and incidentally to assure himself of a minor immortality at twenty.

He sent to the Spectator a letter, signed Peter de Quir, which, after puzzling Steele for months, appeared in the well-known Spectator number 396, and is read with as much amusement now as it was then.

Returning to Melton to teach in the school of his native town, and to become a successful headmaster, Henley produced a long poem which attracted attention, and a grammar in seven languages; then he gave up a curacy under his father to preach in London. Fertile in ideas and in language, he introduced new methods into the pulpit. He acted his sermons, illustrating his utterances with violent gesticulations. The novelty of his methods and the florid wealth of his eloquence impressed the town, drew great congregations and enabled him to raise huge sums for charity. He was rewarded with a living in Suffolk, but on being accused of neglecting his charge he built himself a chapel in London which he called an oratory; hence his title Orator Henley.

Here, in a garish gilded pulpit, resplendent with velvet and other trappings, he preached on Sundays sermons which were occasionally noble and inspiring, always witty, but sometimes marred by eccentricity bordering on ribaldry. Once the bootmakers of London flocked to hear him redeem his promise to teach a new and short way of making shoes. The preacher was as good as his word; he simply cut off the tops of a pair of boots.

During the week the oratory drew crowds for lectures on every subject under the sun, and the presiding genius was one of the foremost figures of his time. But he had once spoken disrespectfully of Pope, and the little poet, with his wrath slowly simmering, boiled up while writing the Dunciad. Three times he dragged Henley in:

> *Tuning his voice and balancing his hands,*
> *Oh, great restorer of the good old stage.*
> *Preacher at once, and zany of thy age!*

The satire likens him to the priests of Egypt, "where monkeys were the gods," and Hogarth, seizing on the idea, portrayed the Orator on a scaffold, with a monkey by his side saying Amen. Pensioned by Walpole for services as a journalist, Henley lost his popularity and died in obscurity in 1756.

The other eccentric clergyman of Melton Mowbray was Dr Ford, who became vicar here in 1773. Though a very pious man, his humour and enthusiasm sometimes carried him away. When he was preaching a charity sermon some huntsmen entered the church very late, and Dr Ford stopped preaching and exclaimed:

"Here they come, here come the red-coats, they know their Christian duties—there's not a man among them that is not good for a guinea."

His great joy was in music, and during the singing of his favourite psalms he would dangle his legs over the pulpit in a paroxysm of delight. He would ride miles to attend a musical festival, especially to hear Handel, whose Messiah would send him into ecstasies. He told a friend that he never journeyed from Melton to Leicester without singing that oratorio right through; so he learned to measure his progress along the road. Beginning the overture as soon as he had crossed Melton Bridge, he found himself in the chorus Lift Up Your Heads when he arrived at Brooksbygate, and at Thanks be to God as he passed through Thurmaston toll-gate.

As the pace of his old horse was pretty regular, he always succeeded in concluding the Amen Chorus at the cross in the Belgrave Gate at Leicester. He died in 1821 and was buried at Bristol.

MISTERTON. It lies secluded on the slope of a hill, contemplating the peaceful meadows and the great park belonging to its hall. Misterton was long the home of the Pulteneys, and there is a tradition that the church was built by John de Pulteney, who was four times Lord Mayor of London in the 14th century and lived in a magnificent house fit for a prince, and was indeed for some time the London residence of the Black Prince.

The church treasures some fine old panelling, loose fragments of carved oak, and a grotesque with protruding tongue on one of its fine 15th century bench-ends. The 15th century chancel has finely chiselled heads of a bishop and a queen on its arch and also enshrines two monuments of the Pulteneys. The earliest is an Elizabethan altar tomb of Michael Pulteney bearing a brave figure in armour and ruff with beard and double chin, dagger at his side, two lions at his feet, and a helmet with a crest of a Moor's head beneath his own. There is also a 17th century altar tomb of John Pulteney, a sheriff of Leicestershire.

The Place of Stone

MOUNTSORREL. Its quarries have paved thousands of our streets, but it is a loveless place. Its own long straggling street has an 18th century domed market-house, its cupola supported on eight pillars and crowned by an urn; it was put here by Sir John Danvers when he removed the ancient cross to Swithland Park.

Standing in this derelict place we see through the columns the proudest thing Mountsorrel has, a granite arch on the summit of its Castle Hill; it is in memory of the men who never came back.

The Castle Hill rises sharply 100 feet high. Here the nephew of the Conqueror built a house which stood 200 years; today the very site of it has been removed by granite quarrying.

Yet this dull place has seen great sights. It has seen five men on horses riding to Doom or Victory. It saw King John, who once slept here. It saw Richard Crookback riding to death and disaster on Bosworth Field. It saw Cardinal Wolsey riding, a fallen and dying man, on his way from Leicester Abbey. It saw Charles Stuart back from Coventry and Leicester, and it saw the great Oliver marching to Preston.

It has an old church and a new one, neither with anything great, and it has a half-timbered house with herringbone work.

The Poet's Sorrow

MUSTON. On the village green stands an ancient market cross, built up anew to mark the coronation of George the Fifth. Peeping above the tree-tops close by is the spire of a church with memories of another English king, and of an English poet.

Except for its 13th century tower and 15th century clerestory the church is chiefly 600 years old, and has preserved a few old benches with poppyheads and a 15th century font with heads of leopards.

The traceried oak screen and pulpit were given by Robert Sanderson, rector here for many years, chaplain to Charles Stuart, and Bishop of Lincoln. When the king was staying at Belvoir Castle he would occasionally ride over to hear the worthy Sanderson preach, for he had a high regard for his chaplain and once confessed that he carried his ears to hear other preachers but he carried his conscience to hear Dr Sanderson.

A simple tablet to Sarah Crabbe recalls the poet who ministered here for several years, more than a century after the royal chaplain had passed on. George Crabbe, "Nature's sternest painter" as Byron called him, came here in 1789, but the place had few pleasant associations for him and enshrined his most tragic memory. In this stronghold of Dissent he was ever at odds with his parishioners because of his violent sermons against Nonconformity, and the tragedy of his married life came as a crowning blow to his happiness. Contented though the couple were at first, his wife fell into despair when five of their seven children died, and on the death of the last her sorrow deepened into melancholy. Poor Sarah Crabbe never recovered her reason, and was an invalid until a merciful death claimed her in 1813. So ill did the bereaved poet become that he asked for his wife's grave to be kept open, but although he recovered his health he never learned to regard this place as anything but a home of sorrows, and when, a few months later, he was offered a living at Trowbridge he gladly left this village, never to return.

LEICESTERSHIRE

Nineteen Children in Eighteen Years

NAILSTONE. It stands high up on the edge of the coalfields, the massive tower and spire of its 700-year-old church dominating both the main street and the neighbouring countryside.

The church has a new font but keeps the ancient one in idleness beneath the tower. It also has an Elizabethan monument showing Thomas Corbet in his slashed doublet and ermine collar. This old gentleman with the long peaked beard, who could proudly call himself Serjeant of the Pantry at the court of four Tudor sovereigns, was at home merely the father of 21 children, 19 of whom had been showered on him by his first wife in no more than 18 years.

NETHER BROUGHTON. The Romans laid a tessellated pavement here, which has gone; the early English builders crowned the low hill with a church which has stood 600 years, with a glorious view of the Vale of Belvoir; and Nature has ringed it round with lovely trees.

The church has been refashioned and has much beauty by craftsmen of our time—two beautifully carved chairs, a pulpit with panel tracery and grape vine trailing round the top, a reredos carved with leaves and grapes, and a heavenly choir of eight angels in stone playing musical instruments.

NEVILL HOLT. A glorious avenue of chestnuts and limes leads to its hilltop, where hall, church, and stone houses are grouped as if by the hand of an artist. The long rambling building of Nevill Holt Hall is set like an age-old story in stone. Now it is a school for boys, but for centuries it was the home of the Nevills. It was a Nevill who in the 15th century gave it a two-storeyed porch, and another who added a lovely oriel window since painted by the lichen and the moss. Some of the earlier generations were responsible for the odd carving. On the buttresses are two lions and an antelope, and above them three men with clubs; the porch has a frieze of angels and odd animals.

The 600-year-old church, whose graceful tower and spire enhance the beauty of the scene, has a battlemented porch built by Sir Thomas Nevill in 1635. The beautifully carved Jacobean pulpit and chair may also have been his gifts to the church of his forefathers.

Sir Thomas has an elaborate alabaster tomb on black marble columns with sword and helmet hanging above. It bears his armoured figure and two cherubs oddly perched on pedestals, little emblems of mortality, one kneeling on a skull, the other standing with a spade. His daughter, Jane Thursby, has a less funereal monument showing her kneeling in prayer while white-winged angels hold back the curtains of her canopy.

NEWBOLD VERDON. It has pleasant cottages and gardens in its curving main street and a plain 18th century hall, partly surrounded by a moat. The church, rebuilt last century, still keeps its ancient tower raised up on a Norman base, an ancient disused font, and an old oak chest with carved foliage. One of the windows has lovely figures of Christ, Joseph of Arimathea and three saints in memory of William Cole, who during a ministry of 41 years worked diligently for the rebuilding of the old church.

In a field close by are a group of ancient earthworks.

The Miniature Church

NEWTON HARCOURT. In a valley stand its oldest neighbours, an attractive Elizabethan manor house and a church which was given a new lease of life last century and has lost most of its ancient aspects and possessions. In the shady churchyard is a striking modern monument in the form of a miniature church with spire, porch, windows, and battlements, set up in memory of a boy of eight, a little shrine not unlike a toy building he himself might have tried to fashion with a big box of bricks. We have come upon no other like it in any of our country churchyards.

Bradgate's Historic Towers

NEWTOWN LINFORD. It is a charming place with thatched and timbered dwellings, a cedar-shaded inn, and a much-restored medieval church in peaceful setting by the stream—nor is this all, for the village is the doorstep to Bradgate Park, one of Leicester's loveliest pleasure grounds and a shrine for pilgrims, for in it are the ruins of the home of the ill-fated nine-days queen, Lady Jane Grey.

We think of her in the village church, where the east window shines in her memory. Given in our day by one of the Greys, it shows Christ among angels, with a colourful crowd of figures below, and has the inscription, Blessed are the pure in heart for they shall see God. An attractive window of red, blue, purple, and green, showing the Angel of Peace with doves and palm and St George spearing the Dragon, recalls those who fell in the war. The modern oak reredos and neat panelling of the chancel are chastely enriched with coloured carving of sprays of honeysuckle, wild rose, hawthorn, lilies, rowan berries, oak and acorn, vine and grape. In the richly carved and gilded medallions of the altar are Passion emblems and the Holy Lamb.

A few steps from the church bring us to the park, where peace dwells in a thousand acres of natural forest scenery. We may ride or walk along the road that wanders through this playground of herds of deer and countless rabbits, between a rippling stream and rocky slopes clothed with bracken and studded with trees. It leads us to the red-brick ruins of Bradgate House, and just beyond to the mere that is so much lovelier than its name (Cropston Reservoir). It was Charles Bennion who gave this park to the people of Leicestershire in 1928, "to be preserved in its natural state for their quiet enjoyment."

Looking out to Old John Hill, with its 18th century prospect tower standing out on the skyline, the old home of the Greys is a place of bitter memories kindly effaced by Time. The fragments of the fine house of early Tudor days are being partly reconstructed with the old material, and as the site is excavated the foundations are being built up, so that it will be possible to form a good impression of what it was like in the days of the tragic young figure whose memory haunts it still.

Of the four towers now more or less complete, three are octagonal and one has eight sides within but is square without. Of the workaday part of the house there are to be seen the well-constructed drains, a massive kitchen fireplace with its broken arch, and two fine baking ovens, between which is a receptacle for the ashes of the wood which heated them. In an isolated wall, patterned in blue brick, is a window which was enlarged in honour of a royal visit to the house.

Near this wall is an ash tree with an amazing branch stretching out for about 17 yards like a huge serpent, propped up almost on the ground. Fine trees here are a background for the forlorn ruins, and beyond a stretch of old red-brick wall is an enclosed garden of fruit trees, one the mulberry tree Lady Jane Grey knew, still bearing abundantly. There is part of the old moat, and a carriage-way paved with stones has been uncovered. It leads to a little bridge over the old mill stream.

It was in one of these towers that Roger Ascham found Jane Grey reading Plato, a child of 13 translating Greek while the rest of the family were hunting among the oaks and bracken. It was said of her that " she had the innocency of youth, the solidity of middle-age, the gravity of old-age, the birth of a princess, the learning of a clerk, the life of a saint," and she was only 17 when she met her tragic fate. In a picture on the stairway of Leicester's fine Reference Library we see her in an interview with Roger Ascham, pointing to an open book.

Of the chapel, whose walls had so often heard her whispered prayers, there remains a small gabled building with a great blocked window. Within it are many old tiles which have come to light, some patterned with roses, a figure in armour on horseback, a thistle, and a stag. But the treasure here is the sumptuous alabaster monument of Henry Grey, first Earl of Stamford, and his wife Anne who was the daughter of the celebrated Lord Burleigh. They lie on a tomb enriched with heraldry, under a pillared canopy surmounted by another great shield. The nobleman (who fought for Cromwell) is in armour with his head on his helmet; his countess wears a jewelled headdress, and her small feet peep from a gown of many folds.

The Bitter Story of Our Nine-Days Queen

LADY JANE GREY, descended on her mother's side from Henry the Seventh, was the eldest daughter of Henry Grey, Marquis of Dorset (whom Edward the Sixth created Duke of Suffolk), and of Frances Brandon, a niece of Henry the Eighth, by which king Jane was named in his will as next in succession to the throne after her cousins Edward, Mary, and Elizabeth.

Her beauty, birth, and intellectual gifts were a fatal inheritance, making her the centre of unscrupulous plots from her childhood up. As gifted as she was winsome, she became under John Aylmer a scholar of astonishing aptitude, and mastered languages with marvellous facility. Such was her charm that she was taken for two years into the home of Queen Katherine Parr, whose second husband, Thomas Seymour, sought to bring about her marriage to Edward the Sixth, or, failing that, to himself when he became a widower; while Seymour's brother, the Protector Somerset, proposed to marry Jane to his own son and his daughter to the dying king.

After the fall of these rivals Jane returned here to her parents, and here it was that, in the absence of the rest of the family in the hunting field, Roger Ascham found her reading Plato in Greek, and enjoyed that interview with her which has an immortal place in the story of our literature. Then it was that she confided to him the story of the tyranny of her parents to her, and of the pleasure and solace she found in her studies.

It was now that John Dudley, newly created Duke of Northumberland, entered into the life of Jane, first by inducing the doomed boy king to set aside Mary and Elizabeth in favour of Jane as his successor, and next by bribing her father to compel her to marry Northumberland's fourth son, Lord Guildford Dudley.

Her resistance to the marriage being overborne, Jane had been a bride only two months when Edward died, and her father-in-law caused her to be proclaimed Queen. Horrified at the dignity so lawlessly thrust upon her, Jane declared it a mockery of God to scruple to steal a shilling and not fear to usurp a crown. Coerced into accepting the throne, she refused to allow her husband to be proclaimed king; that, she said, must be the decision of Parliament.

Jane's unwilling usurpation led to an uprising by the nation, whose sense of wrong was deeply stirred at the sight of a rightful queen dispossessed. Northumberland, at the head of the troops raised for Jane, saw that her cause was hopeless and so declared for Mary, while Jane's own father, hoping to save his life, proclaimed Mary queen and Jane a prisoner.

Placed on trial, Jane and her husband were sentenced to death for high treason, but, Northumberland and two of his confederates having been executed, the young couple were sent back to the Tower with punishment deferred. They might have escaped with their lives but for the fact that Suffolk, pardoned for his share in the plot, took arms again on the rising of Wyatt, and so lost his head and made his daughter's doom inevitable.

Jane and her husband had been confined separately in the Tower, where, on a February morning in 1554, he was led to execution. As Jane followed an hour later, she met his headless body being borne back for burial. At the scaffold she retained her wonted courage and serenity, declaring that she had never wished to be queen, and that, in spite of all pressure and inducements, she died a Protestant.

She and her husband sleep together in that temple of tragedy, the chapel of St Peter in the Tower. One visible memento of them survives, the shortest, saddest, most penetrating of all the inscriptions there—Guildford Dudley's last outpouring of passionate devotion to his bride in the two words, *Jane, Jane*, scratched with a nail on a wall of the Beauchamp Tower where he was a prisoner.

NORMANTON-LE-HEATH. It stands on the edge of a hill looking across wide vistas of the countryside, its spire seen for miles and in its shadow a fine old house that has looked on much of the history of the 14th century church. The windows have beautiful tracery, the old oak screens are adorned with roses, and the font is Norman, the oldest possession of the village.

With Kitchener at Omdurman

NORTH KILWORTH. From its churchyard the green valley of the Avon can be seen spreading away in a gentle panorama. In the church (which though partly modern has an arcade seven centuries old) are inscribed the names of those unreturning brave who left the peace of this place and these fair vistas to make some corner of a foreign field for ever England.

Among these names is that of General Paul Kenna V C. His Victoria Cross had been won in the cavalry charge at Omdurman in 1898 when he was a captain of the Lancers. In the confusion many horses fell, many riders were unhorsed, and the Arabs were quick to take advantage. Captain Kenna first brought back to safety a brother officer who had lost his horse, and then, seeing Lieutenant de Montmorency going to find his sergeant, he galloped back to help. Accompanied by his corporal, de Montmorency found Lieutenant Grenfell on the ground and was trying to place the body on his own horse, when the frightened animal bolted and left him with nothing but a revolver with which to defend himself against a body of 300 Dervish horsemen fifty yards away. At this moment Kenna and his corporal came up, caught the horse, saw Montmorency safe on it and the three galloped back to safety with but a few yards to spare.

NORTON-BY-GAULBY. It is a hamlet of the Wolds, modest and unpretentious, but has a proper pride in its handsome 18th century church. Treasures it has none, nor surprises to warm the heart of an antiquarian, for its beauty is entirely in its outside dress, where the grey stone is enriched with a fine array of carving.

Except for the tower, it is a simple oblong of which the east end serves as chancel, tower and the rest adorned with parapets of open quatrefoils and leafy pinnacles. Bands of varied carving divide the four storeys of the tower, which has fine big belfry windows and a corbel table of flowers and faces. Reached by a flight of balustraded steps leading to the tower, the interior is like a lantern of light with great windows which have quatrefoil tracery. The dado, the box-pews, the west gallery òn fluted pillars, and the three-decker pulpit are all of simple panelled oak.

William Fortrey, who built the church, lies in the churchyard, his great stone tomb surmounted by a pyramid reaching almost as high as the tracery of the east window. By the churchyard is the old red-brick manor house, now a farm.

The Rector's Son and Sir Isaac Newton

NORTON-JUXTA-TWYCROSS. It is a tiny village near the Warwickshire border, unpretentious and remote, but in the 17th century it was the birthplace of two boys who grew up to win some measure of fame. Sir John Moore, who was born here in 1620 and became Lord Mayor of London some 60 years later, founded the school designed by Wren at neighbouring Appleby, and so left his county for ever in his debt.

William Whiston, born in 1667, was the son of a blind, deaf, and lame rector who ministered here for 16 years, valiantly defying his afflictions. The son, who was notorious for his controversies, succeeded to the professorship held at Cambridge by Sir Isaac Newton, and by his lectures did much to make the great man's theories better known. His greater title to remembrance is his translation of the Jewish historian Josephus.

The church where these two clever boys worshipped stands upright and sturdy though six centuries old, with an ancient figure in a niche on the tower, sitting like a weary guardian.

Here Sleeps a Friend of Cromwell

NOSELEY. Here, in a woodland solitude, church and hall stand side by side, companions since Roger de Martival, Bishop of Salisbury, built them 700 years ago. Through all these years of change they have shared the loveliness on every hand.

The hall was made new in Queen Anne's day, but the ancient aspect of the church has changed little in the passing years. A noble

avenue of beeches marches from the hall in rhythmic formation;
by the church is a glorious cedar, and opposite the porch is a curious
beech with a kind of natural crossbar between the branches.

The church has some fine old woodwork, for it is protected by a
carved roof 500 years old, and there is a tradition that the chancel
panelling was made from the oak of the Mayflower. Over some old
traceried desk-ends are oak figures of cocks, there is a venerable
ironbound chest, and the 14th century font is partly enclosed by old
woodwork. In the east window are figures of Apostles and heraldic
glass of the 14th century.

Noseley was the home of the long line of Hesilrige baronets. Set
in the floor are many monumental stones, some engraved with kneeling figures long forgotten, some to their 17th century successors.
There is a canopied altar tomb of Sir Thomas Hesilrige and his wife
Frances, who survived him till after the Restoration; and on the
cornice above them kneel eight sons and six daughters in green
and red robes enriched with gold. One of these sons, Sir Arthur
Hesilrige, appears on another monument with two wives and 12
children, one of whom died when he was only 12, " of incomparable
learning for his age in Hebrew, Greek, Latin, and French." Sir
Arthur, a great friend of Cromwell, played a big part in the Civil
War as an officer and as a statesmen during the Commonwealth, but
his end was tragic. He rests here among his forefathers, having been
for a time one of the most powerful men in the land.

Early left an orphan, Arthur Hesilrige was brought up by Pym
and sat in Parliament as a Puritan. He was one of the Five Members
whose arrest was ordered by the king. He bore his share with Cromwell in the invasion of Scotland. Among Cromwell's letters are two
stirring ones written to Hesilrige from Dunbar, one before the
battle, the order on the day of the victory; brief letters, but compris-
ing a whole volume of military history, and recounting with characteristic modesty a triumph which made Spain recognise the
Commonwealth and Holland hasten to offer an alliance.

Hesilrige laid down his command under the Self-denying Ordin-
ance, and when Cromwell dismissed the Parliament he became
bitterly hostile. After Oliver's death he helped to overthrow Richard
Cromwell, sought a republican form of government, and became a
national leader, but wayward and unstable. He turned from
Lambert to Monk and from Monk to Lambert, distrusted and

Nevill Holt   The Hall and Church

Whitwick   The Modern Abbey in Charnwood Forest

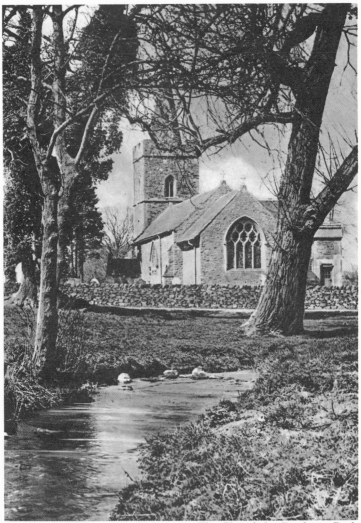

Newtown Linford   **The Church by Bradgate Park**

despised by both, although he was probably honest in intent. Finally he connived at the Restoration on being promised that his own life should be spared, but he was sent to the Tower and there he died.

OADBY. Its houses of many kinds are set in a long broken line, seeming to await the approach of others from Leicester, which has already sent out a tram line to serve them. But in a well-kept churchyard a fine old church is nobly set, with a 13th century western tower crowned by a six-sided spire. The clerestoried nave keeps its 15th century roof, and the windows of the chancel and north aisle, both a century older, have lovely tracery. From its early days the church has preserved a traceried font and a venerable dug-out chest of unknown age.

Husbands and Wives

OLD DALBY. Its popular name of Dalby-on-the-Wolds gives us some idea of its lovely setting. Here it nestles in the deep embowered recess below the cliff, every house with its tree.

The church which grew up in these surroundings was made new last century but has kept some of its ancient monuments. The earliest is a coffin lid with a cross carved on it seven or eight centuries ago. Another is a 16th century altar tomb hardly more than a yard long, with fine figures of a lady in tight-fitting headdress and wide-sleeved robe between her two armoured and bearded husbands, John Hopton and Sir Thomas Tyrull, her three boys and two girls below. A second altar tomb only a few years younger has figures of Andrew Noel, a Sheriff of Rutland, in armour and ruff between his two wives in the same tight-fitting headdresses and loose-sleeved dresses. On the front of this monument are ten children, very small.

Early in the 17th century another Andrew Noel, also Sheriff of Rutland and with the additional honour of a knighthood conferred on him by Queen Elizabeth, came in his turn to be buried here. On his big monument he lies in armour, with a wife who wears the same kind of dress as her gentle predecessors save for the closer-fitting sleeves. Sir Andrew's brother Henry, who was buried in the Abbey, was popular at court and a pensioner of the Queen.

ORTON-ON-THE-HILL. Its medieval church has a graceful 18th century spire looking into Warwickshire and treasures a relic borne with pious hands across the border many centuries ago.

It is the figure of a 14th century abbot who ruled Merevale Abbey long before its dissolution, his hands clasped in prayer and a dog lying at his feet. Other ancient monuments bear it company; there is the stone lid of a priest's coffin carved with cross, chalice, and missal; an old stone tomb with a small figure of a mounted soldier in armour at one end and a Maltese cross at the other; and a 16th century memorial of alabaster with engraved figures of William Foster, his wife in a gown with a jewelled girdle, and three children. In the churchyard is a modern monument to an infant boy with a cherub sitting, wreath in hand and head bowed down.

OSGATHORPE. It is but a bowshot from Charnwood Forest and a mile from Grace Dieu, and it seems to have borrowed a little of the charm of both, for everything about it is neat and comely. Its dwellings repose in a sleepy valley, and its church, carrying its 600 years with such easy grace, seems to keep a parental eye on the young 17th century school and almshouses.

The new apsed chancel was added to the church last century and the medieval chancel now forms part of the nave, the frame of its east window forming the present chancel arch. On a windowsill are fragments of an ancient dial that once stood in the churchyard marking the sunny hours.

All That Is Left

OWSTON. It is set on a hillside that seems away from every- where and is perhaps the most remote village in Leicestershire.

Eight hundred years ago, when church and crown were struggling for supremacy, Robert Grimbald, Chief Justice of England, set on this lonely hillside a small priory named Osulveston. It long sur- vived its founder's family, and, though the Dissolution struck a decisive blow at it, the buildings lingered on till the 19th century. But today Osulveston priory, reduced like its name, is represented in the 600-year-old church only with its ancient font, all that is left.

PACKINGTON. Among its charms it can count many thatched cottages, and even the ancient village lock-up with its mellow red-brick walls and ivied crown. Its church, built anew many times in its seven centuries of service, still has its plain old font and the headless brass of one of its 15th century rectors. There is also a stone with engraved figures of Raphe Leeson with his two wives, all wearing Elizabethan ruffs; and six modern benches with old carved ends, two with Tudor roses and leaves, and a third with the grotesque head of a man. Two of the chancel windows show the Nativity and Our Lord with the disciples in fine modern glass.

Dr Johnson's Bride

PEATLING MAGNA. It is great only in name and pretty only in a small degree, but it has many precious things, and one link with greatness in its little church with beckoning 14th century spire.

In the churchyard is the base of an ancient cross and in the chancel is an Easter sepulchre 700 years old, with a graceful trefoiled arch and musical angels among fragments of 15th century glass. There is a plain 13th century font with a Jacobean cover, a Jacobean pulpit with big sounding board, fragments of a medieval screen resting wearily against the walls, some 15th century benches, and a few Jacobean pews.

Three monuments to the Jervis family are notable. The earliest is an Elizabethan altar tomb to William Jervis and his wife Katharine, with their portraits finely engraved on the top and a happy crowd of 18 children sculptured below. An altar tomb under a 13th century arch has a portrait of another William Jervis who died in 1614, etched with his two wives in rich embroidered gowns, their five children sculptured below. A third William Jervis, who died four years later, kneels on a wall monument with his wife Elizabeth accompanied by a reminder of mortality: *As you are so were we; as we are so shall you be.*

One day in 1689 some other Jervis who, like his forefathers, had dwelt here in peace and plenty, brought his baby girl to the ancient font to be baptised as Elizabeth. She grew up to become the second Mrs Samuel Johnson, the famous Tetty.

She was the widow of a mercer and mother of a daughter and two sons when, in 1735, she married Johnson. Tetty, as the adoring scholar always called her, was a woman of " good understanding and great sensibility, but inclined to be satirical." She was twenty years older than Johnson, and painted her cheeks outrageously, but he was too dim-sighted to see it. He was lean and lank, an ugly figure, his hair straight and stiff, and separated behind; and he often had convulsive starts and odd gesticulations which tended to excite at once surprise and ridicule. He urged his suit like a cyclone, master already of a copious and majestic torrent of language. " This is the most sensible man that I ever saw in my life," said the widow Porter, as she bestowed her hand with her sole property (£800) in it.

Since the death of her husband Tetty had lived at Birmingham, but she was too romantic to be married there; she must mount and ride, nobly squired, all the way to Derby, and there be wedded at St Werburgh's Church.

The marriage proved almost cloudlessly happy. Tetty was saint and Venus to her husband; and to the end, long after her death, he would utter moving and lovely prayers for her soul. She died in the middle of the night, in March, 1752, and was buried at Bromley, Kent, too soon to know the lasting renown which her husband's Dictionary was to bring him.

A Far-Off Ancestor

PECKLETON. Its houses shelter in the hollow; its church stands boldly on the skyline. In the grounds of the hall is a grassy mound in which an unknown warrior of prehistoric days was buried by his sorrowing tribe. In the churchyard is a grand old yew and a slate tombstone with a name of great interest. In this grave lies a far-off ancestor of William Howard Taft, son of General Grant's Secretary for War and himself President of the United States.

Most of the church is 14th century, but its font links it with Norman times. Under an arch in the chancel is the battered figure of an unknown 14th century man in a long gown, his hands clasped in prayer, his head on a pillow; near him is a knight he may have known, lying in armour with his wife. Under the altar table is another old and nameless monument with a roughly carved man's head in a medallion, and on a wall are engraved the portraits of Sir Thomas Harvey in his 16th century armour with two wives in long tight-waisted dresses. The front of an alabaster altar tomb in the south aisle has crude figures believed to represent the six children who mourned him, and on one of the pews is an oak beam thought to have belonged to a medieval rood screen. In a chancel window are two figures of saints 600 years old.

PICKWELL. It has many gabled houses sharing with the manor house a fine view into Rutland. The church is a happy mixture of the ages, with Norman and 13th century arches in the nave, a clerestory and tall chancel windows of the 14th century, and a stately tower of the 15th. In the aisles are five arches for tombs, and there is an arcaded font and a Jacobean altar table. One of the rectors here was the Royalist John Cave, who was in the pulpit one day when Roundhead troops fired at him, and it is said that on another visit they dragged him from the pulpit. His son William, who was born in this village, inherited his father's fondness for the Stuarts and became chaplain to Charles the Second.

The Clerk and the Registers

PLUNGAR. It lies among the farms in the fair green Vale of Belvoir, its little church serene in a churchyard fringed with yew, mellowed by five centuries of sun and rain.

Outside, on the tower wall, are grotesque carvings of a seated horse and a wolf with two men; inside, the tower arch is decorated with leaves and more quaint animals and eight angels bear up the nave roof. The ancient font has a battlemented bowl, and two old stalls have panelled ends decorated with dragons and other fearsome creatures. All the registers before 1754 are missing, and the story goes that the parish clerk, who was also village grocer, took them to wrap up his tea.

Cavalier and Roundhead

PRESTWOLD. It lies enchanting in a sheltered valley, richly wooded and with a stream running through it. The hall, made new in the 18th century, stands on its terrace in a lovely park. At the end of a dark avenue of box and fir, is the church with the monuments that tell the 600-year-old story of the passing generations.

The earliest monument is an alabaster tomb with figures of two unknown ladies in pointed headdress and girdled gowns, angels at their heads and dogs at their feet, and ten monks sitting in panels below. On a 15th century altar tomb are portraits of Richard Neel in gown and coif, with his wife in a close-fitting gown and veiled headdress, angels and monks (two with crutches) sculptured below. After this comes the monument of Sir William Skipwith, knighted by James the First on his way south to become first Stuart King of England. Sir William lies alone on his magnificent altar tomb, a sword by his side, and 15 small angels keeping watch over him. Just below him, on a projecting ledge, is his wife in a mantle, her hood falling back to disclose her comely face. Sir John Beaumont wrote the friendly epitaph extolling Sir William's manifold virtues, and concluding:

All these we never more shall find in one
And yet all these are closed within this stone.

The virtue of loyalty at least descended to his son Henry, who was as attached to Charles as his father had been to James, but his faithfulness cost him his fortune, and he was forced to sell his Prestwold estates. They passed to one of the most vigorous Roundheads, Sir Christopher Packe, Lord Mayor of London and Governor of the Merchant Adventurers. Cromwell knighted him, and he was one of those who petitioned the Protector to assume the crown, so that when the Restoration came many of his honours fell from him and he was fortunate to be able to retire into the obscurity of Prestwold. Here he died and here he was buried under a table tomb which shows him proudly reclining in his mayor's robes.

Many other Packes followed him, and have their monuments here. Charles Hussey Packe, only a schoolboy when he died at Eton in 1842, has as his memorial a charming figure of a sleeping boy by Westmacott; another work by the same sculptor is a marble of Hope in memory of Charles Packe, who died at the beginning of the Victorian Era. To Richard Packe who passed away in his infancy in 1874 there is a memorial relief of Christ carrying a child, by Hamo Thornycroft, and a monument to Colonel Packe who died in the same year has his portrait and attendant angels. Another soldier of the family, killed at Waterloo, is recalled by a relief showing the charge of his regiment.

Two fine monuments of this house have been set up in our own time, one a sculptured portrait of a lady, the other showing Hussey Packe (who restored the church) kneeling before a pedestal with his portrait engraved on it, offering a model of the church to an angel.

The Brass of Margaret Bury

QUENIBOROUGH. A row of creeper-clad cottages in its wide street, with sloping roofs of thatch and a spreading chestnut tree shading the churchyard, are its chief charms, crowned by a slender and graceful spire soaring 162 feet high.

The chancel has Norman walls, a Norman window barely six inches wide, and Norman ornament in a 14th century arch. The arcades and the plain round font are 700 years old, the aisles 600, the tower and clerestory 500. A head carved on a wall is thought to be that of a 14th century vicar. The pulpit is fashioned from old oak seats. Very curious is a 17th century brass showing Margaret Bury sleeping on her tomb under a canopy guarded by trumpeting angels; in her hand she holds a flower, and from her head a ladder rises to clouds inscribed The Land of the Living.

The village has had its stirring hours, for down the street rode the troopers of Prince Rupert, who twice during the Civil War made the place his headquarters. They were not the first warriors to pass this way, for a thousand years before them the Saxons had camped here, and one of their soldiers left a sword that was to lie buried for centuries before it once more saw the light of day.

The Monuments of the Farnhams

QUORN. It bears a name of stirring sound to huntsmen, and it bears also many unlovely marks of industry; yet for those who seek them it has something of the charm of bygone days.

The granite church, with a massive 14th century tower, has Norman stones still in its walls, and in its 13th century vaulted porch a fine Norman doorway with a double row of chevrons. It has two medieval stone screens, of which there are only perhaps a hundred surviving in all England, and it has a plain old font. But its chief possession is the 14th century Farnham Chapel, with the monuments of the Farnhams who have lived here for 700 years. Quorn Hall, built by a Farnham in 1680, still stands with its grove of chestnuts by the Soar, and the 19th century Quorndon House, standing near the site of their ancient hall, is still their home.

The monuments in the chapel do not reach back to the 13th century, but they do proclaim the splendour of the family in Tudor Times. There is a great altar tomb of John Farnham, gentleman pensioner to Queen Elizabeth, who, "descended of an ancient house, with honours led his life." It has a beautiful figure of the gentleman pensioner with his head resting on a helmet, his wife by his side in gown and ruff with her head on a cushion, and a daughter kneeling below. On a wall near by is a panel which belonged to this monument, showing a man in armour conducting a siege of musketeers, and suggesting that John Farnham was a soldier before he became a gentleman pensioner.

Another Farnham monument shows a grave man in fur-trimmed gown kneeling at a desk with four sons behind him, his wife kneeling with two daughters; and on other memorials are engraved figures of 16th century members of the house: Thomas and William in armour, Robert and Francis as men of peace.

In the chancel is a window with figures of Paul and Bartholomew in memory of Thomas Stammers, vicar for 55 years of last century.

Shakespeare's Valiant Man

RAGDALE. On the edge of the Wolds, close to a small tributary of the Wreak, it sees fine views of the rolling wooded countryside. The new hall with its tower and turrets stands back from the road, away from the rest of the village. More friendly, among the farms and dwellings, stands the time-worn church with a fine old cross among the tombstones; and only just a step away is the old hall of brick and stone, pathetic in its faded splendour but attractive still.

This house of many gables, with clustered chimneys and a projecting porch, must have been very charming. Now one half is a farmhouse, the rest forlorn indeed. Over the fine bow window and on the porch are the stone shields of the Shirleys. In the middle of the 16th century the manor came into the possession of John Shirley, who built the oldest remaining part of the house. His grandson Sir Henry, who added the porch, married the daughter of Elizabeth's favourite Earl of Essex, and, uplifted by his marriage, indulged his taste for heraldry and pedigrees.

Proud men were the Shirleys, and none prouder than that Sir Henry who claimed descent from the grand falconer of Henry the Fourth, the " valiant Shirley " of Shakespeare, who fell at Shrewsbury. He once went into the Fleet prison through some trouble he had with the Earl of Huntingdon over the right to hawk. He cared nothing for a lord in England, he said, " except the Lord of Hosts," and it was a fine thing for my lord to deny him hawking in his ground, and he was glad my lord had no more ground to hawk in, that he had a spirit as well as my lord. But after his short spell in prison, Sir Henry, no doubt a chastened man, forgot his hawking quarrels and set about quietly rebuilding his home, " determined not to think of courtly pomp or glory."

We come upon the Shirleys again at Staunton Harold and Breedon-on-the-Hill, and here need only remember Sir Henry's fortunes by noting that his son Robert was seven times imprisoned in the Tower for being too ardent a Royalist, and that his grandson (created Earl of Ferrers in 1711) kept his hawks in one of Ragdale's parlours.

We see their shield in one of the windows of the quaint little church with a squat tower, dwarfed by the size of the old house but snugly sheltered by fine trees. It is chiefly 13th and 14th century, with a chancel made partly new a century and a half ago. A fine old embattled porch and a pleasing doorway lead us inside, where there is nothing older than the charming little arcade with pillars shoulder-high, one of the capitals enriched with leaves and quaint faces.

The fine old font, with a square bowl on four pillars (no two alike), stands on a base of old alabaster gravestones. It is in a pretty corner of the church, lighted by a lancet and a 14th century window, and furnished by three old carved settles. Two faces are carved on one of four old poppyhead benches, and projecting from the inside wall of the tower are two quaint stone heads. Here too is a fragment of stone showing part of a figure with a staff.

RATBY. It lies on the outskirts of Charnwood Forest, its church set proudly on a hill with a venerable yew, all gnarled and worn, to keep it company. By the school in Main Street is an angel of peace which Lord Haig unveiled, not far off is the ancient moated farmhouse called Old Hayes, and Holywell Farm has a Roman encampment of 12 acres. The church, except for its massive 700-year-old tower, is 14th century, with a few fragments of ancient glass in its graceful windows, a richly traceried font, and in the chancel a lifelike figure of Sir Henry Sacheverell in his 17th century gown and ruff.

RATCLIFFE CULEY. It lies in the angle between the Rivers Anker and Sence on the borders of Warwickshire, its church, with a huge wych elm for company, bearing well its 600 years. It still has its plain old font and some fragments of ancient heraldic glass, on which we noticed a solemn owl and a friendly lion.

RATCLIFFE-ON-THE-WREAK. It stands prettily on a hill above the river, abode of both charm and scholarship. The little 14th century church, with a tall modern spire rising above the churchyard, remains still, as do the plain 13th century or Norman font of its predecessor and a small window with all its original 600-year-old glass patterned in rich red and blue.

In the chancel is the 14th century figure of a priest, his hands still joined in prayer though his features are almost worn away; in the nave is a 19th century monument with a praying angel child, in memory of a boy who was killed by falling from his pony.

One of the little-known band of scholars who gave us our greatest book was among the boys who worshipped in this church. He was Richard Kilbye, the brilliant son of humble parents, who became Professor of Hebrew at Oxford and was one of the translators of the Authorised Version of the Bible.

Near the village is a famous Roman Catholic college, founded almost a century ago, and less than a mile to the south is the only Long Barrow in the county. It is 350 feet long, 120 wide, and 40 high, a huge mound raised by the men of the Stone Age.

George Stephenson's Home

RAVENSTONE. This pretty place high up above the River Sence seems as remote from the coalfields as if it belonged to an earlier century. Among its cottages is one of those delightful 18th century almshouses whose charm goes hand in hand with homeliness. Built about a quadrangle, with the Master's lodge and the chapel for its wings, it was founded by Rebecca Wilkins in memory of her son.

Alton Grange, a fine white stone house with graceful cedars in its garden, is associated with the famous name of George Stephenson. He lived here after the completion of the Liverpool and Manchester railway in 1830, and spent much of his time in the development of the mines, but, as Samuel Smiles tells us in his Life of the inventor, "was so much occupied in travelling about from one committee of directors to another—one week in England, another in Scotland, and probably the next in Ireland—that he often did not see his home for weeks together."

Two old yews guard the gate leading to the little church, between six and seven centuries old, and a modern figure of St Michael is on guard outside the tower. In the south aisle is a crudely-carved head of John the Baptist, and on the chancel wall is a tablet set up in memory of his parents by Sir Joseph Mawbey, a native of this village who won a small measure of fame as a politician in the days of Pitt. He wrote much prose and verse, and though Walpole called him vain, noisy, and foolish, a contemporary poet gave him a line in one of his poems, "Sir Joseph is as witty as he's good."

The Clerk's New Coat

REARSBY. By the road where its thatched cottages stand a stream glides by to join the Wreak, spanned by the seven arches of a packhorse bridge which leisurely men with slow-footed beasts have been crossing for 600 years.

A short lane and a yew-bordered path lead from the bridge to the medieval church, with its handsome pinnacled tower. It has a 13th century font supported by four groups of clustered pillars, and a doorway in the north aisle that is perhaps as old. The canopied screen, with symbols of the Evangelists painted on its panels, is modern.

In the churchyard is a slate monument of Cleare Sacheverell, who in 1644 was turned out of his rectory for his Royalist sympathies. His story is not so uncommon as that of his uncle Andrew, who in 1658 was buried here in a leaden coffin, unearthed a century later and sold for 28 shillings to buy the clerk a coat.

Thomas Daffy's Cures

REDMILE. Its poor old windmill is sail-less and forlorn, but its ancient yews still flourish. They stand by the 13th century church, which still has a round Norman pillar and an ancient font with flowers in its panels. An old parson who began preaching here in the year of the Great Fire not only preached the salvation of the soul but sold a medicine to cure every illness. His name was Thomas Daffy, and advertisements of his miraculous elixir were printed long after it had failed to cure him.

ROLLESTON. It has a Tudor hall with an old fishpond in its grounds, close to a church hiding behind a wonderful hedge of yew, 20 feet high. The church lost its antiquity in the 18th century, but among the trees in its churchyard rises the slender shaft of an ancient cross.

ROTHERBY. Trees with massive trunks and spreading branches lean over the stone wall of its curving street, and others screen its pretty 14th century church as they soar above the pinnacled tower and the traceried clerestory.

The church still retains some of the heavy masonry of its Norman predecessor, and the pulpit, the plain altar rails, and the panelled south door are fashioned of oak from the ancient roof. The dim chancel has a 13th century tomb under a new oak canopy adorned with leaves and roses, and a modern reredos with paintings of saintly figures, the Madonna, the Archangel Gabriel, and Hugh of Lincoln among them.

The House of Great Fame

ROTHLEY. Charnwood Forest stretches out its withered arms to the old houses by the stream which runs into the Soar, but Leicester and Loughborough, with the help of the steel arms of the railway, are reaching to these pleasant byways.

The old granite church, founded in Norman days, has a massive 15th century tower, with nave and aisles a century or two older. The traceried screen of the modern chancel is 500 years old, the font with its generous pattern of chevron is Norman, and in a window of the south aisle is a small headless kneeling figure among a few fragments of ancient glass.

Many are the monuments here to the Babingtons of Rothley Temple, who, century after century, father and son, wife and daughter, came here to pray and were brought to rest in peace. In a chancel recess is the 16th century tomb of Humfrey Babington and Eleanora his wife, their figures engraved above those of seven sons and five daughters. On the front of their tomb is the figure of Thomas Babington, kneeling at a prayer desk with his coat-of-arms supported by two baboons on tuns, an odd heraldic pun on the name. Close to it is the 17th century monument of Matthew Babington and his wife, shaking hands. In the north aisle Thomas Babington kneels in his Elizabethan armour, with his wife in a coif and richly embroidered gown, and their five sons and four daughters. In the south aisle is a monument with a shield supported by mermaids.

In the churchyard is a weather-beaten Saxon cross about 12 feet high. Believed to be 1200 years old, it is the oldest relic above the ground of Rothley, but not the oldest found here, for many Roman remains have come to light. More than 200 years ago a Roman pavement was unearthed.

Hidden away in its high-walled grounds near the village is Rothley Temple, famous as the birthplace of Lord Macaulay. On close inspection it reveals itself as one of those fascinating houses of English domestic architecture which have added to themselves through the centuries, the new blending happily with the old. The

Knight Templars founded it as a preceptory in the time of Henry the Third, and their 13th century chapel, with a Knight Templar's worn cross-legged figure seeming to guard the entrance, still stands at the side of the house. It has all its ancient dignity, with the six narrow side windows with trefoil heads which sufficed for the Templars, and a fine 15th century window with fragments of old heraldic glass through which the eastern light falls. In Tudor days it came into the hands of the Babingtons, who surrounded the chapel with the fabric of an Elizabethan house and contentedly dwelt there until mid-Victorian days, allowing nothing to disturb the tranquillity of the old place, save the windows put in to give still more light.

This is a famous description of Macaulay's birthplace by Sir George Trevelyan, who was born at Rothley Temple forty years after his uncle.

Macaulay's Birthplace

ROTHLEY TEMPLE, which lies in a valley beyond the first ridge that separates the flat unattractive country immediately round Leicester from the wild and beautiful scenery of Charnwood Forest, is well worth visiting as a singularly unaltered specimen of an English home.

The stately trees, the grounds (half park, half meadow), the cattle grazing up to the very windows; the hall with its stone pavement rather below than above the level of the soil, hung with armour rude and rusty enough to dispel the suspicion of its having passed through a collector's hands; the low ceilings; the dark oak wainscot, carved after primitive designs, that covered every inch in bedroom and corridor; the general air which the whole interior presented of having been put to right at the time of the Armada and left alone ever since—all this antiquity contrasted quaintly, but prettily enough, with the youth and gaiety that lit up every corner of the ever-crowded but comfortable mansion.

In wet weather there was always a merry group sitting on the staircase or marching up and down the gallery; and wherever the noise and fun were most abundant, wherever there was to be heard the loudest laughter and the most vehement expostulation, Macaulay was the centre of a circle which was protesting against the levity of his remarks about the Blessed Martyr.

The place is full of his memories. His favourite walk was a mile of field-road and lane which leads from the house to a lodge on the highway, and his favourite point of view in that walk was a slight

THE KING'S ENGLAND

acclivity whence the traveller from Leicester catches his first sight of Rothley Temple with its background of hill and greenwood. He is remembered as sitting at the window in the hall reading Dante to himself, or translating it aloud as long as any listeners cared to remain within earshot.

Marvellous Lord Macaulay

WHEN Thomas Babington Macaulay was created a peer it was Baron Macaulay of Rothley he decided to be. Born here in 1800 during a visit of his parents, the eldest of nine children, his father was Zachary Macaulay, a West Indies merchant devoted to the abolition of slavery. His mother was a member of a Gloucestershire family of Quakers.

He grew up at Clapham, where his parents were members of the scholarly and philanthropic Clapham Sect, to whom the slaves were largely indebted for their freedom. Tom was a wonder-child, who could read and expound prodigious books from the age of three, and became poet, historian, and dramatist when very little older; a romantic who saw the Alps in a slight rise on Clapham Common and Mount Sinai in the crest of its island pond; a realist who, when a servant swept away the oyster-shells marking the limits of his patch of garden, burst into the drawing-room with "Cursed be Sally, for it is written, Cursed be he that removeth his neighbour's landmark"; a host who, when Hannah More called in the absence of his parents, startled her by the promise of some old spirits which, he explained, "Robinson Crusoe often drank."

While still a tiny boy he was taken to visit Lady Waldegrave, where his leg was scalded by hot coffee. Asked after a while how he did, he replied, "Thank you, madam, the agony is abated." His language was always mature, his spelling and grammar correct, his memory marvellous; yet his was an entirely simple nature—he was as delighted to help the cook as to commit a masterpiece to memory. He was never allowed to realise that he was clever or exceptional, and grew up to believe that all children knew as much as he.

The child was father of the man. At Cambridge University he proved a magnificent scholar, an unrivalled debater, and notable then, as throughout life, as one of the most brilliant conversationalists of the century. Called to the Bar, which he disliked, he began his career as a writer at 23, by contributing to Knight's Quarterly

Essays and such fine poems as Ivry, The Armada, and Naseby. At 25 began the famous series of Essays for the Edinburgh Review which made him famous in literature. For 20 years this association lasted, his articles numbering only 28, though some extending to more than 40,000 words.

Entering Parliament in 1830, he helped by his splendid oratory to pass the Reform Bill, held various minor offices, and went, at 34, to India as legal adviser to the Supreme Council and chairman of the Committee of Public Instruction, advocating a Western education for Indians. Returning four years later, he immersed himself in politics, became a leading figure of the most brilliant circle in Europe, and began the famous History of the period from the accession of James the Second to the Premiership of Walpole. The work was arrested by his death, the concluding part having to be sketched in by another hand from his notes. No history before ever excited such enthusiasm and appreciation. It has its critics on the score of its intense Whig sympathies, but it remains an incomparable picture of the scenes and personalities of its era.

Macaulay's chief poems, the Lays of Ancient Rome, appeared in 1842, achieving an immediate popularity which has never waned. Such lines as these from Horatius are as well known as Shakespeare:

> *Then none was for a party,*
> *Then all were for the State;*
> *Then the great man helped the poor,*
> *And the poor man loved the great;*
> *Then lands were fairly portioned;*
> *Then spoils were fairly sold;*
> *The Romans were like brothers*
> *In the brave days of old.*

Much of his poetry may be for all time, certainly the tender epitaph on a Jacobite, written when he was 45, with that moving last prayer of the exile who has given all for his king:

> *Forget all feuds, and shed one English tear*
> *O'er English dust. A broken heart lies here.*

A bachelor devoted to his sisters and their children, scholar, statesman, and traveller, Macaulay was an entirely happy man. He died in harness, and an admiring nation laid him in the Abbey with his peers, the poets and statesmen of England.

Hard Times

SADDINGTON. Below its hill spread many green pastures, and set among them is a lake magnificent, a 50-acre reservoir. The church is 700 years old, with a 14th century tower arch and a 15th century clerestory, but much of it has been made new since the day when the record was written of the churchyard fence being broken so that cattle and hogs came in, of the windows being broken so that the starlings came in, of the belfry door letting the wind and weather come in, and of people driven out because their seats were wet with rain.

All that is changed now, and the church is well cared for. The east window has gay glass, and angels guard the chancel. By a strange chance the most forlorn thing is a monument to the rector of the period of decay, Richard Holland; he is engraved on a floor-stone, his features worn away.

King Lud's Entrenchments

SALTBY. It has a little church 700 years old; and on one of its scattered farms is a windmill still turning its sails to the wind in the Wolds; and under its surface a Roman pavement has been found. But life in this village is far older than either windmills or churches or empires. On the high ground of the heath is a long double mound of earth with a tumulus at each end long known as King Lud's Entrenchments.

Lud was the sky god worshipped by the Ancient Britons, and afterwards transformed by tradition into a British king; and it is thought that this place may have been the burial ground of a forgotten chief. It is certain that this secluded spot is of very great antiquity.

The name of Lud is the Welsh form of the British god referred to by Julius Caesar as Nodens. He had a temple at Lydney on the Severn, where a remarkable metal relief has been found showing him standing in a chariot drawn by four horses and with winged figures on either side of him representing the four winds. In British legend he has a silver hand and owned 21,000 cows. The Welsh name for London was Caer Ludd (Lud's Town), and he had a temple on the banks of the Thames as well as on the Severn, Ludgate Hill preserving his name. One legend says that Lud was King of London and brother of the famous Cassivelaunus (uncle of Shakespeare's Cymbeline) who fought against Caesar.

The Lost Castle

SAPCOTE. In feudal days it could boast a castle of the Norman Bassets who came over with the Conqueror and throve mightily in our land.

From this proud castle Ralph Basset, Lord of Sapcote, rode out to fight in the ranks of the barons for Simon de Montfort, and in the next century another Basset went from here to share in the victory of Crecy. Now nothing remains of the castle but traces of its moat, and Sapcote's most impressive sights are the giant craters of its quarries and the grey 14th century church, with a slender spire and a leaf-patterned Norman font.

SAXBY. It has cottages where once were huts of wattle and mud, and a church with a grey tower set where Saxon horsemen rode, for here was a Saxon camp of considerable importance. All traces of the site have vanished above ground, but skeletons of men and horses, bridle bits and brooches, have been found and are now housed in the Bede House at Melton Mowbray, four miles away. Saxby must have been known before the Saxons came, for Roman burial urns have also been found here; but the place has dwindled with the centuries, and today it is a tiny village embowered in trees.

The church was rebuilt in the year of the French Revolution, and has a curious but not unpleasing tower with urns at the base of the spire. One of its 18 round-headed windows has figures of Our Lord and two disciples, and is a thing of beauty.

Mistress Brokesby

SAXELBY. It has the charm of old cottages slumbering beneath their thatch, and a churchyard where yew and lime trees throw their welcome shade and a stream goes rippling by. The 13th century church, crowned by a graceful spire, still preserves its ancient battlemented font and some 15th century benches. The pulpit, adorned with leaves and roses, is also 500 years old, and there is a brass showing Mistress Brokesby in the pointed headdress and girdled gown she wore here four centuries ago.

The Wife's Last Word

SCALFORD. Farmhouses and cottages look up proudly to its church, flaunting its venerable dignity on the brow of the hill.

It is the only church in the land dedicated to the obscure 7th century saint Egelwine, brother of Kenwalch, King of the West

Saxons. Although it has no other link with such remote days, some of its stones have borne their burden hundreds of years, for the arcades are 13th century, the aisles and the big south porch with its canopied niches are 14th, and the lofty clerestory was raised in the 15th. The massive tower was made new in Charles Stuart's day and the chancel, though preserving seven medieval worthies on its arch, is modern.

On a stone standing upright in the vestry is a 16th century brass of a kneeling man; the scroll from his mouth and the portrait of his wife have both vanished, but her scroll remains—a clear case of the lady having the last word. In the churchyard is a fragment of the ancient village cross.

A Lake Before England Was an Island

SCRAPTOFT. Its houses, church, and hall seem to peer over a cliff on to the pastures below. The wooded lands about them were a lake before England was an island, and when the Stone Age men came at last from Europe to find a home on the uplifted bed of that most ancient inland sea, they used its flints for their stone tools. That is the story which the geologists, who have found the flints, would tell of Scraptoft, but our story must begin with the building of its church in the 13th century by true-born Englishmen.

The church still has its 13th century font, and reveals much of its history in its varied monuments. The oldest is the battered figure lying in a recess, of some 14th century prior of Coventry.

In the 18th century the walls of the church became as a book of monuments. On the first page are the canopied busts of Sir Edward Wigley and his wife; then comes an angel leaning on an urn and lamenting the death of Andrew Noel and his wife. James Wigley, who was member of Parliament for Leicester five times before his death in 1765, has a realistic monument with a white marble Britannia, and a smaller sculptured relief showing him instructing his servants in the plantation of his estate. Another figure of a mourning woman laments the passing of Mrs Anne Wigley in 1786, but the most human of these 18th century monuments is that to Ann Firmadge, remembered as a woman with a babe in her arms and two children by her side.

In the churchyard is a 13th century cross with its base clad in moss and lichen, and not far off is the hall made new two centuries ago in the style of Queen Anne's reign, guarded by noble iron gates.

The Adventures of a Family

SEAGRAVE. In this deep valley of the Wolds the Segraves had their manor in feudal days. They came and departed, leaving no more than a name, but their church still stands.

Its fine 14th century tower, with a silver fish for a weathervane, has kept its quatrefoil border below the battlements, and here is the venerable font and the old gnarled chest. It has another curious relic in a musical instrument called from its shape a serpent and mentioned by Thomas Hardy in Under the Greenwood Tree: "There's worse things than serpents; old things pass away, tis true; but a serpent was a good old note." Thus spoke an ancient chorister in praise of this quaint instrument which was invented on the Continent in Queen Elizabeth's day, sounded its note for about 200 years, and then passed into silence.

The most famous name in the annals of the church is that of Robert Burton, author of the Anatomy of Melancholy, and rector here for the last ten years of his life.

The name of the village was borne for two centuries by a remarkable family which came into history as suddenly as it passed out of it. The family grew to note in the 12th century, when Stephen Segrave, a learned monk, turned soldier and, to his great profit, supported King John in his opposition to Magna Carta. Made governor of the Tower, and enriched with wide lands, he proved a ready tool for Henry the Third, encouraging him to flood the country with papal mercenaries, to the sore impoverishment of the nation.

Already sheriff of eight counties, he urged Henry to disgrace and even murder the faithful Hubert de Burgh, on whose fall the monk of Segrave became Chief Justiciar, a post enabling him still further to aid the spoliation of the land by foreign parasites, and to foment the plot which led to the murder of the patriot Earl of Pembroke.

In a fit of cowardly penitence Henry turned on his evil counsellor and confiscated many of his estates; but Segrave endured his punishment meekly, regained favour, and before ending his days as a monk was again at the king's right hand.

His son Gilbert was treacherously seized in France and died there a captive, and Nicholas, the first baron, born about 1238, reversed the ignoble policy of his grandfather by taking his stand for liberty at the side of Simon de Montfort, who entrusted him with command at the battle of Lewes. He was one of the knights who, at the end of Simon's prayer before the battle opened, prostrated themselves on the ground, extending their arms in the form of a cross, and crying, "Grant, O Lord, our desire with a mighty victory, to the honour of Thy name," and he sat in the first true Parliament. In the same year, however, the strife was renewed, and he saw de Montfort slain at Evesham, and was himself taken prisoner. He became reconciled to Edward and accompanied him on the last Crusade; and his eldest son, Baron John of Segrave fought for Edward and was one of the barons who signed the proud defiance of the Pope when he claimed the right to act as supreme authority between the Scots and English.

Many and thrilling were John's adventures in Scotland. His run of victories was interrupted by an ambush in which he was wounded and taken prisoner, but he was rescued by the main body of his army. He broke the resistance of Wallace, whom he brought to London, presiding at his trial, and passing the terrible sentence on the Scottish hero. Then, paid 15s for his task, he carried the body back to Scotland, leaving the head on London Bridge, the right arm at Newcastle, the left arm at Berwick, and the legs at Perth and Aberdeen, only to see Robert Bruce crowned in spite of all. He was then taken prisoner after Bannockburn, but was ransomed and remained closely associated with Edward until his death. His second son John left an heiress whose son married a granddaughter of Edward the First, bringing great estates and dignities into the family and leaving a daughter who married a Mowbray, and so united the Segrave barony to the Earls of Norfolk.

The last of this family to claim attention is Sir Hugh Segrave, a 14th century Treasurer of England. Keeper of castles and forests, and a warrior fighting in France, he negotiated the marriage of Richard the Second to Anne of Bohemia. Among the estates granted him was the manor of Overhall in Essex, the rent for which was a supply of wafers, and attendance on the sovereign at the coronation. He died in 1385, and the male line, which had been in the forefront for two centuries, sank into obscurity.

SHACKERSTONE. The Saxons left here rare beads of amber and glass, but few traces of its antiquity remain. The 15th century church has little record of its past. Most travellers who come this way will perhaps consider (in the manner of Dr Johnson, who thought the best view in Scotland was the road back to England) that the finest thing here is the glorious avenue of beeches and chestnuts leading from the village to Gopsall Hall, the house where Handel stayed with his friend Jennens.

The Three Rectors

SHARNFORD. It climbs up from the River Soar to a hillside church in a churchyard where eight small limes stand like soldiers in a line. Though most of the church is 15th century, its history goes back 800 years, and two heads on the porch are thought to represent the Norman founder (handsome with curled moustache) and the mother of Richard Coeur de Lion.

One of the windows has fine modern figures of Our Lord with Martha and Mary, in memory of Colonel John Watson. His brother was one of three Shearnford rectors with remarkable records. Henry Watson preached here for 54 years, following Joseph Cotman who was here for the first half of last century; but it was an 18th century rector who surpassed even their wonderful records of faithful service. He was John Horton, who was here for 55 years, and liked the place so well that for nearly half a century neither he nor his wife journeyed farther than the four miles to Hinckley.

The Garden Tennyson Knew

SHAWELL. It has a hilltop church and peaceful cottages, with a brook flowing gently by their gardens on its journey to the Avon. It is a scene Tennyson knew well, for he stayed at the rectory more than once, and tradition says that some of the stanzas of In Memoriam came to him when walking in the rectory garden. The tradition may be well-founded, for the poet himself has said that In Memoriam, on which he was at work for 17 years, was written anywhere he happened to be.

Tennyson's hosts were the rector Edward Elmhirst and his wife, who was a daughter of Canon Rawnsley, and as a girl had been a ward of the poet's father. "Your old friend from childhood" the poet called himself in a letter of sympathy on the death of her son. He begged her to believe that the son was more actually living than when alive at Shawell, adding that "if it were not so, that which made us would seem too cruel a Power to be worshipped, and could not be loved." Edward Elmhirst ministered to the spiritual needs of the villagers for 52 years, and the little grey church on the hill, rebuilt in his day, has a window to his memory with the figures of Mary, Simeon, and the infant Jesus.

In a field near the church a little group of elms marks the mounds of an ancient British burial place.

SHEARSBY. It is a pretty village of steep winding streets with a 13th century church perched facing a timbered 17th century house. Much of the church is new, and the 18th century gave it the tower with a curious cap, but a few old dragons and other fearsome gargoyles still guard the outer walls, and in the chancel is an ancient statue of Mary Magdalene. There is a medieval oak screen with modern tracery, a few old bench-ends adorned with quaint dogs and doves, and by the altar two grotesques, half dragon, half frog.

SHEEPY MAGNA. It is an attractive village on the River Sence, with prim cottages in gay gardens, well-ordered byways, and a well-tended medieval church. On the school porch is a sundial admonishing the passer-by to Teach, learn, or depart.

Under an arch outside the church tower is the figure of a 14th century man in cloak and hooded tunic, his hands holding a heart, and his feet on a fragment of a heraldic animal as a token of his worldly importance. The windows are filled with richly-coloured figures of saints and prophets.

By Bosworth Field

SHENTON. South of its peaceful cottage homes, its woods, and the stream that flows swiftly by to join the River Sence, an armed camp rose on a fateful day in 1485, for here on the eve of Bosworth the Lancastrian Earl of Richmond assembled his forces. Twenty-four hours later he had defeated Richard Crookback and the Tudor dynasty had dawned.

Nearly 150 years later, when Stuart had succeeded Tudor, the lord of the manor built Shenton Hall, and it stands today in its park gathering new beauty with the passing years. In one of its four bay windows, which so happily combine stateliness and grace, is a beam inscribed, This house was built by me, William Wollaston, 1629.

The church he worshipped in has been rebuilt by his ancestors, but it still preserves his monument and the font at which his children were baptised. The ancient font is adorned with stars and crosses, the monument has sculptured heads of William Wollaston and his wife Anne, who died in the very year he built a new home for her.

Like a Glimpse of Arcady

SHEPSHED. It now has streets of shops where once were sheep folds, but in the church, with a 13th century tower and a 600-year-old spire overlooking Charnwood Forest, can be seen the sheep's head that gave it a name. The head is carved on a stone in the gallery wall and the sheep's legs and the head of a shepherd are on a corbel of an aisle.

But other fine carvings, less sheepish, adorn the church. In the nave roof are wooden figures of armoured men, and heads of Queen Elizabeth and an unnamed king. Eight old benches have carved poppyheads; the Jacobean pulpit has elaborate ornament with leaves and thistles; and a score of cherubs peep up from the monuments in the chancel. Two sit perilously on the pillars of an 18th century monument to Sir Ambrose Phillipps, M P, and six more smile as they guard the inscription to Sir Ambrose, which tells how, having successfully practised the law for 30 years, he spent his closing years in preventing lawsuits among his neighbours.

A happier and less pretentious monument is an Elizabethan brass showing Thomas Duport kneeling with his wife, four daughters, and three sons, one of whom, John Duport, grew up to become Vice-Chancellor of Cambridge and one of the translators of the Bible.

Not all Shepshed's cherubs are in its church. Many are to be seen in its streets, and over a building occupied by a bank is a gallery of 30 sculptured children representing the seasons. These entrancing infants are shown sowing seed in Spring, playing ring of roses in Summer, picking fruit in Autumn, and gathered round a bonfire in Winter. Amid so much that is ordinary and workaday, it is like a glimpse of Arcady.

Curfew Field

SIBSON. To those who come along the winding lane in search of rest and refreshment it offers an attractive old thatched and timbered inn; to those who seek respite from worldly cares, an ancient church.

Most of the church was made new in the 18th century but its chancel is 600 years old. Under an arched canopy is a stone figure of some 14th century benefactor, his head on a cushion, his feet by an animal, and his hands offering up his heart to God. A splendid 16th century brass shows John Moore in his long priestly gown below a figure of Christ in Glory seated on a rainbow. Another rector, Thomas Neale, whose death in 1859 ended a ministry of 67 years, is remembered by a window and an inscribed brass. The modern reredos has attractive figures of four angels with scrolls and lute and lyre.

Not far off is the Eightlands Field which pays for the ringing of curfew from October to March. It was given long ago by a benighted traveller who, having lost his way, found it again by the sound of the curfew ringing from Sibson's church.

For Fifty-Two Revolving Years

SILEBY. Here among the many unpretentious houses so liberally bestowed upon it by modern industry, the church still proudly stands in all its medieval strength.

The fine tower, the lofty clerestory, and the massive roof with leaves carved on its crossbeams, are all 15th century, but elsewhere the earlier beginnings of the church are manifest, for some of the nave arches and a doorway in the north aisle have fine 13th century mouldings, and the font is as old.

There is a lead wall tablet with a naive inscription: " This was done when Mat Pearson and John Kendall was churchwardens in 1727 by Eli Porter Plumber." A 19th century wall monument, with figures of angels, a woman with a scroll and a man with a sword, recalls John Dudley, rector here for over 60 years.

Close to an ancient elm with a massive hollow trunk is a slate monument to an 18th century rector, on which is written something of the simple annals of the lowly:

For fifty-two revolving years
Devoutly he attended prayers,
With mellow voice and solemn knell,
He sang the Psalms and tolled the bell.

Squires and Spendthrifts

SKEFFINGTON. It was for centuries the home of the Skeffingtons who built the hall, were buried in the church, and were squires or spendthrifts till at last they parted company with the estate. There were gentlemen among them, but the last pages of the story of the Lost Estate are like the Rake's Progress.

The pretty, rebuilt church with pinnacled tower peeping among the trees has a Skeffington Chapel with some fragments of 15th century glass with a figure of the Madonna and kneeling men who may perhaps be penitent members of the family. Here, too, loose in the floor under an arched recess, are kneeling figures of a 16th century Skeffington family.

In the front is Sir Thomas, in ruff and armour—a broad-headed squire with a strong face, looking just the man to muster, as he did in Armada year, 12,000 Leicestershire men ready to fight the Spaniards if they set foot in England. His wife, with a rather tired and patient face, kneels behind him, while his two armoured sons and his two daughters, clad like their mother in ruffs and long gowns, are in the shadow of the arch. Another lady of the family has an arch to herself, and on an early 16th century floorstone are the worn figures of another Thomas Skeffington with his wife and 13 children. Sir John Skeffington, who died in 1651, has a wall monument guarded by golden-haired angels holding back curtains to reveal his epitaph.

Others of the name, which appears at intervals in three centuries of English history, have other resting-places. There was Thomas Skeffington, Bishop of Bangor, a great man who finished the bishop's palace and built the tower and nave of his cathedral where his heart was buried in 1535. Sir William Skeffington, also born here, became master of Ordnance to Henry the Eighth; and his son Leonard, Lieutenant of the Tower, is said to have invented the terrible instrument of torture called Skevington's Irons. John Skeffington, the next direct heir, was killed in a tavern brawl in 1613, and other Skeffingtons took over the broad acres. But they did not keep them, and after their lands had passed by marriage into an Irish family, the last Skeffington wasted the inheritance and sold the old hall and its Old Masters. Sir Lumley of Regency days, the butt of the caricaturists, was, if not the last of the dandies, the last of the Skeffingtons, and by the irony of fate his follies made him the most notorious of them all, Byron writing of his " skirtless coats " and Thomas Moore of his " pea-green coat and rich rouge pot."

The hall where so many of them lived and died is a Tudor stone house, enlarged in prosperous days. It has a great drawing-room, with floors and wainscoting said to have been made from a single oak tree of the park, not one board with a joint in it.

Samuel Granger's Epitaph

SLAWSTON. It stands high above the Welland valley, with more haystacks than cottages, and a 700-year-old church with a spire rising above the churchyard limes. In the tower a clock is ticking in memory of John Morpott who ministered here for 54 years.

In the churchyard is a curious epitaph to two Samuel Grangers. The first Samuel was a carrier who, while on a journey in Hertfordshire in 1787, was run over and killed by his own waggon. In deference to his dying wish he was brought back to this village by his own team in his own waggon, and over his grave was inscribed:

> *Oh sudden change! I in a moment fell*
> *And had not time to bid my friends farewell:*
> *There's nothing strange; death happens to us all,*
> *My lot today; tomorrow you must fall.*

The stone has sunk and the inscription is buried, but its sentiments have been preserved on the tomb of another Samuel Granger who died nearly a hundred years later.

SNIBSTON. It is almost in sight of the dumps and derricks of Coalville, and most of its cottages are the homes of men who go down into the mines. But its church, set on its hill above the secluded valley seven centuries ago, seems to stand serenely indifferent to the destroying march of industry. It boasts an ancient font with a band of foliage, but its pride is to count itself among the smallest churches in England, for it is no more than a nave less than thirty feet long and only half as wide.

The Ride to Khiva

SOMERBY. It stands finely on lofty hill with the spire of its church crowning one of the few central towers in the county, and prominent as a beacon far and wide.

Most of the church is 14th century, but the porch and the south arcade with its graceful capitals are a century older, and the chancel has a Norman doorway. The font, with its little carved heads and canopied arches, is 700 years old; the stone pulpit, with heads of Christ, Peter, and Paul, is modern.

A man of lasting fame baptised here in 1828 was Sir Benjamin Ward Richardson, the physician to whom the 19th century and humanity in general became so deeply indebted for his work in the science of healing and the lessening of pain. One of the 19th century vicars was Gustavus Burnaby, father of that modern Elizabethan, Colonel Frederick Burnaby, whose adventurous life was ended by an Arab spear at the battle of Abu Klea. Frederick Burnaby lies in the Sudan, but both he and his father are honoured by windows in the chancel.

A romantic personality, Fred Burnaby appealed to the ordinary man as a hero who dared and carried through an adventure in the teeth of authority and to the apprehension of a great nation which was causing no little anxiety to England. Burnaby, too, had a racy pen and wrote a book on his Ride which ran into several editions.

The future of India was a serious concern of this country. The Mutiny had revealed a weakness in the British rule there, and Russia was gradually extending her power over the Central Asian States which separated her from the Indian frontier.

Colonel Burnaby had ever a flair for picturesque and hazardous adventure. His post as officer in the Life Guards gave him light duties and ample leave which he used by rushing off to fight in Spain and serve under Gordon in the Sudan. When he heard that the Russians were attacking Khiva he was only prevented from hurrying to its defence by illness. The more he read of Russia's actions in Turkestan the more he longed to get first-hand information as to what was actually happening there. He hated the despotism and the corruption of the Tsar's Government.

The climax came one day in Khartoum, when he read in a newspaper that the Tsar's Government had forbidden foreigners to travel in Russian Asia. What could be the reason ? He asked himself, and determined to answer his question. Hurrying home, he obtained permission from the Russian War Minister to go to India by way of Khiva and Kabul, and on November 30, 1875, he set out on the remarkable journey which has been famous ever since as the Ride to Khiva. The railway ended at Sizeran on the Volga, 300 miles from Orenburg, the border town of European Russia, which he reached by open sledge. At Orenburg he engaged a Tartar dwarf as a servant and drove on to Ursk, where he turned south with the River Ural, being soon in hilly country. One morning he forgot his gloves and, falling asleep on the drive, put his hands in his sleeves. They slipped out, and the pain of frost-bite awoke him. His Tartar servant drove to the next station seven miles off, while Burnaby endured torments, and on their arrival the Cossacks, by applying ice and naphtha, succeeded in saving his hands.

At Kasala, a Russian fort east of the Sea of Aral, the temperature had reached 72 degrees of frost when Burnaby arrived to spend Christmas Day with the Russian Governor. Kasala was a centre of trade and was full of Jews, Greeks, and traders from all over Asia, while the nomad Khirghis had pitched their tents round the fort waiting for spring.

Fearful of being stopped by messages from home, Burnaby made rapid arrangements to go on. He secured two horses and three camels with their driver and a guide, his Tartar servant looking down from a laden camel and saying, Pray God we shall not be frozen to death. Travelling mostly by night, the caravan made for the Oxus River at 37 miles a day. The keen east winds made existence almost unbearable, and the Turkoman guide would eat a four-pound loaf at a meal, and drink out of a bucket the soup which they carried frozen as food for their 14 days journey. At that time no route was marked on any map, and Burnaby wished to avoid the Russian post of Petro-Alexandrovsk, which then dominated Khiva, and to which the Khan paid his tribute, so he made for Kalenderhana, to the west of it. He was now on the borders of his Promised Land, a country to reveal itself as Canaan did to the Israelites after their desert hardships. Here he wrote asking permission from the Khan at Khiva to enter his country.

He now crossed the frozen Oxus, the immortal river of Alexander and Tamerlane, into cultivated country. Many inhabitants of Khiva passed him, some clad in long red cloaks and riding richly-caparisoned horses, some in two-wheeled carts. All gravely saluted the traveller as he passed. Less polite were the people of the first town he reached, Oogentch, crowding round a barber's shop to see their first Englishman. A day or two later two Khivan nobles met his strange cavalcade with a welcome from the Khan and orders to conduct him to Khiva.

Colonel Burnaby described his first sight of the mysterious town as one whose beauty even in the depth of winter enchanted him. It was almost hidden from view by evergreens, only the painted minarets and domes rising above the trees. Within the double walls, sadly out of repair, was a town of 3500 people, with broad streets, nine schools, and a prison with two prisoners. Here the Englishman and his servant spent four days going freely about the quaint town and being treated with honour by the people, who had never seen an Englishman before. The Khan received him, discussing India over a map. Burnaby found it difficult to explain to the Khan the comparative sizes of India and Russia and England.

On the morning after this interview another, far from welcome, took place. Two Russians arrived with an urgent letter from the Commander instructing Burnaby to accompany the bearers to Petro-Alexandrovsk, where a telegram awaited him, a telegram which had reached the outpost by relay of couriers and must have cost a small fortune. Accordingly, Burnaby said farewell to his friendly hosts and went with the Russians. The telegram was from the Commander-in-Chief of the British Army, ordering him home by the shortest route.

SOUTH CROXTON. Standing pleasantly on a hillside road crossing the Croxton stream and climbing upward to the church, it has had the unhappy experience in our time of seeing its steeple struck by lightning, wrecking its 13th century spire and half of the old tower, which was notable for its striking arch. The scene was one not to be forgotten by this small village, masonry crashing through the roof, great stones being hurled into the road, and one falling on a farm building 20 yards away. To the rector, who happened to be looking at the church in the storm, it appeared that the whole structure was enveloped in flame. The church has a Norman font with curious figures and interlaced arches, plain old altar rails, and eight shield-bearers up in the ancient roof.

The Observatory in the Farmyard

SOUTH KILWORTH. It looks into Northants from its hilltop, and through a fine avenue of beeches to Shakespeare's Avon, glistering in the plain.

Much of its church has been made new, but it has kept an arcade with three Norman arches, a 15th century tower with a soaring spire, and a niche enshrining a statue of the patron Saint Nicholas. From its early days it has preserved also a 13th century font shaped like a Corinthian capital, an ancient stone with floral crosses, and the figure of a priest with features worn away by Time.

But its rarest treasure is a 15th century reredos, one of the alabaster carvings for which the Midlands were once so famous. The centre panel is the Crucifixion and at the sides are figures of Mary and John carved with more piety than skill, but medieval.

William Pearson, who is remembered by a tablet here, was known to the village as their parson, but England recognised him as an astronomer of more than common ability, and a true man of science. He made a planetarium, he was one of the pioneers of the Royal Institution and one of the founders of the Astronomical Society of London. In the observatory he built for himself at South Kilworth, in 1821, he did useful practical work in computing the positions of 520 stars. His work is his monument, but if any man should seek another he will find it in his observatory, still standing here in a farmyard.

The Old Familiar Faces

SPROXTON. High up on the Wolds its cottages are set, the church standing aloof above them all, with a strong square tower defying any wind that blows. Seven hundred winters must have tried it hard, but it has been well cared for. Outside its weather-beaten walls stands a stone cross that has survived a rougher treatment, for it was long used as a footbridge across a neighbouring stream, in spite of its carving of rings and wheels.

Inside the church are still many of the faces which peeped out at worshippers in the Middle Ages. Seven odd faces surrounded by foliage look out from the south aisle roof, 16 heads of men and beasts and birds adorn the old corbels in the nave, and eight small heads carved above the flowers in the font have watched the baptism of village children for 700 years. One of the bells has rung the village to church for six centuries. In the vicarage grounds is a curious 18th century hermitage, with a grotesque figure over its entrance and the inscription *Think, and thank God for all.*

The Outdoor Sculpture Gallery

STAPLEFORD. Here, close to the banks of the Eye where the Romans established a settlement and the Saxons also lived, are pretty thatched stone cottages and a thatched schoolhouse, clustered about the deer park of the ancient house.

The hall is a magnificent 17th century stone structure, with high gables and mullioned windows in stately rows. The north wing, which belonged to the early Tudor hall and was made to harmonise with the rest, is remarkable for the outdoor gallery of sculpture on its walls. Some of the sculptures were contributed by the first builders, others in Charles Stuart's time. Each of the three small Dutch gables has a statue in a niche, and below them, in sets of three between the mullioned windows, are 12 more canopied figures of knight and king, six with their names below—Schirard Lord of Castleton, William the Conqueror, Gilbert de Clare, Earl of Gloucester, Bertram Lord Verdun, Walter de Lacy, and James le Brabazon.

Besides the kings and warriors are a number of sculptured panels. Here are two knights jousting and here a swordfight, with a queen and her attendants watching from a tower on one side and on the other a wife praying among her children; here St Martin divides his cloak with a beggar, and there Archangel Michael presides over the weighing of Souls. The Annunciation, the Visitation, the Nativity, and the Adoration, and other sacred scenes are here; and there are panels of Creation, St George and the Dragon, and the martyrdom of Becket.

The people who set this gallery of sculpture on the walls of their house were the Sherards, who for four centuries lived here, their names being writ large in the church.

The church is a bright 18th century building, hidden among the elms and oaks and beeches near the hall, and is decorated with 40 shields of the Sherards and the families into which they married. Their pew fills a gallery at the west end and has a fine Adam fireplace with a panel of the sacrifice of Isaac.

Many of the Sherards who knelt here generation after generation now sleep within these walls. The oldest monument is an unspoiled 15th century brass engraved with portraits of Geoffrey Sherard in armour with his head on a helmet and his feet on a greyhound, his wife in a girdled gown, and their seven sons and seven daughters. Behind an iron railing is a rich 17th century altar tomb of marble which was probably sculptured by Nicholas Stone. It has figures of Sir William Sherard, Lord Leitrim (in armour with a ram at his feet), Lady Abigail beside him in her flowing robe with a greyhound at her feet, and eight of their children kneeling, with three others in swaddling clothes. Over the canopy are the busts of three more Sherards, and above them the head and shoulders of yet one other.

Another monument has upright figures of Bennet Sherard (first Earl of Harborough) and his countess, sculptured by Rysbrack.

The earl, in the classical style of the 18th century, is in Roman costume, with one arm directed towards his wife and his son, a charming little fellow on her knee. On a black pyramid behind them are their profiles in medallion.

The Sherard dynasty ended with the passing of the last Earl of Harborough in 1859, but their old house stands as stately as of old, and by the lake in the park the herons of an ancient clan still dwell.

King Richard's Last Camp

STAPLETON. Long before its little church and cottages were raised in serviceable order about its hill the men of the Bronze Age made here a camp with protective earthworks. Centuries later Richard the Third here raised his standard and pitched his camp. It was a dramatic hour. On the morrow he lay dead on Bosworth Field and a new king wore his crown, the Wars of the Roses that had severed the nation for so many years were ended at last, and the Tudor dynasty had begun.

That is Stapleton's place in a tale of old wars and unhappy far-off days, but there is perhaps a more fruitful memory in the name of Richard Dawes, who was born here in 1708 and who, together with his masters Richard Porson and Richard Bentley, stands as one of the three great Greek scholars of the 18th century.

Saints in Old Glass

STATHERN. Its red and white cottages are as charming as the Vale of Belvoir in which they lie, and its medieval church, in a churchyard with larch and silver birch, is as serene as the smooth green pastures round it.

From its early days the church has preserved a beautifully moulded 13th century doorway and an arcaded 14th century font. In the east window are a few fragments of ancient glass among the new, with St Guthlac sitting at his desk, St Peter kneeling with a crowing cock close by, and an angel before the Madonna. Above them St Guthlac, St Peter, and the Madonna appear again in fine modern glass with Hugh of Lincoln. A lancet window in the tower has a beautiful Baptism.

Colonel Hacker, who managed the execution of the king, lived here for some time before he himself perished under the executioner's axe.

Syston   A Corner by the Church

Stapleford

The Hall and its Sculptured Walls

LEICESTERSHIRE

The Home of the Shirleys

STAUNTON HAROLD. The manor is said to derive its name from Saxon holders in days before the Conquest, but, however that may be, the Conqueror gave it to a Ferrers, and to a Ferrers it still belongs, for the Shirleys who have had it in their keeping for 500 years added the Barony of Ferrers to their title in Charles the Second's day, and have since raised it to an earldom. Their stately house is happy in having preserved a good deal of beauty in its restorations, and especially fortunate in the library front which Inigo Jones is said to have designed, along with the lovely entrance to the park.

The church in the park is architecturally one of the most unspoiled things in Leicestershire. It was built by Sir Robert Shirley in 1653, when new churches in England were rare, and indeed it is believed to have been the only one built during the Commonwealth. An inscription over its doorway, guarded by two angels, tells its story in this way:

In the year 1653
when all things sacred were throughout the nation
either demolished or profaned,
Sir Robert Shirley, Baronet,
founded this church,
whose singular praise it is
to have done the best things in the worst times
and hoped them in the most calamitous . . .

Sir Robert Shirley, who was imprisoned in the Tower many times for plotting against the Commonwealth, died there while still a young man of 28, and was brought from London to be buried in the church he had built. He had built well. The chancel is paved with marble, the boarded ceiling is painted as a cloudy sky, and of the church as a whole it may be truly said that within and without it was built in the best traditions of the 15th century. There is a magnificent screen of ironwork wrought by Robert Bakewell of Derby, ancient banners hang in the chancel, the furniture is richly upholstered with purple velvet, and everywhere is oak panelling.

The monuments of the church are to the Shirleys, the best of them an altar tomb to Robert Shirley, Lord Tamworth, who lies in white marble wearing a wig and a flowing cravat as he was so often seen in the 17th century. The tomb has a background of rich oak.

The romantic chapter of the Shirleys is the story of the famous and infamous brothers—Walter, hymn-writer and friend of Wesley,

o   193

who was born here and was buried in Dublin after an active life as a Methodist preacher; and Laurence who became Earl Ferrers and was hanged on the scaffold, and now lies here. The names of these two brothers were in all men's mouths in the 18th century.

A Peer's Ride to Tyburn

THE silken halter is one of the legends that will never die, but the hanging was actual enough. Its victim was Laurence Shirley, fourth Earl Ferrers.

Lord Ferrers succeeded to the title and estates at 25, sat in the House of Lords, and at 32 married a daughter of an old family from Henbury in Cheshire. He went rapidly to the bad, behaving so outrageously to his wife that she had to divorce him for persistent cruelty. She then married a distinguished lawyer, Lord Frederick Campbell, and in her old age was burnt to death in a fire at Coombe Bank, Sundridge, Kent.

Meanwhile the trustees under the divorce had appointed an old family servant, John Johnson, steward of the Shirley estate, to act as receiver of the rents and to pay to Lady Ferrers the sum due to her under the settlement. Ferrers, who was drinking hard, took a dislike to Johnson, and matters came to a head when the trustees granted the steward the lease of a farm about a mile from Staunton Harold. One day Ferrers summoned Johnson to the house, sent all the servants away, and received the old man in his room, the door of which he locked. Accusing him of various fictitious charges, he shouted, " Down on your knees," and shot him.

Ferrers, after drinking half the night, was besieged in his house the next morning by the villagers, but terrified them by appearing on the bowling green, armed with a blunderbuss, two pistols, and a dagger. All retreated but one, a collier who coolly went up to the maddened nobleman and disarmed him. Brought to justice, Ferrers demanded trial by his peers and defended himself with great skill, but the irony of his scholarly defence was that all his art and intellect were exercised to prove himself mad!

It is often said that he was the last peer to be hanged with a silken cord, but there is no silken halter in the story; it was hemp. Ferrers drove from the Tower to the gallows at Tyburn in his own landau, drawn by six of his superb horses; he was clad in his wedding suit of white silk richly laced with silver, and during a large part of the three-hours ride through the crowded streets he was engaged in theological discussion with the Tower chaplain, and talking to the people. Wesley's doctrine of justification by faith was exciting the world, and Walter Shirley, the murderer's brother, was deeply engaged in it. "I never can believe what some teach, but faith alone will save mankind," said Lord Ferrers on his way to Tyburn. The condemned man was spared the horror of being pushed off the hangman's ladder and cart to dangle from the gibbet, the modern type of gallows being used for the first time for his execution. His body was eventually removed to Staunton Harold, after having lain for nearly a quarter of a century beneath the belfry of St Pancras Church in London.

Pictures in Glass and Brass and Stone

STOCKERSTON. It is a little village of stone cottages, sleeping in a valley near the Rutland border, and has a 15th century church at the end of a lane close to the gardens of the hall. The church has been restored, but has kept many of its ancient treasures.

Some of the windows have glass which has been here 500 years. Here is St Clement with a jewelled tiara, his crozier in his hand, the anchor hanging from his waist; and here, too, is St Christopher. A graphic scene shows Our Lord being nailed to the cross by little men as ugly as the medieval craftsman could make them. A saintly lady in blue kneels in adoration.

The light from the windows falls on an ancient stone engraved with the figure of some forgotten lady of the manor, and near it is a stone coffin lid with the sign of the cross. In the south aisle five altar tombs are joined into one stone table, and resting on them are about 20 old traceried bench-ends. Under an arch is a cross-legged figure in chain armour, his knightly shield and sword by his side, and a dog at his feet. There is another warrior who has fared worse in the war with Time, though his sword is left to him and his hands are still clasped in prayer.

On the chancel floor is a stone with the engraved portrait of Elizabeth Havers in her long flowing Stuart robes, and there are two other memorials in brass, one showing a 15th century knight with his wife, the other a headless 16th century knight with his lady.

The Tale of a King's Crown

STOKE GOLDING. At the end of a byway where a hedge grows over the cobbles a church stands proudly in all its rich medieval splendour. Below the lovely spire is a fine panelled parapet with crowned heads of Queen Philippa and Edward the Third, the 14th century warrior king in whose time most of the church was probably built.

It has a wealth of lovely detail rarely found in a village church. The windows have graceful flowing tracery, and the arcade with its clustered pillars and rich carved capitals is exquisite. The 14th century font has richly sculptured panels of St Catherine and her wheel, St Nicholas raising his hand in benediction, and St Margaret with a vanquished dragon at her feet. There are some plain old benches, a 17th century chest, and a recessed arch said to hold the tomb of Sir Robert de Champaigne, the 14th century founder of the church.

In the vestry is a marble monument to Sir Henry Firebrace, a personal servant of Charles Stuart and one of the men who assisted the king in his attempt to escape from Carisbrooke Castle. This monument is one of Stoke Golding's two links with unhappy far-off days; the other is more shadowy.

Bosworth Field is not far off, and there is a tradition that the crown of Richard Crookback was found in a bush on a hill close to this village. The king wore his crown when he went into battle, but in his last desperate struggle for life it fell from his head into a thorn bush, where it was found later by Sir Reginald Bray, and placed by Lord Stanley on the head of Henry the Seventh. That is the story, and Sir Reginald Bray, who, as the architect of Henry the Seventh's Chapel at Westminster, has a great claim to fame, bore a crown in a thorn bush on his coat-of-arms in token of its truth.

STONESBY. Here among the red-tiled cottage roofs the pale grey tower of the church rises in majestic contrast. It is a tower which would lend distinction to any village, for, though simple and severe, its proportions are those which the 15th century architects of Somerset left as a model to the rest of England.

The church, built two centuries before this 15th century tower, is even more severely plain. It has a Norman font with interlaced arches and sprays of flowers, an old chest with fine rosettes, and two much-worn oak benches with poppyheads and an upturned face on the arm-rests at each end.

A modern stained window in the south aisle is inscribed to Elizabeth Simons, who for 44 years was mistress of the village school. The last tribute of a brother who himself did not live to see it finished, it has pictures of three great Teachers—Christ with the children, Eli with Samuel, and Eunice teaching Timothy.

Hereabouts is an earthwork which Stonesby folk ascribe to Old King Lud, the mythical ruler whose name is preserved in one of London's most famous streets, Ludgate Hill.

Rich on £40 a Year

STONEY STANTON. It is indeed a stony place among quarries, with the shady churchyard like a green oasis among its cobble-paved streets.

The church is mostly 14th century, but has preserved its ancient font, and has over its chancel doorway a Norman tympanum with carving as quaint as it is puzzling. It shows a shepherd with his crook (or perhaps a bishop with his crozier) in the midst of a conflict between a winged dragon and other strange beasts. As though in answer to his entreaties, a dove of peace descends from heaven.

In the churchyard sleeps a saint who ministered here for the first half of the 18th century. John Bold, like Goldsmith's Vicar of Wakefield, was passing rich on £40 a year, £30 being his stipend as curate and £10 his earnings as a teacher at Hinckley. He lived with a farmer, eking out a meagre existence that he might give to his more needy neighbours, frugal living that has been ably described by a later rector:

His daily fare consisted of water-gruel for his breakfast; a plate from the farmer's table supplied his dinner; he took no tea and his supper was milk porridge. He visited all his parishioners, exhorting, reproving, consoling, instructing them, and the effect of his instructions has been visible in my time in the piety, the probity, sobriety, and industry of those who were brought up under him.

John Bold moved among his people giving all he could, asking nothing for himself, and when his days were done, he left a goodly sum to his relations, the farmer's family, and the poor. More than passing rich was he on £40 a year.

A Bullet From the Battle of the Boyne

STONTON WYVILLE. Its few cottages are assembled har-
moniously at the end of a lane with a modest 13th century
church in a shady churchyard.

Among the monuments in the ancient building is one notable for
its sculpture and another for its story. The first is a grand Elizabethan altar tomb with a figure of Edmund Brudenell in his magis-
terial robes, a seahorse at his feet, and Mrs Brudenell (alas, now
headless) kneeling with her son and daughter. By the magistrate's
side is a miniature altar tomb bearing the figure of his infant son in
swaddling clothes, making this monument one of the most pathetic
we have come upon in all our journeyings.

The second memorial is that of a soldier who added new lustre
to the name of Brudenell. It is a marble tablet with an inscription
telling how Thomas Brudenell, who left the law to fight in Holland,
came home with William of Orange, fought many battles in Spain
and Portugal, and eventually died at Gibraltar from the effects of
a bullet which had wounded him at the Battle of the Boyne
17 years before.

The church still has its 13th century font, at which Robert de
Wyville, who went from this humble village to become Bishop of
Salisbury 600 years ago, was baptised.

The Beautiful Cross

STOUGHTON. It lies in the hilly and wooded country a little
east of Leicester, in pleasant lands that once belonged to the
abbey where Cardinal Wolsey lies.

Those who seek its church will first encounter the 14th century
cross in the shade of the limes of the churchyard. It has been called
the most beautiful of all the county's crosses, and there is something
in its fluted slenderness, and the elegant simplicity of the shaft with
its sculptured capital, to justify such praise. It stands like a warden
over the simple memorials of simple folk surrounding it.

The 600-year-old church, made new last century, has in its keeping
many other memorials. There is a fine altar tomb of Thomas Farnham, Teller of the Exchequer under Mary Tudor, showing him as a
solemn bearded man with a chain over his armour, his wife by his
side in embroidered gown, ruff, and cap, their two sons and three

daughters below. One of these daughters appears again on a wall monument kneeling with her husband Sir Thomas Beaumont and ten children, one of whom became the wife of Sir Thomas Richardson, Speaker of the Commons in a Parliament of Charles the First, and set up this monument.

Others of the famous Leicestershire Beaumonts who have marble memorials here are Admiral Basil Beaumont, who was drowned with all the sailors of his flagship when it foundered on the Goodwin Sands in the Great Storm of 1703, and Sir George Beaumont, friend of Dean Swift and M P for Leicester in nine Parliaments. Swift came to see him at his manor house and may have preached here.

The Good and Faithful Servants

STRETTON-EN-LE-FIELD. It is a pretty hamlet close to Derbyshire, with a tiny cluster of houses and a grey 14th century church. The flat oak roof in the nave is 500 years old, the plain font is 17th century, and a recess in the aisle (marked by a stone bearing a cross) is probably the last resting-place of Osbert de Stretton, medieval rebuilder of the church.

Three of the memorials are to old rectors. There is a stone with an engraved figure of Walter Savage of the 16th century, a slate tablet to George Gretton, who was rector here for 44 years and vicar of Marston-upon-Dove for 65, and a marble tablet to John Browne who died after ministering here for 51 years.

The churchyard is bordered by a group of ancient yews.

Looking Down on Bosworth Field

SUTTON CHENEY. It is a place of bitter memories, for it looks down on Bosworth Field. Long ago as that field was fought, small as were the numbers of its combatants, and remote as its issues now seem, thanks to the genius of Shakespeare it bulks more largely in the imagination than many a battle more costly in lives and treasure.

On Ambion Hill, not far from the village, is a small pyramid enclosing King Richard's Well. Anyone may pass it by, yet it is a relic of unhappy far-off days, for where these rude stones stand Richard of York stood to quench his thirst before he mounted his horse and rode to battle. Here it was he drank who drank no more.

The village is a happier place, with antiquity less forbidding. Behind the trees is a stone-framed farmhouse that in Elizabethan days could boast itself a manor, and close by are 17th century almshouses with an end gable curiously holed in rows from top to bottom, as if to shelter pigeons. The church is almost as the 14th century left it, with the tower alone refashioned in new brick.

From its very early days it has kept a plain Norman font and an arcade with one Norman arch and three of the 13th century. Three of its monuments are notable. There is a large alabaster tomb supporting the armoured figure of Sir William Roberts, founder of the 17th century almshouses, his two wives kneeling at prayer desks above him. Opposite them Geoffrey May, the 17th century lord of the manor, kneels on a small wall monument. There is also a tablet inscribed to Thomas Simpson, who made an undesired reputation at Market Bosworth as an astrologer in the 18th century, and had to flee from the neighbourhood, but on coming to London became recognised as a fine mathematician and was elected FRS.

The Immortal Day

Here pitch our tents, even here in Bosworth Field,
Saddle white Surrey for the field tomorrow.

THE ear of fancy still catches the ringing words Shakespeare puts into the mouth of Richard Crookback, as he arrays his forces for his last battle.

It was something more than a dynastic contest at Bosworth Field. Sutton Cheney closed the door on Medieval England, and opened the way to the modern England, into which Marlowe and Shakespeare and all their incomparable company could enter and thrive. The Hundred Years War had ended in 1453 and had brought home to England the nobles and their lawless retainers, who had inherited constant war and plunder as a legacy from their ancestors. Two years after their return they started the Wars of the Roses which, with their 14 important battles, lasted thirty years. Bosworth was the culminating contest in that cruel conflict. Richard, stained with the blood of little Edward the Fifth, of the Duke of York, and nobles beyond memory, was now to fall by the sword to which he had so often appealed. "Is my beaver easier than it was?" he cries; and he needs an easy beaver, for he wears his crown rammed on to it during the fight. After the battle a plundering camp follower wrenched the crown from the head of the fallen king and hid it beneath a hawthorn bush from where it was rescued to be set on the head of the conquering Richmond, Henry the Seventh.

The day was done, the dog was dead. The battle of Bosworth was fruitful of good beyond expectation. It united the houses of York and Lancaster, and with them the entire nation. A century and a quarter of continuous conflict abroad and at home, reinforced by the unresting axe of the headsman, had practically exterminated the fierce and warring baronial families, so that the demoralising fear of recurrent civil war was at last finally dissipated. With the collapse of the great feudal houses the tyranny of Church abuses was broken. Popular freedom dawned at Bosworth.

This one battle ended our civil wars until the Revolution under Charles. With peace at last triumphant, the inexhaustible energies of a splendid people were liberated for the service of learning and commerce, for law-making through Parliament, for the creation of a hospital system, for the erection of noble buildings, for the rapid and widespread diffusion of knowledge which flowed from the books which were now for the first time being printed in England; for the laying of the foundations of a native art to compete with that already glorious in Italy; and finally for the evolution of a seafaring race which was to vie with Columbus, who reached the New World seven years after Bosworth's last blow was struck.

Whoso loves England may fitly pause awhile at little Sutton Cheney to view the ground fought over in 1485 and to bow his head in reverence to the memory of those who died that day to end war and bring a new England to birth.

S UTTON-IN-THE-ELMS. No longer is its regiment of elms encamped here by the Fosse Way. The forest has gone and elms remain as scattered outposts, but among the cottages is a spick-and-span red chapel which will preserve a memory when the last elm is gone. Founded in 1650, though made new in more recent times, it is the oldest Nonconformist chapel in a county which for three centuries has had an abiding Nonconformist strength.

Four years before the chapel was founded in this hamlet John Moore, Bishop of Norwich and Ely, was born here. He was perhaps more famous as a book collector than as a bishop, and George the First did at least one good thing when he bought his library and presented it to Cambridge university.

THE KING'S ENGLAND

George Fox and George Stephenson

SWANNINGTON. By giving its name to the Leicester and Swannington Railway, the first line laid south of Lancashire, this modest town, with a plain 18th century church on a hill above it, won a place in the tale of the Industrial Revolution. It won a place also in the most famous Science Museum in the world, for a piece of the rail, 15 feet long, is preserved at South Kensington.

William Stenson, a coalowner of neighbouring Whitwick, went to George Stephenson in 1832 to propose a line for taking coal to Leicester by rail instead of by canal. Stephenson could not help much with the work, as he was already engaged on the Manchester and Liverpool Railway, but his son Robert and the engineer John Ellis carried it out.

Long before coal came to disturb the serenity of this valley George Fox the Quaker was here seized by his persecutors and taken off to Leicester gaol. In his diary he thus describes his arrest here in 1662:

At night there came one Lord Beaumont with a company of soldiers, and as I was sitting in the hall, speaking to a widow woman and her daughter, they came slapping their swords on the doors and rushed into the house with their swords and pistols, crying, Put out candles and make fast the doors, and they seized upon Friends in the house and asked if there were no more. They asked me my name and I told them my name was G. Fox. I was the man so called and known. Aye, said he, you are known all the world over. Yes, said I, for no hurt but good.

Most of the passenger trains from Leicester to Burton still follow the course of the old railway on which George Stephenson drove the first train on July 17, 1832. The engine was the Comet, brought to Leicester by canal, and the train had a passenger coach and several waggons. A band played as the train made its triumphal progress, and a small cannon was fired at intervals as a sign of rejoicing.

On the earliest English trains a horn was blown by the driver, and it was in 1833, on this little railway, that the first locomotive whistle was used. A train having run down a market cart which strayed on the track, Stephenson consulted an organ builder at Leicester, who took an organ pipe and made out of it a steam trumpet to be worked from the boiler. When it was tested there was heard for the first time the sound which is now among the most familiar, and among the most thrilling, in the world—the whistle of a railway engine.

The tickets for passengers were made of brass and a sand-glass was used outside the Glenfield Tunnel to mark the interval at which trains were allowed to pass into it. There were also primitive methods of signalling, the driver knowing that he was being called upon to stop if he saw a candle in the window of the station.

The White Tower

SWEPSTONE. The white tower of its 14th century church over-looks the valley of the Mease and can be seen like a beacon, far and wide.

Among the monuments are an altar tomb with a battered figure of a medieval Lady Bountiful in tight cap and wimple, with a lion at her feet, and a 16th century figure of William Humpfrey lying in armour with a broken sword, his gauntlets by his side.

From its early days the church has kept a plain font 600 years old, an ironbound chest, and a roughly carved wooden figure of a seated angel. Among its modern possessions are choir stalls carved with angels and monks.

What the Parson Left Behind

SWINFORD. It is a village in the valley of the Avon, close to the county's borders and the lovely glades and avenues of Stanford Park.

Its church, though chiefly modern, has an arcade built at the time when the Norman arch was giving way to the pointed one, and a Norman font of red Warwickshire stone with arcaded bowl supported by twisted columns.

In the churchyard is the railed 18th century altar tomb of William Staresmore, one of those parsons whose eccentricity is his chief title to remembrance. Strange tales are related of him by the old county historian. He locked up his servants every night; he kept 58 dogs, and protected his apple trees by tying a bulldog to each of them. One morning in 1747 the pack overwhelmed him with their boisterous greeting and he fell into the pond; he could not get out any more than his servants could get out of the house to help him. That was his sad end, and his strange ways were even more manifest after his death, for the extraordinary collection of goods and chattels he left behind him included 100 pairs of breeches, 500 pairs of boots and shoes, 240 razors, and 200 pickaxes.

THE KING'S ENGLAND

Sir Joseph Danvers and His Dog

SWITHLAND. Many who do not know Swithland know its slate of soft dark blue, for it covers the roofs of nearly all the ancient buildings in the county, and in the Long Ago it furnished many of the fine tombstones on which generations of Leicestershire carvers lavished their art.

In Swithland Wood, gleaming here and there with silver birches, are small deep lakes made from the quarries in which the slate was worked, and the village still has old stone cottages which recall the heyday of the industry.

On a hill in the park stands Swithland Hall, ancestral home of the Earl of Lanesborough, and on the edge of the park is the church where so many of his forefathers sleep. Though largely modern, the church enshrines many ancient memorials, the oldest being a brass finely mounted on a wall and bearing the figure of a 15th century nun named Agnes Scott, who is believed to have lived in a cave near Leicester called Black Agnes's Bower. Among the most touching are the tablets to two brothers who fell in the Great War, Francis and Brian Butler, sons of the sixth earl. Near them are many brasses inscribed to their ancestors, one giving the pedigree from the time of the Conquest, and here also is some funeral armour, helmet, sword, and gauntlets.

The most curious monument is the elaborate 18th century tomb of Sir Joseph Danvers. On two sides are engravings on Swithland slate, one of a ship in sail and a church below a hill, with the couplet:

> *When young I sailed to India, east and west,*
> *But aged in this port must lye at rest.*

The other has a scene of ploughing and building, with these lines:

> *Be cheerful, O man, and labour to live,*
> *The merciful God a blessing will give.*

It is said that Sir Joseph Danvers would not be buried in the church because he did not wish to be separated from his dog and so had his tomb built into the churchyard wall that the dog, lying in unconsecrated ground, might be near its master. There is also a wall monument in the church to Sir John Danvers, who inscribed on it the history of his family and had it set up in his own lifetime, overcoming the difficulty about the date of his death by saying he departed this life about the 18th century. One who remembered this remarkable Sir John has left us a strange picture of him:

> *He was remarkably fond, like the Chinese, of painting everything red, so much so that every door, window, shutter, and gatepost in the towns of Swithland and Mountsorrel were so decorated. He did not stop here; he adopted it in his own dress; being a big broad-set man his appearance was like that of the Knave of Spades.*

It was Sir John Danvers who removed the cross from the market-place at Mountsorrel and set it in his park. There it is to this day, with carved heads, niches supported by angels, and other crude winged figures at its base.

A Nine-Days Wonder Goes On

SYSTON. It is a railway junction, and the inflexible steel lines that brought to it a new prosperity have taken away much of its rural aspect. But one charming corner remains where old thatched cottages gather comfortably about an ancient church.

The church, made more spacious last century, is mostly 500 years old and has a wealth of carving. High on a buttress of the tower are two curious sculptures of a man and two women, believed to represent the founder and his wives; up in the nave roof are 12 wooden figures bearing coloured shields. The north aisle roof is borne up by modern stone figures symbolising music and prayer, and below it is a wall painting of Christ the Shepherd. The modern pulpit is enriched with figures of six saints, and the oak reredos in the side chapel by three Apostles, Paul carved by a girl, Peter by a workman in a back street of Leicester, and John by a journeyman carpenter. The altar rails, now in their rightful place in the sanctuary, were rescued from a barn where they had lain forgotten many years; but the plain ten-sided font has been here many centuries.

Among the modern monuments is a brass to John Freeman, parish clerk for 58 years, and in the churchyard is an 18th century stone pointing this moral:

> *What I gave I have,*
> *What I spent I had,*
> *What I left I lost by not giving it.*

On either side of the ancient Fosse Way, which follows its straight course near this village, is an ancient tumulus where the Bronze Age men buried the ashes of their dead and Stone Age warriors left their flints. Across a neighbouring brook, tributary of the rivers Wreak and Soar whose waters here unite, a bridge was built in 1797 by three bricklayers and six labourers. For nine days these nine men grappled with thousands of bricks and tons of stone, and then a workmanlike bridge bestrode the stream. Called the Nine-Days Wonder, it stands to this day, a wonder of ages and as useful as ever.

The Almsbox Irresistible

THEDDINGWORTH. It lies close to the borders of Northants, a village with many fine old trees shading street and cottage, and a fine old church with lofty spire that has been a landmark for 500 years.

The early beginnings of the church are revealed more clearly within, for it has an arcade with splendid Norman arches, and a simple Norman font crowned with a modern oak cover nine feet high and richly adorned with angels and a Madonna. Among its other old treasures can be counted a dug-out chest with iron bands, a few fragments of ancient glass, and some 15th century woodwork worked into the pews.

In a side chapel is a fine organ with a silent choir of 16 angels with harp, lute, viol, and trumpet, painted in gay colours on its panels. On a high tomb close to it is the figure of a 17th century man reclining in fur-trimmed gown above his wife and four children, and another 17th century monument shows George Bathurst and his wife, Bible in hand, with 16 kneeling figures below them, all in black. They were staunch Royalists. Six of the sons fell fighting for Charles, another became Chaplain to Charles the Second, and the youngest became Treasurer to the last of the Stuarts, Queen Anne.

A peculiar monument shows the rector Slaughter Clark in his gown standing up to preach, while his wife sits leaning against an urn, looking somewhat bored.

There is a touch of humour as well as an irresistible appeal in the lines on the almsbox:

> *If aught thou hast to give or lend,*
> *This ancient British church befriend;*
> *If poor but still in spirit willing,*
> *Out with thy purse and give a shilling;*
> *But if its depths should be profound*
> *Out with thy purse and give a pound:*
> *Look for no record to be given*
> *But trust to thy reward in Heaven.*

The Yew and the View

THORNTON. Its churchyard has one of the county's finest yews and one of its grandest views. The yew, ten feet round, was planted in 1723; the view is of a lake winding below in the eastern valley, one of the big reservoirs from which both Leicester and Nuneaton draw water.

A pretty avenue of beeches leads down to a little church 600 years old save for the 15th century tower, on which the spire is set so gracefully. The wooden porch shelters a massive door with 13th century ironwork, said to have come from the ruined priory of Ulverscroft. There is a traceried 15th century font decorated with Tudor roses, the base of a painted medieval screen, some 16th century pews with linenfold, a 16th century pulpit, and a curious triangular window in the north aisle.

The Flight into Egypt, the Wise Men, and the Madonna and Child are portrayed with great simplicity in fragments of 14th century glass, and the Madonna is shown in a 17th century altar painting by an unknown Spanish artist, appearing again finely carved in wood on the modern lychgate.

St George's Dragon Sleeps

THORPE ARNOLD. It is gathered about a hilltop near Melton Mowbray, with a 14th century church set among elms that rise above the tower. In the modern roof of the nave are some old stone grotesques, a cow, an ape, and a bearded man among them; on one of the capitals of the arcade are the smiling heads of a man and two lions; and two angels are on a 19th century wall monument to John Cleathing who ministered here for 50 years, one of the longest records of service we have found in the county.

But the most remarkable carving in the church stands out boldly on the Norman font, where a quaint St George is attacking a snorting dragon. Behind the saint the dragon appears again, sleeping peacefully after the combat, and two ornamental crosses with heads at their centres complete a Norman sculptor's work. It is the only time we have seen two dragons with one St George.

By the porch is the base of an ancient cross, and not far off are earthworks thrown up in a shadowy past as an encampment for some British tribe.

The Tragic Bell

THORPE LANGTON. It is a tiny place with a cheerful air and a church to match, with flowers nodding gaily in its churchyard and stone faces smiling from the venerable walls. Most of the church is 14th century, but its tower and spire are a century older and the clerestory a century younger. The font, the oak pulpit, and some of the woodwork in the screen are all 500 years old.

A tragic little story is told of the belfry here. One night in 1782, after the other bellringers had left, one of them stayed behind and left the tenor bell delicately balanced upside down, thinking it would turn over in the night and wake the village. It did not turn over in the night, but it turned the next morning and killed a carpenter.

Charles Booth Explores the Slums

THRINGSTONE. It is a colliery village with little charm and less antiquity (save for the moated farmhouse called Stordon Grange), but in its modern church sleeps a man whose work for humanity is bearing fruit still.

Charles Booth, who was laid to rest here in 1916, was a Liverpool shipowner who, after half a lifetime in the world of shipping, devoted the second half to investigating human shipwreck. He was unsparing in giving money for the collection by a band of inquirers of every fact which could have a bearing on the origin and malignant influence of slums. In this inquiry he himself took an unwearying part, and the outcome was his work on Life and Labour. But this was only the beginning of more elaborate volumes directed to show how regular earnings and a comparative comfort reduce poverty, misery, and depravity. For this purpose it was necessary to describe the general conditions under which each class lives. This new survey of London in 17 volumes with tell-tale maps showing every street in relation to its poverty was like a modern Anatomy of Melancholy, giving material of an entirely new character for the information and guidance of social reformers. Charles Booth gave these facts to the world at his own cost, opening closely-shuttered windows with his understanding, and letting light and air into the dark recesses of suffering and want.

THRUSSINGTON. It has an old bridge of two arches across the River Wreak, from which we see the tranquil picture of its red-brick cottages and the 700-year-old church of yellow stone

Stoney Stanton   Carving over Doorway

Thorpe Arnold   St George and the Dragon on the Font

Sapcote   Font   Swinford   Font

NORMAN TREASURES IN LEICESTERSHIRE HAMLETS

Woodhouse Eaves   The Mill above the Village

Ulverscroft Priory   The Ruins by the Farmhouse

crowned with white battlements and pinnacles. On the porch of the church are the heads of a bishop and a queen, and on the ancient font is a curly-headed man. At this font in 1582 was christened Sir Thomas Hayne, who was to become a schoolmaster at Merchant Taylors in London but did not forget his old village, for he left his money for the education of ten poor children here.

Hugh Latimer's Village

THURCASTON. Any one will point out to us the decaying timbered house on the Rothley Road, for it is everywhere known as the house (or the site of the house) where was born Hugh Latimer, the yeoman's son who said to Ridley, when the fires of their martyrdom were kindled at Oxford:

Be of good comfort, Master Ridley; we shall this day light such a candle in England as I trust shall never be put out.

It is one of the proudest memories of this proud county.

Here somewhere among the old cottages we are sure Hugh Latimer was born. In the fields near by is a bridge over which he must often have walked. In this valley by the Rothley Brook he played, and looked on the trees of Charnwood Forest, much thicker then than now. This was the first church he ever saw, its Norman doorway the first through which he passed, and its tower has the grinning gargoyles he may once have gazed upon in child-like wonder.

The nave has a high-pitched 15th century roof unlike any other in the county, supported by eight grotesque corbels. It has also a rare screen with a row of open arches 700 years old, one of the oldest screens in England.

What else is here that young Hugh Latimer knew ? There is the font with a shallow bowl at which he was baptised, and high in the tower is a bell he often heard, with the crowned heads of Edward the First and Queen Eleanor and the Madonna and Child upon it. There is a 15th century brass of John Mershden in his richly embroidered cope as Canon of Windsor, which he saw, and the east window has some cleverly grouped fragments of glass with figures of angels, heads of men, and a little praying man in red and blue (thought to be John Mershden) that may once have shed an illumined light upon him.

P

On a wall is a modern tablet bearing his portrait, for the name of Hugh Latimer, written in letters of gold in the annals of the English Church, is nowhere more cherished than in this little place, where he murmured his first prayers, and where the divine spark that was in him first kindled.

His Words Still Ring Through England

NO one did more than Latimer to establish Protestantism as the prevailing form of Christianity in England. He did it by his life, his preaching, and his death.

At first he was "an obstinate Papist," till he became friendly with a Norfolk man, little Thomas Bilney, who was an earnest student of the New Testament, and who led him to found his faith on that book. Bilney remained an orthodox Roman except on some points, such as circulating the Bible and not praying to the Saints as mediators between man and God, and for these deviations from orthodoxy he was burned at Norwich, 24 years before Latimer's martyrdom. Latimer went on building his faith on what he found in the New Testament until he was alienated from the beliefs and practices of Romanism and began to denounce what he regarded as its superstitions and abuses.

Fearless, independent in character and thought, ready in speech, full of humour with a tinge of satire, he remained throughout his life the most popular preacher of his day.

Of course he was beset by enemies. The Bishop of Ely attended at Cambridge to hear him as a university preacher. Seeing the bishop in the congregation he changed his text and pictured what Christ would have been as a bishop. The bishop thanked him and asked him to preach a sermon against Luther. Latimer replied that Luther's works were prohibited, and so he had not read them, whereupon the bishop banned him from preaching in his diocese. But Wolsey gave him liberty to preach throughout England, and Henry the Eighth made him one of his chaplains, giving him a quiet living in Wiltshire.

Latimer believed in preaching, and blamed the bishops for not preaching themselves instead of harassing those who did. His own preaching was practical, with direct bearing on life, but he was incessantly harassed, called up for rebuke, imprisoned, and only released by the king, whose supremacy over the Church in England had now been acknowledged. When Cranmer became Archbishop of

Canterbury Latimer's position was altered. He was allowed to preach anywhere in the province of Canterbury, and was a frequent preacher before the king, and in 1535 he was made Bishop of Worcester.

For four years Latimer served as bishop and was active in preaching, in circulating the Scriptures, and in taking part in conferences that were too theological for his taste, till in 1539 the Act of the Six Articles was passed, the first providing that anyone who did not believe in transubstantiation should be burned. Then Latimer resigned his bishopric. He was ordered to stay in custody of the Bishop of Chichester and so remained for a year. Little is known of him for the next six years, but at the end of that period he was sent to the Tower for encouraging "the folly of preaching." While he was awaiting his trial there Henry the Eighth died and the accession of Edward the Sixth brought him freedom. His fame spread farther and wider, and his popularity grew among the people. He resumed his preaching to great crowds at St Paul's Cross and in the country, but declined to return to Worcester as its bishop, though specially asked by Parliament.

Six weeks after Mary Tudor became Queen he was called to London and committed to the Tower, old and ill. Two years of examining and badgering followed in London and Oxford before he, unswerving in his faith, was brought out as one of Mary Tudor's 300 victims and burnt in the name of Christianity, cheering his fellow martyr Bishop Ridley with the message that will resound throughout England as long as England lasts.

The Ancient Knights

THURLASTON. Its pleasant street, two or three timbered cottages, and the church are all that is left from the spacious days when the Turvilles were lords of the manor there. Their house has been pulled down, but their names live on in the neighbouring hamlet of Normanton Turville, and Thurlaston church still has their monuments.

A modern lychgate shaded by a lovely lime points the way to the church. It has been made new but still has the arcade built when the English pointed arch was coming in. The chancel has old choir stalls and modern wall-paintings, but the chief treasures of the place are the sculptures of knight and squire and lady, Turvilles of the long ago.

The first Turville lies under an arch, a bearded cross-legged civilian in a long belted robe. The altar tomb of Hugo Turville, who died in 1347, shows him in tunic and hood, holding his heart in his hands, and beside him is the battered figure of his wife. An armoured knight of the 15th century lies on an altar tomb adorned with angels, his head on a helmet, a lion at his feet, and his lady beside him in tight-waisted robe and ornaments, with angels supporting her cushioned head.

Two other memorials of the Turvilles are notable, one with the heads of Edward Turville and his bonneted wife, the other the head and shoulders of Elizabeth, a child brought to rest in Cromwell's day.

The Old Milestone

THURMASTON. When the Emperor Hadrian visited Britain in the year 120, he made a triumphal entry into Leicester, and because he had passed Thurmaston on the Fosse Way the Roman milestone there was dedicated to him. It recalled his imperial dignity, mentioned the names of his father and grandfather, and stated that Ratae was two miles away. Some 1650 years later the milestone was found by a workman digging for gravel, the first of its kind discovered in Britain. Having suffered many vicissitudes, including that of being threatened with employment as a garden roller, or of being broken up for road material, and having actually served for nearly half a century as the base of a lamp-post, it now stands in dignified security in the museum of the Roman town of Ratae and the English city of Leicester, to which it pointed the imperial way.

The milestone is the most important stone in this old place's history. It may have had others, for during seven centuries Thurmaston maintained two chapels of ease. The 13th century one remains as a ruin in the vicarage garden; the other was rebuilt.

THURNBY. It has a hilltop church with a 13th century nave and a central tower on massive arches built when the Norman style was changing into English. The rest of the church is chiefly modern, but it still keeps a 13th century pillared font, an old and battered ironbound chest, and a few stones carved by either Norman or Saxon masons.

Ice Age and Bronze Age

TILTON. It is Tilton-on-the-Hill, and the road climbs past the cottages and the trees, past the farmhouse with its fragments of the old manor, past the ancient church, and still higher to Halstead, the highest hamlet in the county. This great height (700 feet above the sea) probably remained above the ice-cap of Britain in the Ice Age, and ages afterwards served as a signpost along the trackway through the forests by which the Bronze Age men threaded their way from sea to sea.

Tilton's church of golden-tinted stone comes chiefly from the three medieval centuries, though there is earlier work in the base of the 14th-century tower with its graceful spire of the same time. With the tall broken shaft of the old cross for company in the churchyard, it is a fine picture outside. Its embattled walls are adorned with leafy pinnacles, and with an interesting array of carvings. All round runs a corbel table of flowers and queer faces and there are many queer gargoyles. Faces enrich the windows, which are a pleasing feature, especially the big ones of the 15th century clerestory, and the 14th century ones of the south aisle, which are framed inside by arches on slender pillars.

The most striking of the gargoyles are on this aisle, their curious feature hidden from the casual eye. One is a grotesque scaled animal, and as we stand beneath it we see a small human face breaking into a smile. The other is a grotesque with human head and wide-open mouth, and between its feet is a little human head, upside down. One of the great gargoyles on the clerestory is a lion; a second is a figure on another's back, holding its mouth open.

This carving in stone continues inside. Heads are everywhere, holding up the roof beams, adorning the fine arcades; some wear medieval headdress, some have curling hair, some are smiling, others are pleasantly grotesque. A fine big head (with open mouth showing teeth) holds up an arch with tiny hands in buttoned sleeves.

Four angels with outspread wings encircle one or two fine capitals in the north arcade. The other is most striking, for round it creep a fierce lion, a meek lamb, a grotesque with battered head, and a fox running off with a goose. The chancel has some of the old roof beams, and bosses showing faces in foliage.

The charming tower arch, with its mouldings on detached shafts and capitals carved with simple leaves, saw the dawn of the 13th century. The doorway to the tower stair is as old, and the west lancet has a very deep splay. The Norman font has a square bowl on a stout central pillar and eight small shafts.

There are tombs of the Digbys who lived here for three centuries. The last of them are not here, for Sir Everard was executed for his share in the Gunpowder Plot, and his brilliant son Kenelm, the Admirable Crichton of his age, was buried at Christ Church, Newgate. But here lies Sir John Digby of 1269, sculptured in stone, more than lifesize and crosslegged, clad in chain mail with a sleeveless surcoat. His great shield is carved with fleurs-de-lys; his feet rest on a splendid lion which holds a man's head between its front paws, while its hind paws are clasped round the tip of the knight's sword. Under the next arch of the arcade lies Sir John's wife Arabella, worn but graceful in draped headdress, the fold of her mantle caught up on her arm, a lapdog at her feet. Sir Everard Digby of 1509 is also in stone, wearing armour; a lion is at his feet. A nameless tomb with shields stands in the middle of the chancel, where, on the wall, is a quaint 17th century monument with figures of Augustin Nicholls and his wife with their 12 children, three in swaddling clothes.

From Sheep's Back to Peer's Back in a Day

TUGBY. Much of its ancient church was made new last century, but happily the remarkable character of its tower was left undisturbed. The tower has four storeys, the top two Norman, and the lower ones, with the little doorway and the window, Saxon, one of the rare examples of their work remaining in this county. The work of the Normans can also be seen in the south doorway. Among the other notable possessions of the church must be counted a 14th century paten engraved with the head of Christ. In the nave is a wall monument with a lengthy inscription to Henry Skipwith, equerry to Queen Elizabeth.

Here is told a curious tale of the Sixth Lord Berners, to whose memory are a set of windows of the Beatitudes. It is said that he appeared at a dinner of the Leicestershire Agricultural Society dressed in a coat made with wool which that very morning had been growing on one of his sheep at Keythorpe Hall, a mile away.

The Glowing Glass from Sainte Chapelle

TWYCROSS. Its ancient church stands boldly on a hillock among its retinue of yews. It is like a plain stone casket of glittering gems, for its east window is aglow with glass 700 years old.

When the French Revolution threatened the lovely Sainte Chapelle in Paris, much precious glass was taken for safety from that Gothic shrine and bought by a wealthy Englishman. It was presented to our William the Fourth, who gave some to Earl Howe, and he it was who found a fitting sanctuary for it here.

In its beautiful colours the window shows the Last Judgment with a seated figure of Christ, an angel and a kneeling penitent, and a number of other sacred subjects. Here a woman touches Jesus as He speaks to the multitude, and here the widow gives her mite. There is the Presentation in the Temple, Our Lord being taken from the cross, a father bringing his son to be cured; Mary Magdalene bowing her head; the spies carrying the grapes from the Promised Land; Moses with the Tables of the Law; and Solomon in his glory. It is all rich and rare treasure to come upon in a humble village church.

TWYFORD. It lies in a lovely valley below the commanding height of Burrough Hill, with its little church in a churchyard shaded by chestnut and sycamore. The church is dedicated to St Andrew, whose figure, austerely carved on a buttress of the 15th century tower, looks out above two vacant niches. The nave has a Norman arcade with rich capitals and a 13th century font.

The Glory is Departed

ULVERSCROFT PRIORY. It is perhaps the loveliest ruin in the county, beautiful in decay. Sheltered in a valley in the heart of Charnwood Forest, it stands by a brook rippling among the trees.

Much of the moat which surrounded the Norman priory still surrounds the ruins of the priory raised in 1361, the 14th century tower of the priory church dominating the scene. Its high pointed arch and its decaying sides are enclosed and protected by a loose stone wall.

By the tower stands a wall of the chancel, the old stone seats still with the tracery a 14th century carver lavished on them. Part of the refectory is here, with the pulpit and the guest house (now a barn), with 13th century windows and a massive 15th century roof. At the neighbouring farmhouse, with its medieval windows and doors, and walls that stood two centuries earlier round the prior's dwelling, is enshrined a remarkable old collection of tiles, carvings, and fragments of 14th century glass, the flotsam and jetsam of the foundered priory.

These ruins that have so lingered through the centuries seem to whisper something of the priory's story, of its builders and bene-factors, its splendour and decline. At the height of its prosperity the priory of Ulverscroft kept open house for any wayfarer, suc-coured the needy, comforted the weary, and maintained the poor in villages for miles around. Their income was nominally small, but they farmed on a large scale and at one time had 300 beasts, 1000 sheep, and 60 pigs ranging through the forest. Another glimpse of their importance is afforded by their possession of a falconer, huntsman, and ranger, and the man who cut the firewood for the house. All these disappeared at the Dissolution, and on their fate the poet Montgomery wrote:

> *Thy glory hath departed, Ulversdale,*
> *Thy glorious pageant of monastic pride,*
> *A power that once the power of kings defied.*

Roman, Saxon, and Norman

WALTHAM-ON-THE-WOLDS. High up on the Leicestershire Wolds it stands, with a black smock windmill and a lofty spire. Roman pavements and Saxon stone coffins found in its soil testify to its great antiquity, and the church itself, though chiefly 13th and 14th centuries, has precious links with Norman times.

Two Norman doorways have survived (one of plain solid work-manship, the other with zigzag on its capitals), and the font (with interlaced arches and sprays of foliage) is one of the finest Norman fonts in the county. The nave arcade is adorned with many carved heads, grave and gay, and above them angels and grotesques support an ancient wooden roof, decorated with figures bearing shields and scrolls. Ten angels support the chancel roof, and on the modern choir stalls are small canopied figures of the Four Evangelists.

The reredos, with a Last Supper in rich mosaic, keeps green the memory of Gabriel Gillett, who ministered here for 40 years last century, and a lovely figure of St Michael in a red cloak pays tribute to one who did not return from the War. In the vestry is a charming list of rectors, each with an oak panel to himself, his name in letters of gold above his brightly painted coat-of-arms.

Hobart Pasha

WALTON-ON-THE-WOLDS. It has a little church refashioned in the 18th century, a modest house of prayer with one old possession, a beautiful carved organ seat that was once a choir stall in Peterborough Cathedral.

Behind the church, looking on to smooth lawns and a dark hedge of yew, is the rambling old rectory. Beside the house is a noble cedar planted by a 19th century rector, father of Augustus Hobart-Hampden, better known as Hobart Pasha.

Born in this mellow old rectory in 1822, he spent his early years in the serenity of this old garden, and began his career by entering the Navy when he was 14. His craving for excitement led him to serve against slavers in Brazilian waters and he was in the Baltic during the Crimean War; but when these days were over the Navy had not enough adventure for him, and he became Captain Roberts, blockade runner in the American Civil War. Then the name of Hobart-Hampden was expunged from the Navy list, but later it was restored, only to disappear again when this descendant of the Elizabethan sea-dogs helped the Turks by checking blockade runners to Crete. After these activities he became Hobart Pasha, Admiral of the Ottoman Fleet and Commander of the Turkish Black Sea Fleet in the Russo-Turkish War of 1878.

He lived a life of strange adventure, but it must be said of this son of the rectory that wherever he went, whatever he did, he remained an Englishman in the heroic tradition.

The Oldest Words on a Brass

WANLIP. Here in green pastures a Roman built his house beside the Soar, setting in it a tessellated pavement to remind him of the home of his fathers far away by the Tiber. Hundreds of years later the pavement was unearthed with fragments of broken urns and coins of Constantine. All these, alas, have vanished from the scene, but the secluded 14th century church has its own store of antiquities in a few fragments of old heraldic glass, three bells that rang out before the Reformation, and a brass to the church's founder.

The brass is notable, for it has the earliest prose inscription in English on any brass in the land. It is dated 1393 and shows Sir Thomas Walsh as a knightly armoured figure with a lion at his feet, his wife beside him in cloak and embroidered cap with two dogs by her feet. She was the lady "whiche in her tyme made the Kirke of Anlep and Halud the Kirkeyard." Few medieval churches can point with such certainty to the monument of their founder.

The Poor Squire

WARTNABY. It is a pleasant village on the Wolds, with a church that has served its people for seven centuries and more. It has a Norman arcade still bearing dim traces of painting set there by some devout 12th century monk, a plain but ancient font, and two simple old benches in the chancel. A brass in memory of Rosamund Bingham, who worshipped here last century, has an engraved figure of a saint.

At the neighbouring Wartnaby Hall, which hides its ivy-mantled charms behind a screen of trees, Charles the Second, while on a royal tour, took breakfast with the squire John Hacket. It is said that the gay king found such a boon companion in his host that he offered to knight him on the spot, and it is also related that the squire's finances would not permit him to accept the honour.

In more recent years the village had another distinguished visitor in Sir Rider Haggard, who, during the travels of inquiry which led to his valuable book on Rural England, came here and was shown how to make Stilton cheeses, being told that, apart from making no noise, they were more troublesome than babies.

Mary Edwards Comes to Town

WELHAM. It is near the southern border of the county, a placid group of cottages, a wayside inn, and a little grey church 600 years old.

The church has a huge monument to a generous squire, Francis Edwards, who at the beginning of the 18th century built new houses for the villagers and rescued their church from decay. The monument standing 18 feet high and decked with urns and pedestals, was put up in 1728 by the squire's daughter Mary.

In later years Mary Edwards forsook this quiet village of her childhood, took up her abode in Kensington, and there aspired to play grand dame. But her eccentric ways made her the laughing

stock of society and she avenged herself by commissioning Hogarth
to portray the absurdities of the fashionable dress of the day.
Hogarth carried out her wishes in the picture he called Taste in
High Life, and Mary Edwards, having made her little storm in the
society tea cup, came home again and now sleeps by her benevolent
father in the quiet of this place.

The V C Postman

WHITWICK. It is set where the county seems to divide, with
the coalfields and a dusky population on one side, and on the
other the blue-eyed, rosy-faced people who live on the outskirts of
Charnwood Forest.

The brook flows about the oddly-shaped mound which is called
Castle Hill, and past the steep churchyard, one branch of it coming
darkly from the coalfields and the other through an outskirt of the
village long called the City of Dan. Here, below house and church
and chapel and brook, the geological bed of greenstone intervenes
between the coal measures and the New Red sandstone. In one of
the shafts of the nearest colliery it is 60 feet deep.

From that remote period we may move on to one when Whitwick
was on the trackway through the forest by which the salt was brought
from Cheshire's salt mines to the south, and it may be that Castle
Hill (on which the Earls of Leicester planted the castle) was originally
one of the guiding marks through the primeval forest. Not far
away is a natural monolith, a relic of the glaciers of the Ice Age,
the Swanimote Rock where the old Swanimote (or Moot) was held.

In the steep sloping churchyard rises a 14th century tower, grey
and massive, impressive in its strength. In the church is the 14th century font and the 14th century tomb of Sir John Talbot, with a
battered figure of an armoured knight over seven feet long as
Sir John was when he lived 600 years ago. Nothing else of him is
known, and according to a local couplet,

> *Nought remains in Talbot's name,*
> *But Talbot's wood and Talbot's Lane.*

Even these are not now to be seen. There are two modern windows
which claim attention. One has the Crucifixion scene in memory of
the men who have lost their lives in the neighbouring coalpits and
granite quarries; in the other the church tower and the old castle
appear as a background to a fine picture of Bishop Grosseteste of

Lincoln, restoring to church and priest the great tithes of part of the ancient parish.

Many heroes in lowly walks of life have lived in and round Whitwick. Not least among them was the village postman Thomas Ashford, who won the Victoria Cross in the Afghan War. During a sortie from Kandahar he rescued a wounded soldier when under fire of the Afghan snipers. Having carried a comrade to safety and himself into immortality, he came back to England to carry on his work, delivering letters here and walking 20 miles a day.

Up in the hills, hidden among the trees of Charnwood Forest, about a mile from the village, is the Abbey of Mount St Bernard, handsomely designed by the elder Pugin. It has church and cloisters, chapter house and refectory, museum, library, and guest house, and a farm for lay brothers and a house for the poor. Founded in 1835, it was the first Roman Catholic Abbey so built and used in England since the Reformation. Those who live there have a well deserved name for hard work and good works. Ambrose Phillipps de Lisle, who was largely responsible for the foundation of the abbey, was buried in its church; he appeared as Eustace Lyle in Disraeli's Coningsby, but has here a surer title to remembrance.

The Mother of Dean Swift

WIGSTON MAGNA. Wigston Two Steeples is its older name, for, though it has grown up with industry along the railway and the canal, it has been distinguished by having two churches, each with its steeple, for centuries.

The more stately of the churches is All Saints, six centuries old. Its spire is one of the best in the county, its tower rests on three massive arches, and the capitals of the nave arches have curious medieval grotesques as well as floral ornament. The handsome screen is 15th century, and under a deep sepulchral arch is a 13th century coffin with a cross and a headless figure carved on it.

The other church, in a pretty churchyard shaded by chestnut, yew, and lime, still has its lovely 14th century steeple, but for the rest has been made new, and is chiefly notable as the only church in England dedicated to Wolstan, the 11th century Bishop of Worcester whose inspired preaching of the Word, unwearying devotion to the lowly, and constant care of the needy caused him to be venerated as a saint in his lifetime.

Wigston may claim to have been an important place in Saxon days, for many ornaments of wealthy thanes have been unearthed here, and here alone, in a county so devoted to the horse, have been found Saxon horse trappings.

It is thought that Abigail Herrick, mother of Dean Swift, was born in this village, and if it be true then Wigston must have been dear to the heart of her famous son. It is pleasant to recall that Swift, whose pen was so often dipped in gall, wrote a tender tribute to his mother when she died. "I have now lost my barrier between me and death," he records in his diary. "God grant I may leave as well prepared for it as I confidently believe her to have been. If the way to Heaven be through piety, truth, justice, and charity, she is there."

The Village Thankful

WILLESLEY. It is one of the little group of what we have called our Thankful Villages, 31 of them, whose men all came home from the war. It is the only village in the county with this proud distinction. Three went out and three came back.

The hall with a lovely lake in its grounds, the church beside it, and a few neighbouring farms—these are Willesley. The hall is an imposing house of red brick with a profuse array of Tudor gables, capped by four little towers. The church is 600 years old and has a few fragments of ancient heraldic glass, one with a figure of a knight kneeling before a castle. In the chancel are two 16th century floor stones with figures worn by the footprints of time, showing John and George Abney, each with his wife. In the floor is another worn stone with the figure of Sir John Wilkins, a medieval priest.

The Mark of the Axe

WISTOW. It has little more than its hall and church, reached by a field path from Kilby, along which we may often walk and meet nothing more than a rabbit.

The Elizabethan hall, standing serenely by a lake, was the home of many generations of Halfords. It is a peaceful country house, yet it must have witnessed many stirring scenes of civil war. Its most tragic visitor came to it at a turning point in history, when the Battle of Naseby had been lost and won, and, from the stricken field King Charles came to shelter here under the roof of his loyal supporter Sir Richard Halford. It was the great day in the annals of this house, and the house treasures still the decorated saddle and stirrups of the king who came riding in the hour of his doom.

Hiding among the trees near the hall is the little 700-year-old church, where many Halfords lie. Chief among them is Charles Stuart's supporter Sir Richard, whose monument shows him in armour, his two sons at his head and feet. This is his inscription:

Weep not to read so many worthies dead,
But weep to see so few left in their stead.

It is interesting to recall that, though Sir Richard and his son Andrew (who hanged some Parliamentarians he captured in a skirmish) were sentenced to death, both were freed by paying ransoms and both died in their beds.

Mourning figures and other memorials recall the Halfords who worshipped here in the 18th and 19th centuries, and quietly played their parts in public life. The most notable of these is a sculpture of a doctor giving medicine to a sick man, a last tribute to Sir Henry Halford, who was famous as a physician during the first half of last century. Sir Henry, who as a doctor attended four English monarchs, was associated in a curious way with the ill-fated king for whom his ancestors fought. He was present when Charles Stuart's coffin was opened at Windsor in 1813, and managed to procure a piece of bone bearing the mark of the axe, which he would exhibit for the entertainment of his friends at the dinner table.

The Smiths

WITHCOTE. It is pleasant to find a way here by a footpath wandering through the countryside near the Rutland border, crossing a stream of the Chater by a footbridge and leading into the park where those good companions, the hall and the church, stand so serenely. The orange-coloured hall was long the home of a family with one of the oldest and most widespread English names, the Smiths. The mounds on Castle Hill are all that remain of Sauvez Castle.

The little 15th century church, standing in the leafy shade of slender trees, is like a small college chapel, a single pinnacled and battlemented chamber. Although for the most part it is adorned with 18th century work in wood and plaster, it has windows remarkable for their wonderful display of German glass. Although 500 years old, it is splendidly preserved, its 18 figures of saints and holy men including Bartholomew, Simeon, Thomas, Christopher, David, Joel, Daniel, Andrew, James, and Peter. Another treasure is the reredos, with a copy of Murillo's Holy Family.

Of the Smiths who lived so long at the hall there remains part of a monument to the Ambrose who died in 1584, with a guardian angel holding an inscription "Live to die, die to live," one of the oldest of Christian moralities. The Henry Smith, born here about 1550, whose preaching made him renowned throughout the countryside as Silver-Tongued Smith, sleeps at Husbands Bosworth 20 miles away. Another Henry Smith was on the side of the Parliament in the Civil War and signed the death warrant of the king but when the Restoration brought him to trial he pleaded that from first to last of these unhappy wars he had been a man of trouble and sorrow and knew not what he had done. His estate was confiscated and he died a prisoner in the Tower.

Old Stones from Watling Street

WITHERLEY. For 500 years the lofty spire of its 14th century church has soared up proudly overlooking two counties, for the River Anker which runs so prettily by the churchyard is the boundary of Warwickshire.

The church has a 14th century font, a lovely figure of the Madonna among some fragments of 15th century glass, and a 16th century roof with grand oak beams. The modern chancel has a lovely altar table and finely carved stalls, and a tablet pays tribute to the memory of Isaac Whyley, who died in Trafalgar year after ministering here for almost half a century.

By the pathway from the porch are some kerb-stones brought here from an 18th century bridge which carried Watling Street across the Anker not far off.

Robert Herrick's Uncle William

WOODHOUSE. Delightful stone cottages line the byways in its glorious countryside, for Woodhouse is on the fringe of Charnwood Forest. One of its enchanting vistas is of the red-brick manor house peeping through a long double avenue of lofty elms; the house has the shadow of antiquity over its gables, oriels, and clustered chimneys, but is actually modern.

Beaumanor, serene in a setting as lovely as its name, has an association which must make it for ever a place beloved by all who love English poetry. For centuries it belonged to men of high lineage, until in Elizabeth's day it passed from nobleman to merchant, and became the property of Sir William Herrick, uncle of the poet, and for some years his guardian. William Herrick was sent as a boy to serve his apprenticeship to the poet's father, a goldsmith in Cheapside. When he was able to set up a business for himself he became jeweller to the first two Stuart kings, and was soon one of the richest merchants in London. He bought Beaumanor from the Earl of Essex when he was 32, lived there till he was over 90, and was buried in the Herrick chapel of St Martin's in Leicester.

The hall of this famous house has among its historic possessions some rare and curious treasures. One of the rooms has part of the massive bedstead in which Richard the Third rested his uneasy head before his death on Bosworth Field. There are chairs said to have been fashioned from the wood of old London Bridge, and in the hall is one enormous chair without a nail or a joint, hewn in the 17th century from the heart of a giant oak in the park.

The small 15th century church, with a slate-capped tower, has many monuments of the Herricks, and still keeps a little of the richness they bestowed upon it. There are fragments of old heraldic glass and a Jacobean pulpit given by Sir William in 1615. The screen in the north aisle has a panel bearing the initials of the poet's uncle, and three others with texts.

The churchyard has some grand old yews and glorious views of the slopes of Charnwood, of the windmill crowning the heights above Woodhouse Eaves, and of the soaring height of Beacon Hill, second highest point in the county.

On the Edge of Charnwood Forest

WOODHOUSE EAVES. It has magnificent vistas of the countryside rolling away in rocky and wooded splendour, for it is on the edge (eaves) of Charnwood Forest. School, vicarage, and the modern church with its many lancet windows, stand on a rocky perch, and near them is a cross of memory with the names that live for evermore inscribed on a stone in a rock garden below. On a neighbouring hill stands a gleaming white windmill with a view of Charnwood Forest spreading away in a distant panorama.

LEICESTERSHIRE

A Great Church Rescued From Neglect

WYMESWOLD. It was once a market town, and many pros-
perous-looking houses in its streets bear witness to its thriving
days. The church, built on a large scale in the 14th and 15th
centuries, has clearly been a prosperous place, but is much restored.

Dean Alford found it in a sorely neglected state, with tallow dips
in sticks set in the pews for lighting, and parish meetings permitted
within the altar rails. In his 18 years here before he became Dean
of Canterbury he raised £3500 and put matters right. A vigorous
Christian and a busy parson, he found time to do all this as well as to
follow those Greek studies which enabled him to produce his famous
edition of the Greek New Testament and other scholarly works.

The east window has modern glass with figures of Jesus, the
Madonna, and Apostles. Among the few antiquities preserved are
some fragments of old woodwork with leaves and Tudor roses,
probably once part of the medieval screen now hanging on the
walls. There is also an ornate marble monument to William Leeke,
Serjeant-at-Law under Charles the Second, who, as his epitaph
records, resigned a judgeship as soon as he received it. Here also
lies Thomas Russell Potter, historian of Charnwood Forest.

The Church Rich with Carving

WYMONDHAM. It is an old market town close to the Rutland
and Lincolnshire borders, with a broad street and a byway
running down to a noble church. Sir Charles Sedley, the depraved
companion of Charles the Second, was lord of the manor and stayed
here when the plague was raging in London. It was an earlier
Sedley who, in 1637, founded the grammar school standing by the
lychgate, a plain stone building housing no scholars now and used
as a reading room.

The handsome cross-shaped church, with a 13th century tower,
15th century belfry, and a tall spire, has some splendid carving.
Its 700-year-old arcades have finely carved capitals, one adorned
with winged angels and another with merry faces, heads of oxen,
and ballflower. On the walls are 30 corbels with heads of bearded
men and angry men, and fearsome monsters, and in the south transept is some fine old oak carving. There is a small cupboard carved
with the Annunciation and the Baptism, and on the wall above is
some rich panelling with cherub heads and scriptural scenes.

On an altar tomb lies the 14th century figure of Sir John Hamelin, cross-legged and in chain mail, with a battered frog squatting near his sword and a tame lion at his feet. There is a 16th century brass of Dame Margery Berkeley, in a veiled headdress and a girdled gown, and in the bell tower is a patronising memorial to James Woolman "for meritorious conduct as a ringer and respectful demeanour for 40 years in this parish."

In the churchyard, where the stem of an ancient cross now serves as a sundial, is a 19th century tablet to Richard Craggs, 52 years parson and nearly 40 years master of the grammar school.

RUTLAND

The Child of Our Counties

PERHAPS we may call it the Little Brother of the Shires. Hiding between three counties, with Leicestershire next door and Northants and Lincolnshire on its borders, Rutland is the smallest of all our English counties. A rough triangle 63 miles round, with an area of not quite a hundred thousand acres (about 150 square miles), it would take more than three hundred Rutlands to make up England, and forty to make up Yorkshire. Its population of about 17,000 is in keeping with its size, and there are over a hundred English towns with three times as many people as this county.

Rutland is not in the Conqueror's Domesday Book as a county, for when that survey was made the Rutland we know was grouped partly with Northants and chiefly with Notts. Among the many explanations of its name is one that in Saxon days the Ratae tribe came in through the Fens by the River Welland and gave their name to it before passing on to Leicester. However that may be, it was the royal domain of Roteland in the Confessor's day, and he bequeathed it to his wife Edith, whose name is remembered in the village of Edith Weston. But the earliest mention of Rutland as a county was seven centuries ago, in the days of King John.

Rutland has no natural features distinctly its own; it blends into the landscape of its neighbours. The north part of the county is a fertile plateau of grassland, and its general slope is from the Leicestershire Wolds on the west to the lowlands of Lincolnshire on the east, and the River Welland which separates it from Northants on the south.

It has none of England's grandest scenery, but is a truly fair county, and from its high places are many delightful vistas of green pastures stretching to far horizons. Within its borders we may find all the charms of gentle wooded hills, fertile valleys, and tranquil villages with thatched cottages, and none of the ugliness industry has bestowed too freely on some of its neighbours.

Chiefly an agricultural county, with an unusually large proportion of its area under cultivation, its only considerable industry is in the limestone quarries. The stone from Ketton quarries is known far and wide, having been used for many churches in Norfolk and Suffolk, as well as for York Minster and Exeter Cathedral. The stone is also front-page news in Fleet Street, where St Dunstan's church pays tribute to its qualities.

The county's only important towns are Oakham, its capital, and Uppingham, famous for its public school. Oakham, surely the quietest county town of the 20th century, has a quaint marketplace with the butter-cross and the stocks still there, a Norman castle with a remarkable collection of horseshoes significant of one of our ancient customs, and a lovely church with a weathercock as old as Agincourt. It is a tiny place of tranquil streets (in which we found growing perhaps the greatest wistaria we have seen).

These are its two chief centres of population, but there are many attractive and surprising villages in the 320 miles of Rutland's highways and byways. Five of them have still among their treasures the work of Saxon carvers or masons, and more than twenty proudly display the master hand of the Norman craftsman.

Tickencote has a magnificent Norman shrine, the carved vaulting of its chancel roof unlike any other in England except in the choir at Canterbury, and its chancel arch has five richly carved orders as noble as in any Norman church. Great Casterton, where John Clare first met Sweet Patty of the Vale, has an even older heritage, and many relics of the Romans and the Stone Age men have been found there. At Market Overton, the home of Sir Isaac Newton's mother, the stocks and whipping post are kept in token of the bad old days, and here we found a 13th century font on a base thought to be Roman, a Saxon arch in the tower, and a sundial said to be the gift of Sir Isaac

Newton. The village of Wing has an interesting survival from Merrie England in a turf maze forty feet across, one of the best preserved of all these entertaining survivals of the countryside. Liddington has a charming Bede House, and what could be more surprising than to find at Preston an almsbox from a church in Asia Minor, two pieces of mosaic from a Constantinople church destroyed 500 years ago, candlesticks from Damascus, and yews from the Garden of Gethsemane?

But it was the village of Teigh, a little place on the Leicestershire border with ivy and wistaria draped about stone houses, which gave us one of the happiest memories of our tour of Rutland. It is one of England's small group of Thankful Villages where all came back safe from the war, and in its curious church is a brass inscription set up in thanksgiving for the return of eleven men and two women, the Lucky Thirteen.

That is Rutland's most thankful village, but surely all these villages must be thankful for the peace that is theirs in our bustling and hustling century.

Our smallest county has no particular heritage of great names, and few poets have sung its praises; but Rutland needs no poet to sing, for it is a county with no masses of chimneys, no black spots, no distressful areas, and in a world where so much changes for the worse Rutland changes only for the better. Serene and tranquil, wrapped in a cloak of sweet content, she lives in rare simplicity at the heart of England, and we who know too well the stress and strain of towns may envy those who can say each day:

> *These simple joys that never fail*
> *Shall bind me to my native vale.*

The Parson's Victoria Cross

ASHWELL. It abounds in natural charm and has a fine old church, with a pyramid cap peeping out of the trees as we come from Oakham. Green hedges and ivied stone walls line the roads. Opposite the church is the Old Hall made partly new, set off by smooth lawns.

Looking its best outside, the church is chiefly 14th century, with earlier work in the arcades, which continue into the chancel and open to chapels. One of the arches is Norman, and nail-head ornament enriches the capitals.

The windows are a charming feature, some of them adorned with frames of ballflowers, and most of them having delightful little faces on their hoods. Dainty indeed is the hood of ballflowers over the charming east window, spoiled only by the stone panels filling the base. On each side wall of the chancel is a corbel table of ballflowers alternating with little faces of animals and men.

There is a double piscina in the chancel, and a fine piscina niche in the south aisle. A flower-shaped drain is in a windowsill of one chapel, and in the other a bracket piscina, a niche, and a carved bracket.

The very fine wooden figure of a 14th century knight, thought to be Sir Thomas Touchet, lies in the south chapel. His head rests on cushions, his hands are at prayer, his legs are crossed, and his features are worn, but every detail of his costume is clear—his chain mail, his tunic, the sword with a broken handle, the girdle, and the spurs.

On the top stone of a 15th century tomb near the wooden knight are engraved the lifesize figures of John and Rose Vernam, their hands in prayer. John wears the everyday garb of a medieval citizen, with a tasselled purse, and his dagger at his side; she has a flowing headdress. One dog is curled up at her feet, and another, alert, is at John's feet. The great stone is covered every inch with the initials of louts, some cut three centuries ago.

The stately alabaster figure in the other chapel is supposed to be their son John, rector here. He lies in his finely draped robes, his feet and his hands broken. His guardian angels are battered, and the lion at his feet has lost its head.

Here, far from war's alarms, sleeps a very gallant figure, Parson Adams, who came as rector and was the first clergyman to receive the V C. An Irishman of Herculean strength, he was said to be the strongest man in Ireland in his youth. He consecrated his physical prowess with all the energy of his heart and mind to the service and salvation of his fellows. Going out to India in 1866 when still on the right side of thirty, he became a model padre, toiling unremittingly for the troops and carrying his message far into the jungle, where his strength enabled him to reduce forest trees to logs and raise logs to temples.

As war blazed up, Adams was called to serve with a field force under Lord Roberts, and his courage and devotion made him an almost legendary figure. The great testing time came at Villa Kazi when Adams was forty. A number of men of the 9th Lancers were trapped in a muddy watercourse and in danger either of drowning or of death from the spears of Afghans. Under heavy fire the padre dashed single-handed to the scene of danger and rescued the men. It chanced that Lord Roberts himself was a spectator of this thrilling incident, and in his despatches home he begged that Adams might receive the V C.

He had many years of military experience in the East, and again and again was under heavy fire. Nothing daunted his spirit, nothing dimmed the sunshine of his nature. He left India as the idol of the Army and was for several years a rector in Norfolk, and a royal chaplain before he came here as a man of 62, with the hope of years of service before him. But his constitution had been undermined, and he died little more than a year after reaching Ashwell.

A Green Field for the Poor

AYSTON. It has a goodly heritage, rich with trees, a hall in a beautiful garden and springy lawns, and a church that has stood about 700 years. It has still its 13th century nave arcades, its tower is 14th century, and its chancel 15th. Its sundial has looked down on many generations. The church has a fine possession and a curious fragment.

The fine possession is in its windows, which have 500-year-old glass showing the Crucifixion with the Madonna and St John, and below it figures of priests and a crowned head. In another window is ancient glass brought from the hall, showing the Wise Men at

Bethlehem, the Presentation in the Temple, the head of a monk, and a white hart.

The curious fragment is a piece of ancient sculpture which keeps alive the story of two sisters, one-armed twins. They appear to have been industrious cripples, busying themselves in much good work and making money by their spinning so that they earned enough at last to buy a field, which they left as a legacy to benefit the poor of Uppingham. The ancient sculpture is fading away with the centuries, but we can still see that the craftsman was moved by the story of these devoted sisters to give one of them two hands, that he might show them clasped in prayer.

The Chalice in its Ancient Case

BARROWDEN. The pride of Barrowden is its delightful church, the interior of which had seen four centuries when Wren began to build St Paul's. There were no architects until centuries after its erection, and its dimensions suggest that the Norman master mason went astray, so great is the contrast between the breadth and the length. But the men who gave Rutland her churches built with beauty as with strength. The south doorway's carving, the 14th century tower and spire, the 13th century nave arcades, all proclaim a splendour from which the glory is not entirely departed.

A relic of the days of chained books is a glazed case with a chained book in it still; it is made from an old Jacobean lectern and pulpit. One fine panel has inlaid flowers. There is a curious leather receptacle in which the chalice is kept—a remarkable survival, for it is said to belong to the 14th century.

It was surprising to discover, when we called, that the ancient practice of rush-bearing survives at Barrowden, a reminder of days when feudal lords held their estate on the payment of dues in rushes for the church or for the king's castle.

A King in His Flight

BELTON. It is fair to see, with a Tudor farmhouse which was once the old hall of the Verneys, an ancient church, and much natural charm.

The Norman church has marks of a fire of 700 years ago; we trace evidence of the flames on some of the piers in the nave. Not all was lost. The fine arcade of pink stone is Norman, and a 12th century trefoil window still lights part of the nave. The battered font is 13th century.

It would seem that Gothic humour ran riot with the 15th century masons of Belton. The men who carved the piscina arranged for the water to drain down the throat of a grim monster, and the craftsmen of the fine embattled tower left it bristling with gargoyles peeping and leering over the countryside. We may wonder if any medieval son of Belton could have doubted the reality of demons.

On one of the tombs are 16th century alabaster figures of Sir Thomas Haselwood, his wife, and their eight children, but the most intriguing stone in Belton is the plain base of the peace memorial, which sends us away wondering, for tradition says it is the stone on which Charles Stuart rested on his flight from Naseby.

The Saxon Doorstep

BRAUNSTON. It has sunken roads and ancient earthworks which take back its human record thousands of years; and its church preserves a link with the Saxon forerunners of its Norman builders. Outside the west end is a crudely carved stone which for generations served as a doorstep. One day it was turned over, and underneath was found a primitive carving of the figure of a woman, believed to be Saxon.

The church has a massive Norman doorway, a Norman font, and Norman work in the chancel arch. The clerestory, like the tower, is 14th century. There is a stone coffin whose history is lost, a brass portrait of Kenelme Cheselden who died in 1596, and windows of St George, St Martin, and St Dunstan. There are still faint traces of the colour which once made the church gay with glowing scenes from the Bible, the villager's only art gallery in the Long Ago.

Sir Andrew Goes Empty Away

BROOKE. A little group of homesteads now, it has known more bustling days. The green mounds on Priory Farm outline the buried ruins of the priory founded here 800 years ago; the solitary arch and the deserted pigeon cote are all that survive of the magnificent house built on the ruins in the days of the great architectural revival called the Renaissance.

The church with a 13th century tower, graced by slender columns on each side, comes from a period of changing architecture. The south doorway is Norman yet has an English arch, and we see the passing from one style to another again in the chancel, in certain arches, and in the aislé. The font is pure Norman, a square bowl with three arches on each side.

Brooke has a fine legacy from wood craftsmen who were taking up their chisels when Shakespeare was laying down his pen. They fashioned this admirable pulpit, the reading-desk, the altar rails and two altar tables; they carved the chancel screen, the choir stalls, and some old box pews. But older craftsmen still were here, for the church has an ancient chest hewn from a tree, and ancient ironwork on the doors.

There is a pathetic memorial to five women and one man; he was Henry Rawlins and all five women were his wives, all dying within 13 years, as the stones in the chancel floor tell.

The chief treasure of sculpture here is the elaborately carved tomb of Charles Noel, who lies in armour on a pallet of straw, wearing his wig and ruff. He was a younger son of Sir Andrew Noel, an Elizabethan knight who represented Rutland in Parliament, a man of much distinction in his day, with three daughters who married peers. The story is told that he was so enterprising as once to return himself for Parliament without the aid of the electors, and the House of Commons, unmoved by the assurance that Rutland would have none other, refused to receive him and sent Sir Andrew empty away.

The Great House

BURLEY. It was part of the grandeur that was Rome, for Romans were here. It knew rough Saxon lords and stern Norman masters. It became the seat of men who helped to make and mar our history, the holiday haunt of kings, and the scene of civil war.

The house that makes it famous is Burley-on-the-Hill, standing in a finely timbered park of 1000 acres, surrounded by a wall about six miles long, with gates wrought by the masterly hand of Jean Tijou, the Frenchman whose example inspired English craftsmen to an era of genius in ironwork that they never excelled.

The original house was owned by Sir James Harington, to whom James the First came as a delighted guest. He returned in 1621 more enchanted still, for now his Steenie, the profligate Duke of Buckingham, was lord of Burley. The lavish host commissioned

Ben Jonson to write a masque for the occasion. Next Charles Stuart with his queen was here, and it was for their entertainment that the redoubtable dwarf, Jeffery Hudson, was served up in a pie.

Battered down by the Parliamentary Army, the house has been rebuilt and burned down and rebuilt again ; today it is a noble English home, with a magnificent Doric colonnade extending nearly 200 feet along the north front.

> Kings have on this spot made their abodes ;
> Tis fitted now to entertain the gods.

A covered way leads from the house to the Norman church, with its lofty and richly decorated 14th century tower. The north arcade is Norman with finely carved capitals; the south arcade is 13th century. The 15th century font is rich with tracery and has sculptured heads at the corners. There is a charmingly carved reredos, with Christ and six of the Apostles in delicately wrought niches.

Near the tower arch are alabaster figures of a knight and his wife who died before Agincourt; their name and fame have vanished like the memory of the peasant who tilled their fields.

> The knight is dust,
> His good sword rust;
> His soul is with the saints, we trust.

We have no doubt as to the cenotaph by Chantrey in the choir. It is a beautiful sculpture in memory of Lady Charlotte Finch, governess to the children of George the Third and Queen Charlotte. We meet her often in the Court pages of Fanny Burney's Diary, where a strange story tells of an attempt to stab the king, and the queen, finding Lady Charlotte in tears, said to her in a frenzy of emotion, "I envy you—I can't cry!" The monument here shows Lady Charlotte as a lovely kneeling figure, but she lies at Ravenstone in Buckinghamshire. A 19th century member of the family with a monument here is Emily Finch, who has a sculpture charming with carvings of cherubs and angels.

One of the vicars of Burley looking down from the walls in a photograph was here for half of the 19th century; he was John Jones.

Jeffery Hudson

THIS is the story of the little man who was put in a pie. It is curious that the smallest of our counties should have produced the smallest man who has come into our history. He has come into our literature, too, as the dwarf concerned in the plot in Scott's Peveril of the Peak.

Jeffery Hudson was born in 1619, the son of the tall broad-shouldered drover who had charge of the animals George Villiers, Duke of Buckingham, used for bull-baiting. While his brothers resembled their father in stature, Jeffery, though perfectly proportioned, was only 18 inches high when he was nine years old.

The Duchess took a fancy to this pretty little fellow, and dressed him in silks and satins, in which he made a bright little ornament in the grand rooms of Burley-on-the-Hill. One day Charles Stuart and Henrietta Maria came to stay here and a big pie was placed on the dinner table, and, when it was cut, out jumped sprightly little Jeffery. The queen was so delighted with the dwarf's quaint ways that the duchess gave him to her.

His portrait was painted by Van Dyck in a picture of Henrietta Maria which is now at Petworth in Sussex, and he was so petted and spoiled that he grew proud and refused to recognise his father, an offence for which Charles Stuart ordered him to be punished. He was a great friend of the king's giant porter. In 1630 he accompanied the queen's dancing master to the French Court, where he received £2500 in presents. Flemish pirates, however, robbed him of this on his journey home, and carried him off to Dunkirk.

When the Civil War broke out Jeffery was made a Captain of Horse, but there is no record of his having taken part in any battle, though he had the courage of a grown man. He accompanied the Queen on her flight from Pendennis Castle in 1644 and shared her unhappy days at Paris. Here in 1649 he had a quarrel with Lord Crofts and challenged him to a duel; they fought on horseback and Lord Crofts was killed. Hudson was banished and took ship for England, but Turkish pirates captured him and sold him as a slave in Barbary. He was forced to work very hard and was cruelly beaten, and it is strange that the little man of 30 then began to grow, and reached three feet and a half.

At last he was ransomed and returned to Oakham, where the Duke of Buckingham gave him a small pension. But he longed for the silk and satin life of the Court again, and went to London, and as a Roman Catholic he came to be suspected of complicity in a Popish Plot. He was imprisoned in Westminster Gatehouse, and soon after his release he died, aged 62.

Where the Roman Temple Stood

CALDECOTT. Speaking the tongue of Virgil and Cicero, Caldecott was Roman before it was English; it may be presumed that the Roman settlement running 500 yards along the river will one day yield rich treasure for those who seek it in this village of charming thatched cottages. But not all Roman Caldecott is underground, for the walls of the old church are rich in Roman tiles.

There are those who believe that the church stands on the site of a Roman temple, and the church itself takes us nearly halfway back to the Roman days. It comes from the 13th and 14th centuries, the chastely carved font having been made about 1300. The charming porch has stood since 1697, just a hundred years before lightning set the spire on fire but left the five melodious bells still ringing. They are as old as the porch, and one of them has on it, "Peter Browne gave me to this town."

Shattered in the Wars of the Roses

CLIPSHAM. All Rutland knows Clipsham stone; here it is at home. Clipsham Hall, glorified by its yew hedge, stands handsome and durable in it, a fine advertisement of local products.

The church, bordered by splendid limes, has a finely decorated 14th century spire, with miniature crosses and mimic battlements. The arches of the north aisle are Norman; the children's little pews stand by the Norman font. The venerable roof timbers are elegant with their tracery, and the brackets rest on beautifully carved heads. There is an attractive modern reredos finely carved with scenes of the Ascension, the Last Supper, the Transfiguration, the Nativity, and a New Testament scene from Egypt.

But the most precious possession of Clipsham is the heraldic glass in the north chapel, for it was part of the ancient church at Pickworth and was shattered in the Wars of the Roses. This glass through which the light is falling was in those wars which drove the Plantagenets off the throne and put the Tudors in their place.

Peter Gunning's Prayer

COTTESMORE. Bronze Age, Roman, Saxon, and Norman—all were here. Burial places rich in relics of peaceful folk and warriors have been found, with shields buried as an expression of the old belief that the departed heroes would fight in another world with the weapons of this. The story of Cottesmore is 5000 years long.

Cottesmore   The Cottages by the Church

Barrowden   South doorway   **Empingham**   Old Dovecot

Egleton   Norman Tympanum

Manton   Almsbox   **Morcott**   Norman Capital

A splendid Norman doorway survives in the church, but most of it inside is from the 14th and 15th centuries. The finely carved pulpit is Jacobean. The richest treasure of the church is the font, with its arcaded bowl of the 14th century resting on a base much older, with primitive carvings of the Crucifixion and an abbot with his staff.

There is a memorial to William Brereton, who was rector here for fifty years; and another which says:

> *Beneath this stone lies a dutiful son,*
> *What faults you have seen in him take care and shun;*

and another on the coped tombstone of William Westbrook Baker, of whom we are told that he originated a small allotment system in 1830 and invented a plough.

Here in the days of the Stuarts lived Peter Gunning, whom we meet much in the diaries of Pepys and Evelyn. A great scholar of his day, he owed his immunity to the tolerance of Cromwell, and though he used his power to persecute the Nonconformists he is remembered by one of his prayers that has become immortal, *For all sorts and conditions of men.*

Labourer and Philanthropist

EDITH WESTON. It is Edith Weston because Edward the Confessor gave his Queen Edith this western part of Rutland. The shaft of a cross in the centre of the village seems to link us with those days. It is all a delight to those who love our old thatched cottages. The Hall, with its wide lawns and stately trees, stands by the 12th century church. The tower and spire, 500 years old and a model of grace, well justify the proud rhyme inscribed in the church below:

> *Crown of all the neighbouring lands,*
> *High and lifted up it stands.*

In truth pretty rolling country never was better capped.

The spacious church is noble with the massive strength of Norman builders, rich with their carving on the chancel arch and in the beautiful north arcade, of which the deeply cut mouldings of the round arches are a joy to the eye. The south arcade is 13th century but keeps the Norman arch. From the same century comes the lofty arch of the tower. The reredos is by one of our fine modern sculptors, Sir George Frampton, and shows Christ on the throne with a kneeling angel on one side and a woman on the other.

Two things stir our imagination here. There is still ticking away a venerable one-handed clock under the tower, which we were told has come down from the Commonwealth and has chimed away the hours for many generations in this place. The other is the memory of William Lloyd, a labouring man at Edith Weston in the days when the life of a labourer was almost beyond endurance, for he lived at the middle of the 19th century, and in his lifetime he gave his savings to this church so that the interest might be given to the poor. William Lloyd had saved £100, and we wonder if any other church has known a man like this humble toiling philanthropist.

EGLETON. The Normans built here a great and imposing church; their successors have reduced it to a nave and chancel. The English builders deprived the church of its aisles and today we see the splendid Norman pillars of the nave arcade incorporated in the wall, but much of the work of the masters remains.

There is a splendid Norman doorway, with an elaborately carved tympanum showing a dragon and a lion tugging at a cable within a cable border. Beautiful Norman decoration enriches the chancel arch, and the font has the Norman craftsman's crucifix and wheels on its four faces. In the tower arch is a charming 15th century screen, and among the pews four carved bench-ends add their touch of ancient dignity.

The Great Family

EMPINGHAM. Set among fine limes and rich with an avenue of beeches and sycamores, with a river running drowsily by, it has one of the most beautiful churches in the county. Its 14th century tower has battlements and pinnacles, and a spire ornamented with arcading. The richly detailed west doorway has deeply cut mouldings and graceful columns. The arcades have round and pointed arches built when the Norman was passing into the English style.

The chancel and the south transept are 13th century; the building of the aisles was spread over another two centuries. Peeps of old wall paintings and old glass strengthen the impression of past glory. The pulpit is 300 years old, and we imagine that Thomas Lovick Cooper, remembered on a wall tablet, must have preached from it to boys and girls who were still listening to him when they were old, for he was rector here for 60 years, from 1831 to 1892. He was born in the first year of the century and lies in the churchyard.

There is a finely carved tomb built into the wall under the tower, but the most interesting grave in Empingham is the tomb in the north wall of the transept, supposed to contain one of the bodies of the Normanvilles, lords of the manor from soon after the Conquest to the 13th century. They were scholars, preachers, soldiers, crusaders, diplomats; one is on the roll of benefactors of Battle Abbey, and one defended Kenilworth for King John. They were part of the backbone of Norman and Plantagenet England, blazing up and burning out in the long baronial wars. Today one of them lies in the tomb in this beautiful church, but who he was and what he did apparently no man knows.

In a field hereabouts is a magnificent round dovecot built of stone; it has over seven hundred nests.

The Old Home of the Cecils

ESSENDINE. Once a battlefield for Danes and Saxons, it links us with Elizabeth and the great Lord Burleigh. All that is left of the old home of the Cecils is buried in the green mound and moat stretching from the church to the river. Defended by a deep moat in which the water still remains, a formidable castle towered where these ruins hide their heads in the turf.

The church has a fine avenue of limes, with an ash tree seeming old enough to have sheltered the great Burleigh himself. The church forms a venerable background, with a wonderful Norman doorway which some believe to embody Saxon work. The arch of the door is pure Norman, but the tympanum is held to be earlier. It is rudely carved to represent Christ with His left hand resting on the Gospels, the right hand raised in benediction, and angels attending.

The doorposts are curiously wrought with animals and human figures, worn out by the passing of the centuries from Saxon England. The hand of the Norman can be traced in the chancel arch.

A Group of Fine Monuments

EXTON. One of the few miles which brings us here from Oakham is the straight mile of Barnsdale Avenue between splendid chestnuts, limes, ash and birch trees, beeches and sycamores. It ends at the gates of Exton's thousand-acre park with its fine lake and noble trees. Another mile beside the park ends at the village, a delightful corner of England where roads thread their way among stone dwellings in haphazard array, with gables and dormer windows peeping out from thatched and tiled roofs. There are old-world gardens, peeps of green hills, and a simple peace memorial opposite a green shaded by 14 sycamores. This village of stone and greenery is a place of twists and turns, with a pretty picture at every one.

By the charming well with its stone roof on eight brick pillars is the school. It was summer when we came, and children were at their lessons in the playground. One boy was by the roadside with his board and easel, sketching the school; another was painting a picture of the thatched cottages.

Here in the park are the ruins of a noble house of Elizabeth's day, the fine 19th century home of the Earls of Gainsborough, and an old church which is one of the finest in Rutland. They make a fine group seen from a gate near the church—the church with its glorious tower, the new hall with its stone walls and curved gables, the windows gleaming in a frame of trees, and the fine ruins of the Old Hall softened by their mantle of green. The old hall was destroyed by fire; the new one has many valuable pictures, a fine library, and a small Roman Catholic chapel with fragments of rich old glass.

One of the glories of the much restored medieval church is its tower and spire, a lovely composition. The tower and its corner turrets are embattled, as is the eight-sided lantern resting on it. From the lantern rises a graceful spire with two tiers of gabled windows. Stately arcades with richly moulded arches on round and clustered pillars divide the nave and aisles, one of the capitals carved with grotesque faces. The lovely chancel arch rests on foliage capitals, and the corbels holding up the roof are carved with angels. Crested helmets, gauntlets, and flags hang in the nave. The flag of St George is near the peace memorial, and in the vestry is a tin hat, another reminder of the war. A great treasure is the 14th century font, an eight-sided pillar enriched with recessed arcading and heads of men and women.

Exton is famous for the monuments of the Noels and the Haringtons, but older than these is Nicholas Grene's medieval stone tomb, enriched with tracery, on which rests an alabaster stone carved with a Calvary. The 18-year-old James Noel of 1681 is a lifesize figure in elaborate dress with wig and cravat, standing against a pillar on which are two cherubs. Young as he was, we read that he was grave, discreet, and wise. Nollekens was the sculptor of a monument in the chancel, showing Lady Gainsborough pointing to medallions of herself and her two husbands, one of whom was Baptist Noel of 1751, the 4th earl. Another monument by Nollekens (to Lieut-General Bennet Noel of 1766) has a figure leaning on an urn on which is his bust.

The most astonishing of all the Noel monuments is one to Baptist Noel (3rd Viscount Campden, of 1683) and his fourth wife. Impressive in its size (for it reaches the roof) and in its elaboration, it is the work of Grinling Gibbons, showing two full-length figures, and groups of small figures in wreathed panels and medallions. The long inscriptions tell us something of Noel's life, of his loyalty to two sovereigns, of his imprisonment in the Civil War, and of the spoil and havoc of his houses.

Of our own day is an inscription to Tom Cecil Noel, who was only 20 when he found a soldier's grave in Flanders. The tower screen, on which are four musical angels with golden instruments, and a charming figure at an organ with golden pipes, is to two of the family who died in 1931, one of them all but a century old. The figure at the organ is an extraordinary surprise.

Carved in white marble on her great tomb of alabaster and black marble lies the shrouded figure, in peaceful sleep, of the young Lady Anne Bruce, wife of Lord Bruce of Kinlosse, who died in 1627.

Exton was long the home of the Haringtons, who came here in the 15th century. On a beautiful alabaster tomb with tracery and heraldry lie John Harington of 1524 and his wife Alice, their hands in prayer. He is in armour with a fine collar; he has a sword and dagger, and his gauntlets are by his side; his feet are on a lion, and under his right foot is a battered little figure with beads. His wife is a slender, dainty figure in kennel headdress, with a mantle held by a tasselled cord; she has a tiny rose and a cross on the chain round her neck; and two little belled dogs are holding the folds of her graceful gown. Two angels are at her head.

We see Sir James Harington of 1591 and his wife Lucy in a fine pillared monument with coloured shield in the chancel; they are kneeling at prayer on red and green cushions, he wearing armour, she a draped mantle with a ruff.

Most charming of all in this delightful group is the great monument to Robert Kelwey, who has been sleeping here since 1580, a man who loved retirement and lived a beautiful life. He lies under a magnificent canopy, wearing a fur-lined gown and a flat hat. He was the father-in-law of the first Lord Harington, who with his wife

Anne raised this handsome memorial; we see them kneeling on cushions beside Robert Kelwey. Lord Harington is in fine chased armour, his wife and their daughter Lucy are delightful figures in flowing mantles and pretty headdress. Between his parents and close to his grandfather is the quaint figure of Kelwey Harington, lying on a lovely little table tomb two spans long. Only 21 weeks old when he died, he wears a long gown and a round hat; his head rests on an embroidered cushion, and at his feet is the head of a lion. All the figures wear beautiful ruffs at neck and wrists. The detail in the monument is exquisite, both in the figures and in the rich adornment of fruit and flowers and festoons.

It was this Lord Harington who entertained James the First at Burley-on-the-Hill not far away, and helped to wreck the plans of Guy Fawkes by carrying off Princess Elizabeth before the conspirators could abduct her. From 1603 till his death John took care of the princess, who was often at Exton. He saw her become Queen of Bohemia on her marriage, and gave her so much of his money that he became very poor, and was given royal permission to coin farthings. He sleeps at Exton, as does his son, the 2nd Baron, a great scholar and friend of that brother of Charles Stuart whose death brought the doomed king to the throne.

GLASTON. A compact and snug little place, it has a hall, a church, and a few cottages. The church is one of the few in Rutland with central towers, crowned with a Peter Pan of spires that seems never to have grown up quite high enough to give the church true dignity. Outside the west window are two charming heads of winged cherubs. The arcade of the nave is 12th century, the three-seated sedilia and a marble coffin are 13th century, and in the chancel lies Walter Colley, the 14th century lord of the manor.

From the Stone Age to the Tudor Age

GREAT CASTERTON. It has been here for thousands of years; it was a Stone Age settlement, and the skeleton of a Stone Age man has been found this century with his tools and weapons about him, a grinding stone and implements for making needles from bone and horn.

Here, too, the Romans came, leaving the village a Roman name and much Roman workmanship—coins, implements, and tiles from their heating chambers. The defensive ditch and bank of their camp are here, under and below the ground, and a piece of the Roman road is laid bare. It was here that Ermine Street entered Rutland, the Great North Road with its coaches succeeding the highway built for Roman chariots and marching legions.

The church stands where the Romans built, and the soil is sown with fragments of their structure. The stately 13th century building has Norman arches in the nave with beautifully carved capitals; the original clerestory and lancet windows; and an impressive font probably Norman, square, with a rudely carved diamond pattern, and altogether unusual. The pulpit is Elizabethan. There is an ancient door with fine ironwork.

A tomb set in a niche was probably 400 years old when Elizabeth was born. Wonderfully preserved, it shows the figure of a priest in his vestments. Outside, under a recess in the same wall, is another venerable monument, the work of some freakish sculptor of olden time. It has the figure of a woman, but as only her head and her feet are shown, the remainder of the stone being left uncarved, she appears to be occupying a bed too short for her.

Above her, on a window bracket, is a carving of a woman with a curious 13th century headdress; and in a niche in the outer wall of the chancel is a statue of Paul. Quaintness and charm blend everywhere about this unspoiled church. The capitals of the porch columns are finely carved with foliage, and over the porch is an old sundial.

It was to this place that there came tramping one day from Northampton two men seeking work on the land. One of them stayed and settled down at a farm, and here he met a village maid who lives in English poetry. She was Sweet Patty of the Vale, for the labourer was none other than John Clare, the peasant poet of Northampton over whom sorrow was to brood to the end. He saw Patty Turner here one autumn day two years after Waterloo, a farmer's daughter of 18, and he wrote these lines:

> *And I would go to Patty's cot,*
> *And Patty came to me.*
> *Each knew the other's every thought*
> *Under the hawthorn tree.*
> *And I'll be true for Patty's sake*
> *And she'll be true for mine,*
> *And I this little ballad make*
> *To be her Valentine.*

The poet married the pretty maiden, and this is their love-story.

The Love-Story of Patty Clare

SHE met him walking to Stamford with a fiddle under his arm, to play while the lime-burners danced. He looked at her and stopped. She smiled at him, and that loosened his tongue. He asked might he walk with her, and she said Yes. He said he was John Clare, and she said she was Martha Turner. Presently she stopped in sight of a cottage with a barn and said this was her home and he must go.

John found his way there again. Whenever Patty saw him coming she ran to her gingham frock and hurried into it. He was an amazement to her, this young man in ragged clothes who worked at the lime kilns. She had never heard anyone talk as he could. The shoemaker was poor stuff in comparison. John told her he could write poetry and had written a poem about her, and with his arm round her he repeated: "My love, thou art a nosegay sweet."

After some weeks Patty's father found out about John and denied him the house. John was in despair, and his fortunes sank still lower. He lost his work and was obliged to apply for parish relief. He had hoped to publish a volume of verse, but not enough subscribers were found. Then one day a bookseller in Stamford came across one of his poems, written in pencil on a dirty bit of paper, and he knew that here was a genius. He used influence with a London publisher to produce a little book of poems by John Clare.

Then Patty turned the shoe-maker away for good and her parents had to make the best of it.

After some ups and downs they were married, and a gentleman offered the poet a little annuity to help him on. For a time Patty lived on at Casterton, and then settled with John and his parents. She was now the wife of a poet who had been to London and seen great people; but he was the same John Clare who worked in the fields and scribbled verses on rough bits of paper, and he was a faithful husband to Patty.

After a time she found his fame rather a trial. She had got quite used to footmen in splendid livery coming to the cottage to bid John Clare go to visit this nobleman or that; she got rather tired of strangers stopping at her door to ask: Does John Clare live here? John was called in from his work in the fields to be looked at by grand people from London.

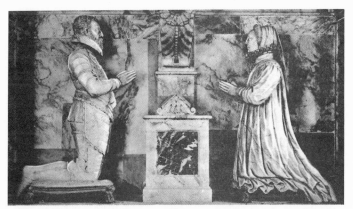

Sir James Harington of Elizabethan Times, with his Wife

Panel of Viscount Campden's Memorial by Grinling Gibbons

Robert Kelwey with his Daughter and Son-in-law
THE SPLENDID MONUMENTS OF EXTON

Exton   The Medieval Church

Exton   A Village Byway

Great Casterton   **The Village Street**

Burley   **15th Century Font**

Exton   Figure on Tower Screen   **Tickencote**   **13th Century Font**

Uppingham
Historical Windows in the School Museum and Dr Thring's Monument

Great Casterton   Norman Arcade   **Burley**   Norman Arcade

Unfortunately he was but a nine-days wonder. The day came when he had to hawk his poetry about the countryside. Patty never had enough money for food and clothes for the children. Years passed with changing fortunes, all to little effect. It is no wonder if Patty became a little hard.

Owing to excessive poverty when he was a child, to malnutrition and labour beyond his strength, John had no constitution. He had early contracted fen fever, and this was liable to recur at any time. His health was weakening; and there was worse than that, guessed at by Patty with terrible foreboding. It was no comfort to her that just now he was writing really lovely verse. The climax came when, after ill-health, debts, disappointments about published work, a well-meaning friend set Patty and John and their six children in a cottage about three miles from Helpstone. John was pulled up by the roots when he could least bear it. He lapsed into weeks of melancholy and designed a gravestone for himself: *Here rest the hopes and ashes of John Clare.*

During that terrible winter Patty had her seventh child, and soon after it was born she knew her husband was losing his reason.

At last a good friend sent him to a private asylum, and Patty, grim of face and sharp of tongue, faced the prospect of bringing up the seven children. John escaped from the madhouse and presently was sent to Northampton Asylum. He was carefully treated, and given considerable freedom in his sane spells, when he would sit in the church porch and watch children playing. He could also write poetry, some of it very lovely. He lived there 22 years. Once his youngest son came to see him; Patty never went—she could not bear it. Before he died all but his dreams had passed away. He only wanted to see the sunshine and the clouds.

He is sure of his immortality. Some of his work is pure poetry. We remember him in these lanes of Rutland, and we like to think now and again of poor Patty, who bore the hard burden of life in his name, and went to an unremembered grave.

The Sheep-Dip in the Street

GREETHAM. It will not permit us to forget the old saying that England has been carried on the back of its sheep, for its farmers find their sheep-dip in the stream which winds through the village street.

The 14th century tower of the church is richly decorated with traceried windows and rows of stone faces. A 13th century font has a head at each corner. But the oldest things here are Norman mouldings and Saxon carvings; they are from the vanished church and are built into the wall. They have quaint figures of an angel driving Adam and Eve from the garden, the dove bringing back the leaf to Noah in the Ark, the Prodigal Son returning to his father, Moses striking the rock, Daniel among the lions, and a man sacrificing a bull on the altar. There are also heads of saints, flowers, and various forms of decoration, all among the earliest carving in the county.

Greetham has not forgotten its children, who have their own little pews, five of them rising in tiers, a very pleasant sight.

The Spreading Beauties of the Vale

HAMBLETON. Proudly poised on a hill, it looks out on the spreading beauties of the Vale of Catmose. Snug below lies Nether Hambleton, which has in its Old Hall as charming an example of a 17th century house as the county can show. Time has brought a change of status for it, and it is now a farmhouse, distinguished looking. It has still its noble gables; its wings are joined by colonnades on which are balustraded balconies; and on the roofs are parapets of open arches. There is a fine Jacobean staircase.

The church has a Norman door with deep moulding, a masterly work. In the nave some of the 12th century piers have been made new; but the font is ancient, and two tombstones, each showing the head and shoulders of a figure with the hands clasped in prayer, are old beyond knowledge. A massive iron-bound chest has held the secrets of many a century within its sturdy embrace.

The Stones of Ketton

KETTON. The stones of Ketton have reached Fleet Street; they are in the Tower of London and in York Minster; they are part of Exeter Cathedral and in a host of churches all about. Ketton Hall, of course, is built of them with the imposing wall round its handsome park. The Romans must have known of them; one of their fine tessellated pavements was found here.

The lofty and graceful church has a 13th century tower and a 14th century spire that are among the architectural glories of the county. The tower is pierced on each side by a delicate window with slender columns; the spire has three tiers of dormer windows and four stone canopies sheltering saints. The richly moulded west doorway, its door hung on magnificent hinges, is famous. This Norman doorway has on each side of it a blind arch—English pointed yet rich with Norman carving, an admirable example of the merging of Norman into Gothic.

Much of the quaint interior has vanished, but there are fine traceried windows, and a 14th century font carved with foliage.

Simon Langham's Village

LANGHAM. Here on Ranksborough Hill lived the Romans; a small bronze statue they left is treasured at the British Museum. At the eastern foot of the hill the village lies, widely spread, proud of its 17th century hall and still more of its church.

The church, a comely building, has a good 13th century tower and a 14th century spire, with pinnacles and gargoyles garrisoning the roof.

Like no other entrance we have seen is this pinnacled porch, for it has a high stone platform which was once part of an upper chamber. The time-worn stoup remains, and traces of colour on a niche suggest a picture of ornate richness in olden days. The tower arch, part of the chancel, and the handsome piscina are 13th century. The rich decoration of the 14th century is in the arcades, the clerestory, and a beautiful transept window.

The font is 15th century—as old as the roof, which is supported on brackets with carved heads. A carved figure on the bracket of a north aisle window shows us that the humorous mason did not exhaust his fancy on the goblins outside, for here is an impish figure crouching on hands and knees with his tongue out. On an alabaster stone in the transept is engraved the figure of John Dickenson in a 16th century merchant's gown; his wife has her purse, and their eight children are with them.

An odd little possession from the 16th century, set in a frame on a wall, is a counter found in the churchyard in our time; it was made for reckoning on a counting board when the multiplication table was less familiar than it is today.

In one of the windows are modern paintings of St George slaying the Dragon, St Martin dividing his cloak with a beggar, the Martyrdom of St Sebastian, St Michael and his Dragon, St Maurice,

St Adrian, and St Oswald, the Christian king of Northumberland. The window is in memory of Sir Henry Clarke-Jervoise, who is shown kneeling with St Hubert and the stag.

The peace memorial has been fashioned from an old carved chest; it is an altar, and with it are photographs of the Langham men.

A pretty little custom has come down from ancient days and is preserved in the village, which owns a plot of land, given centuries ago, on which is grown a crop of hay for strewing the floor of the church on the Sunday after the Feast of St Peter. Often the floors of churches were strewn with rushes; Langham does it still with hay.

The Second Founder of Westminster Abbey

IN this small place was born Simon de Langham, who grew up to be Lord Chancellor and Archbishop of Canterbury. He was a stern disciplinarian, insisting on all the observances of his order, and rigidly conscientious over the administration of funds. So it was that some of the older monks at Westminster Abbey hated him, and he had "many ill tempers to deal with, some being insolent, others old and particular, some extravagant, others perverse." But from the better sort, the wiser and understanding, he earned the title by which we honour him, of Second Founder of Westminster Abbey.

Simon was born here early in the 14th century, but his father, obviously a layman, was buried in the nave of Westminster Abbey, where his son became a monk early in life and quickly revealed those qualities of mind which by 1349 made him prior.

Edward the Third was given more to militarism than to monasteries, but Simon won him to a recognition of the splendour and romance of the old building, and secured from him various gifts. The warlike king found in Simon an able and honest minister, and made him Chancellor of the realm, in which position he played an important part in state affairs for some years, especially in his stout resistance of papal power in England.

There came a phase in the relations between Edward and Simon when the Pope made the abbot Archbishop of Canterbury, but the king had not been consulted, and he resented the affront. The Primate, having already given the king a lead in this direction, resigned his primacy.

Not to be intimidated by Edward's disapproval, the Pope next made a cardinal of Simon, who, grieved at his sovereign's displeasure, retired to the Continent. He was quickly restored to royal favour and had a leading part in the affairs of the nation. He had long before this resigned the abbacy of Westminster, but his heart yearned towards it, and at his death at Avignon in 1376 he decreed by will that his body should be buried in the "West Monastery, near London," and after a temporary interment at Avignon he was brought home and buried in the splendid tomb in the Chapel of St Benedict, the first of the great ecclesiastical sepulchres in the Abbey.

The Beautiful Bede House

LIDDINGTON. Spreading itself through a picturesque valley, it is rich with a fine old church and its famous Bede House.

The Bede House stands little changed since its foundation by John Russell when the Battle of Bosworth was an event of yesterday. The home of bishops for over a century, it was refashioned by Thomas Cecil, the son of Elizabeth's great Lord Burleigh. He fought against the Armada, but the Bede House is the work he would wish to be remembered by. He converted it into an almshouse for a warden, 12 men, and two women, adding to it for the comfort of the pensioners the stone-roofed verandah running along the north side. A picture of rare charm, the old house is domestic Gothic at its best.

Its most conspicuous note of splendour is the banqueting hall on the upper floor, where handsome windows overlook the quiet churchyard. Here is a 400-years-old ceiling fit to grace a royal palace; it is of panelled oak with richly carved tracery, a noble example of old English craftsmanship. The windows have heraldic glass, and over the fireplace are carved three roses. At the end of the hall is the warden's room with another fine Gothic fireplace, and a window with a kneeling bishop. The staircase has two richly moulded doorways, one door keeping its original ironwork. The bishop's quaint lookout tower at the corner of the garden wall is as he left it, projecting over the pavement, with a public path running through.

It is but a stride to the lofty and dignified church with its 14th century tower and spire. The chancel, which has been here 600 years, has still in its walls the old earthenware jars that were built into church walls in those days to improve the sound, one of the first experiments in acoustics, a primitive sort of loud speaker.

Quaintly carved heads, those on the south side all smiling, support the roof spanning the tall arcades. Two coffin lids are 14th century, one with an ornamental cross, another with carving of head and hands in a sunken panel. Of two brasses, one to Heleyn Hardy, who died in 1486, is a work of beauty, showing her in a butterfly headdress and the costume of a widow who has taken religious vows; the other is that of Edward Watson, who died in 1530, and is shown in a furred gown with his wife and 15 children.

The old screen has on its panels traces of the rich colour of medieval days. The square font and its carved cover are both Jacobean. The altar, brought forward into the chancel, is surrounded on all sides by rails made in 1653, reminding us with special emphasis of Archbishop Laud's edict that the communion table should be in a place apart.

The Norman Craftsmen

LITTLE CASTERTON. Embowered in splendid trees, the 13th century church keeps something of the Norman church before it. It has a Norman tympanum fixed to a wall of the aisle, rescued from serving as a windowsill in the early years of the century. Here also is still the Norman craftsmen's picture in stone of the Tree of Life, with wheels signifying Eternity and the Trinity. There are Norman capitals adorning 13th century stonework, and the beautiful piscina has a 14th century canopy carved with faces. There is some 14th century glass, and in the modern glass of the east window is Our Lord in glory, with St Hubert and the stag and St Francis with his little brothers the birds.

The fine oak roof is borne on brackets with figures and shields, its bosses being carved with foliage and heads, one being of Christ wearing His crown of thorns. The lower half of the carved Tudor screen survives, and there is some good Jacobean panelling.

In the chancel is one of the finest brasses in Rutland, representing Sir Thomas Burton of Tolethorpe, who died in 1381. He is with his wife, and is wearing chain mail with a lion at his feet; a lap dog lies in the folds of Dame Margery's ample skirt.

An arched recess has under it two ancient tombstones with beautiful crosses; one is thought to be the tomb of the founder of the church; the other is interesting to antiquarians because it seems to have been used, as brasses and parchments were sometimes used, a second time.

There are two charming heads of angels carved in our time by Captain Harrison in memory of himself and his wife. They lived at Tolethorpe Hall, close by, which rests on ancient foundations and has still a 14th century gateway.

The Vicar of Wakefield's Hero

LYNDON. Here sleeps a famous scholar, in a hamlet with a 17th century hall and a 14th century church with a single treasure—a Norman font that was lost and has been found again. An ancient cross which has kept it company most of its centuries rests broken in the porch, its base and socket ruined in the churchyard, where sleeps William Whiston.

The hero of Goldsmith's Vicar of Wakefield is, of course, the vicar, but, the vicar in turn had his hero, and that enviable man was another vicar, William Whiston, who lies beside his wife in this little churchyard. It was not the mathematician in Whiston that stirred the reverence of the Vicar of Wakefield, not his varied scholarship, his whimsicality, that convulsed the Court and confounded men of learning; still less was it the translator of Josephus who appealed to the Vicar of Wakefield. Whiston had pronounced it unlawful for the clergy to marry a second time, and the second chapter of Goldsmith's immortal novel tells us to what astounding purpose good Mr Primrose turned the ruling.

As with the Vicar of Wakefield, so it was with the contemporaries of Whiston—the one thing by which he is remembered, his Josephus, was then of no account; the endless controversies in which his rapidly changing theological views involved him were everything. Born in 1667, he was a Fellow of Clare College at 23 and sought by learned labour to prove mathematically the truth of the Bible. He succeeded Sir Isaac Newton as Professor of Mathematics, on Newton's own recommendation, but later the great man objected to the heresies of Whiston, who complacently explained that it was all because he would not do "as his other darling friend did," and learn of him without contradicting him. Newton could not in his old age bear such contradiction, said Whiston, "and so he was afraid of me for the last 13 years of his life."

Mr Whiston's courage was equal to his great industry. The story is told that he was once in company with Addison and Steele, Sir Robert Walpole, and Mr Craggs, who was Secretary for War, and the question arose whether a Secretary of State could be an honest man. Being pressed for his opinion, Mr Whiston said he thought honesty the best policy, and if a Prime Minister would practise it he would find it so, to which Mr Craggs replied that it might do for a fortnight but not for a month. "Have you ever tried it for a fortnight?" asked Mr Whiston, and there was no answer. It is also told of him that once in a conversation with Queen Caroline she asked him what the people said of her faults, and, she insisting, Mr Whiston said that she did not behave with proper reverence at church. She replied that the king would talk with her, whereupon he said that a greater than kings was there to be regarded. The Queen acknowledged it and asked for her next fault, to which Mr Whiston answered "When I hear your majesty has amended that fault I will tell you of your next."

Whiston was an ill-balanced genius, naïve, honest, candid in the most distinguished company, a parson always at odds with authority. But he did in the end give us a masterly translation of the great Jewish historian, and his book, now two centuries old, still holds the field unchallenged. He died here in 1752 while staying with his only daughter, who was married to Samuel Barker of Lyndon Hall.

MANTON. It has a Norman church rebuilt 600 years ago, but the bells still ring from the Norman tower, and the children of Manton are still baptised at the Norman font. One of the windows has a little ancient glass showing a woman at prayer, and there is an ancient stone coffin with a beautiful sculptured cross. A carved almsbox is very quaint; it is from the days of the Stuarts. A window at the west end is one of the narrowest we have seen, suggesting the eye of a needle.

We walk to the church through flowers, roses all the way.

The Saxon Clock

MARKET OVERTON. It has great possessions, rich in treasure and in memory, for it is Roman, Saxon, and good English too. The Romans camped where the church now stands, and their coins have been found in thousands here, covering 350 years of Roman history.

The Saxons were buried where the Romans had camped, and they left behind an urn a foot high, a magnificent brooch, and one thing truly wonderful—a Saxon clock which has been found here and is

The Garden Tower

The Cloistered Verandah

The Great Hall and its 16th Century Ceiling
THE LOVELY BEDE HOUSE OF LIDDINGTON

South Luffenham   Medieval Capital of South Arcade

Cottesmore   Carving on Font   Tickencote   Carving on Arch

Tickencote   Wooden figure of 14th Century Knight

now among our national antiquities. It is a primitive but thrilling thing, a simple form of the clepsydra of the Egyptians, common in Greece and Rome and known to our bronze-working British ancestors. The Greek clepsydra was pierced by holes through which a measured quantity of water escaped in a known time; in the one found here the principle was reversed. The saucer-shaped bronze vessel, pierced by a single hole, was placed on the surface of the water, so that it gradually filled and sank. The time taken for the filling of the Market Overton clepsydra is just over 62 minutes, a very good guess at an hour.

One other notable thing the Saxons left here, the only Saxon tower arch in Rutland. Two great stones that kept it company in the ancient belfry now welcome us at the churchyard stile.

The church has a remarkable font, standing on a base believed to be Roman, made up in the 13th century from two capitals, and therefore linking up a period of a thousand years of craftsmanship. The door of the church has been swinging on its hinges for over 600 years; it is older than the nave, which is late 14th century.

There is a stone coffin in which a little child once lay, a wooden cross from France, and a tribute to one who was a friend and doctor in this place for half a century.

On a corner of the church tower is a sundial said to have been given by Sir Isaac Newton, whose mother came from Market Overton. Harriet Ayscough left here to become the wife of Isaac Newton the elder, and was a widow in six months, three months before her illustrious son was born. He was so small that she used to say he could have been put into a quart mug, but he was sedulously nursed, and when his mother married again it was his kindly grandmother from Market Overton who took him in hand and set his feet on the path that was to lead to glory.

Under a group of trees on the village green are the stocks and whipping-post which were still in use when Newton was a little boy.

The Beautiful Arcade

MORCOTT. Morcott has charming old houses and the picturesque ruins of a windmill, and the church has one of the finest arcades in Rutland, standing as the Normans left it and rich in moulded capitals—Norman craftmanship unsullied. The tower arch has capitals with serpents round them. The lower part of the tower and the south doorway are Norman. The chancel is 15th century but keeps its 13th century arch, and has a 14th century tomb in which lies William de Overton under a sculptured cross and a dainty moulding of flowers. The Jacobean pulpit is beautifully carved, and the ancient sanctus bell remains for all to see, resting on the battlements of the tower.

A Hero of Jutland

NORMANTON. Its church stands with the 18th century hall in a park of 500 acres. They are all that Normanton has. The modern church, harmonising in design with the hall, has a portico and an open bell turret, is light and dignified, and has a handsome pulpit of iron and bronze.

The oldest stones of Normanton lay on a windowsill when we called, a carved head and other fragments of the 14th century church which once stood here. An old chest and some chairs belonged to the vanished shrine. There is a thrilling remembrance of the most dramatic days of our time in a tablet memorial to Victor Ewart, a lieutenant on the battleship Queen Mary, and an only child. At the Battle of Jutland he commanded a turret on the Queen Mary, and, having fought his guns to the last, he surrendered his slender chance of life by returning into his turret to help his men.

A wall sculpture by Rysbrack shows a cherub holding a medallion of Sir Gilbert Heathcote, who built the hall. He governed London as lord mayor and sat for it in several parliaments. For two centuries Sir Gilbert has slept peaceably here after his stormy life.

He Set Trade Free With the East

PERHAPS we remember Gilbert Heathcote best as one of the founders of the Bank of England, but he lives as a courageous figure standing at the Bar of the House of Commons, throwing down the gauntlet of British commerce in defiance of the richest monopoly of the age.

The Old East India Company treated the traders of England as Spain and the Pope had sought to treat the rest of the world in regard to the discovery of America. It hunted down independent merchants, arrested them, confiscated their goods, and treated them as pirates, simply because they offered for sale English goods in an English sphere of influence; and Sir Gilbert Heathcote brought matters dramatically to a head. He bought a fine ship, the Redbridge, loaded her with a rich freight, and despatched her, nominally for the Spanish port of Alicante. Here the Company committed its final blunder. Arrests of ships on the high seas and of free citizens in foreign ports thousands of miles away were long in coming to a hearing at Westminster, but now they induced the Admiralty to pounce before the Redbridge left the Thames, an act of high-handedness which set political London blazing.

The issue was fought out largely on political lines, but it was as a citizen and a merchant with argosies in many seas that Gilbert Heathcote took his stand at the Bar of the Commons. Advocates of the Company asked him point blank whether he could deny that the Redbridge had been fitted out for the Indian trade, and his answer was memorable: "It is no sin that I know of," he said, "to trade with India; and I shall trade with India till I am restrained by Act of Parliament."

Parliament declared that the arrest and detention of the Redbridge was illegal. Within a few days a vote made it for ever the law of the Empire that no power except that of the whole legislature can give to any person or to any society an exclusive privilege of trading in any part of the world.

As a founder of our national bank, as a financier, as a far-trading merchant, as a promoting member of the new East India Company, as a member of Parliament, as a bulwark of the military defences of London, and in many other capacities, Heathcote was a notable figure, but it was at the Bar of the House that immortality found him.

Echoes of Long Ago

NORTH LUFFENHAM. It has a Saxon graveyard in its midst, the ruin of an old hall, a church with many treasures, and a magnificent walnut tree overhanging its graveyard. Digging here for sand some years ago, builders brought up spear-heads and arrow-heads with metallic fragments of shields, urns, buckets, bronze ornaments, glass beads, and fine brooches.

Down in the valley are fragments from a nearer Past, two moated enclosures which have lost their Middle Age strongholds. Here once stood the old hall; in the wall that flanks the path to the church is a curious hole through which, it is said, the owners of the hall used to pass food to the poor. A dry ditch survives to remind us of the siege of 200 royalists in the old hall during the Civil Wars. They held out against 1300 Parliament troops until cannon were brought up, when the house was shot through and through. Its owner was taken to London, where he died in captivity.

The church is 13th and 14th century, with a fine tower and spire and impressive battlement roofs. The nave arcades are bold and fine. The roof rests on carved stone corbel heads, and there are figures of angels in wood and a Jacobean pulpit. The east window is modern, but the rest of the windows are 14th century, and there is some original glass still in them; on it are painted the figures of Mary Magdalene, Edward the Confessor, and St Barbara. There is also some ancient heraldic glass.

Here lies a very great friend of learning, Robert Johnson, founder of Uppingham and Oakham Schools. He has an elaborate wall brass in this church where he was rector 300 years ago. There is a bust of Susanna Noel showing her in 17th century costume, with the pathetic inscription that she had only one daughter, a little Susanna who died the third day after she was born. There is a touch of pathos also under the coat-of-arms of two men of long ago who sleep here: "two loving brothers, Jonathan and John Barker, Gents."

In the 17th century the fame of a native here spread through England on almanacs he devised with learning and imagination.

A Forerunner of the Quack

HE was Vincent Wing, a forerunner of the astrological quacks of Fleet Street, with more excuse than they. While other men more fortunate sought the society of men of science at the universities, he laboured unaided at his studies here, became a firstrate mathematician, and acquired a good working knowledge of the classics.

Before he was thirty he thrilled a credulous England with predictions which made its flesh creep, in a volume of forecasts called A Dreadful Prognostication, whose dire portents, he assured his public, were "drawn from the effects of several celestial configurations." That was the head and front of his offence as an astrologer in an age when astrology and astronomy ran in double harness, but his labours in his quiet home here made Vincent Wing a serious astronomer, and he performed a service of national value by issuing year after year, an astronomical almanac. He had a complete grasp of the Copernican System, and his writings had a great part in familiarising the nation with a celestial philosophy at which many scholars still boggled. For twenty years Wing's almanac was a standard authority in England; it had the approval of the Astronomer-Royal, and a sale of fifty thousand copies.

We may regard the astrologer of North Luffenham as a quack, but with his fanciful predictions there was this solid knowledge, a real contribution to public learning of which our modern star humbugs have nothing to boast.

Rutland's Great Little Capital

OAKHAM. The biggest town in England's smallest county, it is as charming a place as we could wish to find. It is the very heart of Rutland, spacious though small, with wide streets and fair gardens, with trees shading old houses, with peeps of green hills and woods, and lanes and wooded paths running from its very marketplace. Here is something very few capitals possess, a peacefulness unruffled by the 20th century.

It is famous for its magnificent church, its old school, and what is left of its castle. It gave us one of the meanest men in the world and one of the smallest. The mean man was the wretched Titus Oates, born here in 1649; the little man was Jeffery Hudson, who first opened his eyes in an old house here in 1619, and nine years after hopped out of a pie into the presence of Charles Stuart:

> *O was not that a dainty dish*
> *To set before the King?*

A knightly father and son of Oakham, Sir John and Sir William Brown of Caxton's day, were lord mayors of London.

Who does not love its gracious marketplace? It has fine trees, old houses, and a splendid school. A curious old butter-cross has an ancient sundial, and near it is a shelter with a fine roof on eight posts. It is all quaint and beautiful; and a traveller here could hardly be surprised to see a prisoner in the five-hole stocks, for Oakham's small square is still like a piece of 17th century England.

Near by is almost all that is best in the town. We cross a wide street and come to Flores House with an ancient doorway between two faces, and a piscina with a head carved among foliage. It may have been the home of a group of priests in the 13th century, and it was certainly the home of Roger Flore, who put the top on the church spire. In Northgate is a house with a piscina centuries old, and not far away is the tiny chapel of St John with stone faces that were here 400 years before the railway came. This simple building is all that is left of a hospital founded by William Dalby of Exton, and it has a scratch dial, two doorways through which no one has passed for centuries, a stone owl in a corner, and splendid roof timbers. At Oakham Lodge are some of the finest cedars in Rutland, and a well as old as anything in the town, once a place of pilgrimage.

A stone's throw from Oakham's famous school, and overlooking the quiet marketplace, is something no traveller should miss. We come to it up a little lane from the market, through old gates in the shadow of a great chestnut tree. Here is what has long been known as Oakham Castle, part of a 12th century manor house of which the timber buildings and most of the fortifications perished long ago. We see it today as a court-house 60 feet long and 40 feet wide, its gables crowned with curious carvings, its handsome aisles and decorated doorways fascinating the lover of fine places. The round stone pillars, supporting ornamented arches as beautiful as anything built in Norman England, have remarkably fine capitals, with foliage that has been compared with Canterbury Cathedral carving. Among the carvings are curious figures of animals playing musical instruments.

But the remarkable sight which summons the traveller here is a collection of horseshoes. If there were any truth in the saying that a horseshoe brings good luck, Oakham should be the most fortunate town in England, for here are marvellous shoes of all sizes and all kinds. Some are rusty and some brightly gilded; some are very small and some over a yard high, much too big even for the famous horse of Troy. Many of them have crowns, and all have the names of their owners. Through many centuries it has been one of Oakham's quaint customs to take a horseshoe from every peer passing through the town, a custom, perhaps dating from the time when the Conqueror's Farrier lived here. His descendants built this hall. Among the shoes on the walls is one said to have been given by Queen Elizabeth, and the Earl of Sandwich had left one just before we called.

High above Oakham's lovely church, with big windows, handsome pinnacles, and richly buttressed canopies, is something we see wherever we go in these old streets. It is Cock Peter, watching over the town, a weathervane which must be one of the oldest in England, for it is said to have shown the way of the wind to men who went to Agincourt. It is still the highest and proudest thing in Oakham, and is known all over Rutland.

Peter crowns the graceful 14th century spire, the glory of Oakham's noble tower, which has two saints and a figure of Christ. There was a church here in Norman times, and of the one built in the 13th century there still remains the chancel arch, the south doorway, and a spacious porch carved with animals, and with the Crucifixion on an elegant cross. But most of the church is 14th century, and as good as anything of its kind for miles round. Splendidly lighted, unspoiled by restorations, beautifully furnished, it is one of the best of the many proud churches of this little county. Its roofs have hundreds of panels, those in the sanctuary richly carved.

The nave is its great pride, its arches resting on slender clustered pillars, the admiration of all who come to see their astonishing capitals. Here are angels singing, a fox running off with a goose, a monkey with a heavy weight round its neck, the crowning of the Madonna, a beast playing an instrument, a man with foliage springing from his mouth, an angel driving Adam and Eve from the Garden, and a man with a broom. Added to this noble sculpture gallery is a remarkable company of about 40 corbel heads in stone, and many queer wooden faces among the rough old beams in the roof. Some of these are 500 years old. There is a bracket with what is thought to be the head of Henry the Sixth, a rich alabaster reredos of the Ascension, a fine brass eagle, and a cornice in the chancel with flowers that may have been carved in honour of Roger Flore, to whom the church owes much of its beauty. There is an ancient tomb without a name, and an old font (from the first church) with arcading by a Norman workman; its base is part of the old churchyard cross. One of the memorials has an inscription to John Bullivant, proudly telling that he was with Sir John Moore at Corunna; a tablet tells us that Robert Adam and his wife worshipped in these pews through more than half the 19th century, and another records three generations of one family of parsons from Napoleon's schooldays to his fall at Waterloo; the grandfather would hear of his rise, the grandson of his defeat.

Four things will long be treasured in this fine church. Two are exquisite Elizabethan chalices; one is the Oakham Bible written on vellum, perhaps a year or two older than Magna Carta; the other is a small alabaster figure of a little maid of 15, Anne Burton. She died at the beginning of the Civil War, and we read of her that

> She was a flower of matchless price
> Transplanted hence to Paradise.

We found in this town so like the country an entrancing natural wonder, the biggest wistaria we have seen in our journeyings, blooming in Spring and in Autumn too, a sight not to be missed by anyone travelling herabouts. It rises from a stem about four feet round; it covers most of the front of one house, and runs under the thatched eaves of another, past a row of nine doors and windows and creeping up to the chimneys when it has nowhere else to go. It can have but poor stuff to spring from, for it is rooted in the pavement, but there seems no doubt that if an arch were built for it to bridge the gap it would run to the end of the street and become one of the seven wonders of the natural world.

Oakham's famous school, founded in 1584, has been sending a fine type of boyhood into the world since the days of Queen Elizabeth. Founded, like Uppingham, by Robert Johnson, it has a simple memorial chapel, one of the finest of its kind in the Midlands, its west front enriched with carvings showing the sacrifice of our Motherland in her darkest days, the work of F. W. Sargant, brother of one of the headmasters.

Two of the school's original buildings are here still. One, a vicarage in the 16th century, has a fine doorway; the other is a plain building in the churchyard, for 300 years the only Oakham room where lessons were taught. It was here before the Armada came, and though it has been restored it has still its fine old roof, and inscriptions in Hebrew, Latin, and Greek. It is now a museum, and has treasures from the country round about, but perhaps its most prized possession is the original charter granted by Elizabeth, with its seal for all to see. One of the striking things which delighted us when we called was the series of fine and vigorous wall paintings by the sister of a headmaster, telling the story of Gareth and of the Death of King Arthur.

> Among all the headmasters of Oakham School, none is more affectionately remembered than Edward Vere Hodge.

On the Castle Gable   Medieval Capitals in the Church

Norman Work in the Castle hall
THE ANCIENT CARVINGS OF OAKHAM

Oakham   **The Norman Castle**

Oakham   Medieval Church

Ryhall   Church and Dovecot

Preston   Manor House   **Tickencote**   Norman Church

Oakham   The Quaint Marketplace

Tickencote   The South Side of the Church

Tickencote   The Wonderful Norman Chancel Arch

Edward Vere Hodge

HE came to Oakham in 1879, and ended the century here. The school numbers had fallen and its reputation was growing dim. It did not seem as if the old grand days could be brought back by such a man as Edward Vere Hodge, for he could not even look severe! But the wiseacres were wrong.

One day when the school choir was rehearsing festival music in the parish church, and many others were there to listen, a terrifying thing happened. The whole church rocked, and a ball of fire fell whirling from the roof, struck the floor, and exploded loudly. The spire had been struck by lightning.

Edward Hodge stepped forward in a leisurely manner and said in his usual quiet tones, reminding us of the still small voice: "I hope you will not fail to appreciate the extraordinary beauty and interest of this phenomenon."

Certainly he was the right man to be a headmaster. In a very short time he had revolutionised the school, numbers were mounting rapidly, and a fine type of boy was asking to come in. The gentle Head ruled by love, and it proved more effectual than fear.

There was steel under the gentleness of Edward Hodge, however; he was strong and of good courage, and nothing could daunt his spirit in adversity. As the years drew on they brought the dread disease of arthritis, and he became a cripple. Then he talked cheerfully of the pleasure to be had from books. His eyesight failed, and he said that wireless had just come in time for him. He could always find something to be glad about; he never whined or whimpered.

Then, a few years before we called here, he passed away, mourned all over the world by his old boys. One of them has said:

I have had to face situations of terror on both sides of the Earth, and I have been horribly afraid. It has helped me and saved me from disgrace to remember E. V. Hodge. I guess that there are hundreds of old boys who have been similarly saved.

It is the glorious epitaph of a little quiet man who ruled by love.

The Battle and the Poet

PICKWORTH. The Wars of the Roses are commonly held to have had little effect on the life of the country, but a 14th century arch with carved capitals, standing bare and melancholy on the hilltop here, contradicts the comfortable legend. The arch is all that remains of Pickworth's old church, and if local history is correct it was the soldiers at the Battle of Losecoat Field, in 1470, who destroyed not only the church but the village.

A wood of veteran oaks on the Great North Road marks the scene of the twelfth of the 15 battles of the Roses, after which the defeated Lancastrians threw off their coats to escape detection. The tide of national affairs receded from ruined Pickworth, where to this day fireplaces, floors, and other remnants of former houses are brought to light. The surviving villagers had no heart to restore their fallen church, which crumbled till the steeple was taken down in the 18th century and used in building bridges. A farmhouse near a ruined arch is built from the stones of the lost shrine.

Here we cross the track of poor John Clare, the rustic poet who lived sadly at Pickworth. A solitude of huts and farmhouses it was to him. It was while here that, by saving pence from his scanty wage, he made up the sovereign demanded by the printer for publishing the prospectus with which he hoped to get subscribers enough to pay for the printing of his poems.

The Stones from Constantinople

PRESTON. It has the picturesque gabled houses built when the Stuarts were on the throne, and it has stones in its church which stir the imagination of any traveller.

The church is Norman and English. Its tower was built when Chaucer was riding with his pilgrims down to Canterbury. The chancel, the south arcade, and the font are all of the same 14th century. There are handsome canopied seats for the priests which have been here 600 years, all the time with the light falling on them through these traceried windows. The windows of the clerestory are the youngest part of the structure, 15th century. The north arcade of the nave is the oldest part, being Norman.

To this small shrine has come an odd collection of treasures from the far-off world. There are lamps and candlesticks in the sanctuary from Damascus; an almsbox from a church in Asia Minor with St George and the Dragon painted on it; and two pieces of marble floor mosaic on either side of the chancel step which were in the church of John the Baptist destroyed by the Turks when they took Constantinople. They were part of the great event which brought the Turk to the gates of Europe. The stones had been here but a few years when we called, taking their place again in a Christian building after lying despised since 1453.

Thrilling it is to see these stone fragments here, far from the great highway of the world to where they once belonged. They were part of the splendour of Christianity in the days of its conquest by the Turks; as we go through the churchyard we think of Christianity's earliest days in Palestine, for the yews here were brought from the Garden of Gethsemane.

The Griffin and the Lion

RIDLINGTON. This village of golden-tinted stone, where houses are roofed with thatch and tiles, and grassy banks lend charm to the roads, lies on a ridge above the River Chater, seeing a fine view of the wide valley.

A fine copper beech is seen from the churchyard, and roses climb the walls of the church. Much of it is made new, but remains of medieval building are in the arcades, the chancel arch, and the tower, which was rebuilt early this century. A reminder of its early days is the seal of Robertus de Brachele, first rector of Ridlington in 1217; it is in a glass case with that of the rector of 1920. In another glass case are the old musical instruments used by the choir. There is a curious pulpit, and we remember the font for having a three-sided bowl.

The treasure here is a Norman tympanum over the vestry door inside the church, a vigorous piece of sculpture showing a griffin and a lion attacking each other. Round the stone is a band of plaitwork, and beneath the lion is a wheel, supposed to symbolise the unending struggle between the forces of good and evil.

On a monument on the chancel wall is the kneeling figure of James Harington of Exton near by, where in the church we see fine monuments of others of this famous family. James died in 1613, and here his wife kneels with him. They had 16 children.

The Men Who Lost the Battle

RYHALL. It bestrides a little river and has a church with a legend. Here St Tibba, niece of King Penda of Mercia, is said to have lived in a cell 1300 years ago, on a spot now covered by the church. St Tibba, whose body was transferred from her cell to Peterborough in 936, is the patron saint of falconers.

The 13th century tower and spire are among the chief beauties of the county, and along an outside stringcourse runs a host of grotesque figures. The south doorway, with its border of floral moulding, has over it a priest's chamber which has been a school. The chancel arch, the pillars, and the lofty arches of the nave are 13th century. In the north arcade is a crouching stone figure of St Christopher, wearing a coronet of fleur-de-lys. The font and the sedilia are 700 years old.

There is a touch of pity and a fragment of literature on the chancel wall, in an epitaph that might have been written by John Evelyn for his extraordinary little son. It tells us of one small Samuel Barker, who died in 1696, " a child of admirable sweetness of temper, of an erect and comely body, of a most poignant wit even beyond what could be imagined at the age of 2 years and 15 days."

Here, too, is a touch of history, for here, while the church was rising, lived Hugh le Despenser, last Justiciary of England; warrior, diplomat, and lawyer, who accompanied the only English King of the Romans to the Continent, but, quarrelling with him, burned down his royal patron's castle at Isleworth. A close ally of Simon de Montfort, Despenser sat in the first English Parliament, and was with de Montfort when the great Simon fell on the battlefield of Evesham. Having himself refused to quit a losing battle, de Montfort urged Despenser to escape and continue the struggle in better days, and, on his refusing to escape, answered, "Come, then, let us die like men." They were among the 160 nobles who fell on that disastrous day.

One more link with fame has Ryhall. John Clare worked as a labourer on one of the farms. He lived at Pickworth three miles away, and it was here that he would sit in the hedge and write his poems. Once he went to the post office hereabouts but was unable to post his packet to the printers as an extra penny was wanted because it was past posting time. John Clare managed to save enough money from his weekly wage of nine shillings to buy a notebook. In this he wrote poems describing rural life and scenery. The publishers of Keat's poetry saw them and published them in 1820, the little book achieving immediate success.

The village is much as he saw it, though only the old inn, with its 13th century cellar, now marks the site of the ancient manor house.

RUTLAND

The Coeur de Lion Chest

SEATON. It has a towering viaduct over which the railway runs, with 82 arches 70 feet high, each one costing a thousand pounds. Perhaps there seems something of Roman vision and efficiency in this imposing work; it rises, indeed, in the very place where Roman builders were building 17 centuries before the railway came; the bronze brooch of a Roman lady has been found.

The church, with ancient tombstones built into its outer walls, has a 14th century tower and spire, but the inner doorway is Norman, the chancel arch is Norman with splendidly carved capitals, and part of one of the arcades is as the Normans left it.

A great ironbound chest, a storied receptacle, was made to receive contributions for the crusade of Richard Coeur de Lion. He could not speak the tongue of his native land, and lived among his people hardly a year, but this colossal almsbox speaks eloquently for him. It has not suffered the indignity of the ancient font, which we found made into a seat.

The Archdeacon's Extraordinary Son

SOUTH LUFFENHAM. It is on the River Chater, with a ford and a small footbridge, and with something linking it with imperial affairs and classical scholarship.

There is a 14th century tower with a curiously crocketed spire; and of its four bells one is the earliest dated bell in the county, 1563. Two tiny niches are carved above the porch. The north arcade is Norman, the capitals beautifully decorated with foliage and carved heads. The lofty chancel and the south arcade are 13th century. A 14th century tomb in the chancel has the Culpepper arms, and the sculptured figure of a woman lying under an elaborately carved canopy. There is a dug-out chest five feet long. The windows are chiefly 14th and 15th century, but one in the south aisle has an inscription linking Luffenham with stirring events. It reads:

In pious memory of the Venerable George Hodson, M.A., Archdeacon of Stafford from 1828 to 1855, and of his son, Major Hodson, Commandant of Hodson's Horse, killed at Lucknow, 1858.

Another name of fame, honoured by scholars throughout the English-speaking world, is among the rectors; Robert Scott was here four years before leaving to be Master of Balliol. He and Henry George Liddell produced the great Greek Lexicon.

But it is the name of Archdeacon Hodson's son that stirs the imagination of visitors here. He was one of the many sons of the parsonage destined to carve out great careers in India. He arrived there when 24 years old, and by his conduct in the Sikh war made the lifelong friendship of Sir Henry Lawrence.

He was as unconventional and intolerant as General Gordon, and quite as indiscreet. The enmity provoked by his brusque attitude possibly had something to do with his being charged with complicity in the murder of a British officer, with unlawful imprisonment of a native chief, and with dishonesty concerning regimental funds. He was acquitted of all imputations, but throughout his career the same kind of charges recurred with regard to his attitude towards life and property.

Still suspect and deprived of certain of his functions, Hodson seemed on the brink of ruin when the Mutiny enabled him to re-habilitate himself and win immortal renown. One of his feats was a magnificent ride of 72 miles with vital despatches, through country alive with enemy cavalry. He was permitted to raise a body of irregulars called by his own name, and he performed prodigies of valour at its head. Perhaps the finest swordsman in India, he was a born cavalry leader and intelligence officer. It was said that the only reason for his not receiving the Victoria Cross was that he earned it every day. His gallantry and genius had a foremost part in saving the British cause from overwhelming disaster in India.

He still had, however, the defects of his qualities, and marred brilliant achievements in the field by methods savouring of medieval days. One of his sensational feats was to ride out of Delhi with a handful of men to a point six miles away, to arrest the last of the Mogul rulers, and calmly to disarm a multitude of rebels. Next day he repeated the ride and captured three native princes. As his return journey was menaced by hostile forces, he shot his prisoners dead, although in one case he had given a written guarantee of safety. He also shot a native money-lender, on the vaguest rumour, it being found afterwards that Hodson was in his debt. Grave charges of looting were also made against him.

He died as he had lived, a fearless man; he was shot at Lucknow, while leading an attack on a defended house. An extraordinary character, in money matters reckless, if not criminal, he died poor and left a widow almost beggared.

The Wonderful Norman Columns

STOKE DRY. Like a small window of the countryside, it has noble and spacious views of the valleys of the Welland and the Eye, the old forest of Rockingham, and a noble church. Though a 17th century belfry crowns the 14th century tower, the church has the ancient Norman strength, and the rebuilding of the 13th and 14th centuries left us something of the splendour of its creators. Very imposing, too, is the remarkable oriel window with heavy mullions over the north porch; behind it is a room said to have been used for discussing the Gunpowder Plot.

But the treasure of the church is in the famous Norman columns of the chancel arch. The two slender pillars have graceful carving of figures and foliage, among which we recognise the eagle of St John. One capital has a figure holding a book. A man at a bell rope is one of the earliest examples of bell-ringing in England, a very vivid piece of crude sculpture. The columns are crowded with strange animals, people, and grotesque ornament. They are among the most vigorous examples of Norman sculpture in any of our churches. Other Norman fragments are on the string course in the chancel and in the 14th century chantry.

One of the nave arcades has clustered columns of the 13th century; the other has plain round pillars. Little of the old frescoes survives, but in the chancel is something left of the crucifixion of St Andrew, with the saint kneeling at the foot of the cross. The chantry has also fragments of wall paintings showing the martyrdom of King Edmund with a Danish archer still clearly outlined, the martyrdom of St Christopher, and what may have been the murder of Becket.

There is a carved and canopied screen of the 15th century believed to have come from Lyddington, and the chancel has a finely carved old chair.

The monuments remind us that Stoke Dry was long the home of the Digbys. There is an engraved portrait in alabaster of Jaquetta, widow of the Everard Digby who was killed at the battle of Towton in 1461. Jaquetta survived her husband 36 years and is here with their 14 children. In the chantry is a massive tomb with the headless armoured figure of another Sir Everard, who died in 1540.

A handsome table tomb has the elaborate figures of Kenelm Digby in 16th century armour and his wife clasping a book. Her head rests on a gilded and coloured cushion; his is on a helmet. Grouped round the base are quaint figures of their 11 children, two in swaddling clothes.

The fine Digby home is no more, but some of its material is in the wall of the rectory garden. Here was born that Everard Digby who fanaticism involved him in the terrible Gunpowder Plot.

The Terrible Plot

SIR EVERARD DIGBY is perhaps the saddest illustration of the terrible crimes that fanatical men have planned in the name of religion. He was born on May 16, 1578, and both by inheritance and marriage he was a very wealthy man. Everyone admired him. He was tall, handsome, brave, and thoroughly trusted, a fine gentleman of the sporting type. He had been brought up as a Protestant, but was converted by a famous Jesuit priest, John Gerard.

When the Stuarts came to the throne with James the First a certain section of Roman Catholics conceived the wholesale murder of the King, the Lords, and the Commons. They thought the Romanists were much greater in numbers than was generally supposed, and that in the confusion a successful Revolution could be achieved and Romanism again established in the land.

A man named Robert Catesby carried out the arrangements of this Gunpowder Plot for the murder of the whole body of the rulers of England, but the real leader was Sir Everard Digby. He found most of the money needed. His share of the work was the organising of the Revolution in the country when the slaughter was completed. He was to call together for a great hunt on Dunsmoor Heath, near Rugby, a concourse of Roman Catholic gentry on November 5, 1605, the day when an explosion would have destroyed all leadership, and left England paralysed by the shock.

About fourteen people were active participators in the Plot, and they worked at it for more than a year. They brought over from the Netherlands a fanatical desperado named Guy Fawkes to fire the 36 cwts. of gunpowder which they had placed in a cellar under the House of Lords, hidden under coal and blocks of wood. The preservation of secrecy was amazingly sustained. The midnight between November 4 and November 5 was reached, and Guy Fawkes was hiding in the cellar ready to lay a trail of gunpowder and blow the King and Parliament sky high. But at that quiet hour the

Ryhall
St Christopher

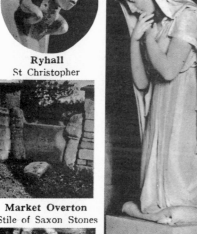

Market Overton
Stile of Saxon Stones

Burley
Lady Finch, by Chantrey

South Luffenham
Corbel

Market Overton
Font of Roman Stones

Stoke Dry

Norman columns and Oriel over Porch

Empingham
The Handsome 14th Century Tower

Tinwell
The Tower and its Saddleback Roof

Wing   The Ancient Maze

place was surrounded by soldiers, Fawkes was captured, and tortured till he revealed the names of the plotters. In the meantime Catesby and other conspirators, who were on the watch, perceived that the plot had failed, and galloped out of London to Digby's rendezvous 80 miles away in the Midlands. By breaking into stables and seizing fresh horses the conspirators made the 80 miles journey in eight hours. On meeting Digby they found that he had not been successful in gathering a substantial number of sympathisers, and those who had come began to disperse. Riding on towards Wales, they were still unable to persuade their friends to take the risks of a rising, and the sheriffs of the counties were now out in pursuit of them. Digby ordered them to scatter and save themselves, but all were captured. Several, including Catesby, fell fighting, and the rest, including Digby, who pleaded guilty and expressed his regret, were tried and hanged in St Paul's churchyard.

A clue to the plot had come into the hands of the King's Council ten days before Guy Fawkes was arrested. Lord Monteagle received an anonymous letter warning him, as he valued his life, to make some excuse for not attending the meeting of Parliament, for it would receive a terrible blow, and the members would not see who hurt them. Monteagle took the letter to the King's Council and the King's advisers decided from this wording of the warning that it foreshadowed an explosion of gunpowder. They therefore postponed the search to a late moment to catch the conspirators at their murderous work, and this they did.

On the scaffold Sir Everard Digby declared that Father Gerard, their most trusted Jesuit adviser, did not know of the plot. " I never durst tell him of it," he said, "for fear he would have drawn me out of it." Fanaticism blinded their eyes to the difference between pure religion and hideous crime.

The Bad Duke Humphrey

STRETTON. It has fragments of coffins 800 years old at its church door, and the Norman doorway has a tympanum made from what is believed to be a Saxon coffin lid. One of the arcades is 13th century with clustered columns and handsome capitals, a Norman arch remains unspoiled in the south transept, and the rough square font is Norman. A recessed tomb in the chancel is 14th century; the chest was made in 1662.

This was the church at which Cuthbert Bede was rector for 12 years, during which time he successfully strove with his pen to restore its decaying fortunes. Cuthbert Bede was Edward Bradley. It was with the Adventures of Mr Verdant Green, a laughing fantasy on Oxford University life, that he established his reputation. He wrote much and lectured throughout the Midlands to raise funds for his church, and one of his pen-and-ink sketches hangs here, showing the chancel before he restored it. Another of his drawings shows us a wall painting discovered in the church and lost again. But the figure of abiding interest here is Humphrey, Duke of Gloucester, whom three Shakespearean plays make immortal. He lies at St Albans, but here he was lord of the manor 500 years ago and he remains the most illustrious figure in its story.

Youngest son of Henry the Fourth, he combined the qualities of his grandfather with something of the personality of Henry the Fifth, but with an instability of character and a faithlessness to women which make it difficult to accept Shakespeare's portrait of him as a single-minded patriot. His title of the Good Duke Humphrey was a tribute not to his moral probity but to his patronage of scholarship. Described as "the most lettered prince in the world," his benefactions formed the nucleus of the first Oxford library, which has now developed into the Bodleian. All his life he was a student, and all scholars were his friends.

Humphrey was a good soldier. He commanded one of the three divisions at Agincourt, where he was desperately wounded and saved from death by the valour of Henry the Fifth. When a peace conference was proposed and John of Burgundy dared not be present unless Humphrey was handed over as a hostage, Humphrey rode into the sea at Calais and surrendered himself a prisoner. As a statesman he was grasping, prone to quarrel, and consumed by ambition. His marriage involved war with Burgundy, but he cruelly deserted his wife, and on the union being annulled by the Pope he married Eleanor, daughter of Lord Cobham. For many years he quarrelled with Parliament as to his powers as Protector, but he stood to the nation as the embodiment of patriotism, and in spite of his avarice he was generally beloved.

With the decline of his power he saw his wife condemned for witchcraft without raising a finger to save her; and the pathetic scenes between them in Shakespeare, seem to be based on authentic detail. Shakespeare represents the Duchess, having been banished, walking in a white sheet with a taper burning in her hand, when the Duke appears:

DUCHESS: *Come you, my lord, to see my open shame?*
Now thou dost penance too. Look how they gaze!
GLOUCESTER: *Be patient, gentle Nell; forget this grief.*
DUCHESS: *Ah, Gloucester, teach me to forget myself!*
For whilst I think I am thy married wife
And thou a prince, protector of this land,
Methinks I should not thus be led along,
Mailed up in shame, with papers on my back,
And followed with a rabble that rejoice
To see my tears and hear my deep-set groans.
Sometime I'll say I am Duke Humphrey's wife,
And he a prince and ruler of the land :
Yet so he ruled and such a prince he was
As he stood by whilst I, his forlorn duchess,
Was made a wonder and a pointing-stock
To every idle rascal follower.

Humphrey, who had already been impeached for treason, was summoned to appear before the King and Parliament at Bury, and on arrival was arrested. He died five days later under circumstances that gave rise to grave suspicion. Shakespeare represents him as murdered, but the truth seems to be that the shock of his arrest was too great for a shattered constitution. Buried in St Albans Abbey, where he had already prepared a grave, his body was seen, in 1703, in a leaden coffin, but it is there no longer.

The Lucky Thirteen

TEIGH. A pleasant little place on the Leicestershire border, it has stone houses, draped with ivy and wistaria, grouped about a little church made almost new except for its medieval tower.

Apart from the tower, it is only a simple oblong of which the east end serves as a chancel, but we remember it for two things—the curious arrangement of the pulpit, and a brass inscription set up in thanksgiving for the return from the war of all the thirteen who served from the village, eleven men and two women. For this is one of the 31 Thankful Villages where all came back, the only village in the county with this distinction.

The chief entrance to the church is by the tower and under the pulpit, which projects from a kind of oak screen filling the space of the tower arch. The upper part of the screen is painted to represent a leaded window with trees showing through. The pulpit is so high that the parson looks down about 13 feet, and below it, on each side, is a reading desk, one for the parson and one for the clerk. It happens, of course, thanks to this peculiar arrangement, that much of the service is conducted at the west end. The pews face each other, arranged in tiers on each side of the little nave.

Here lived John Benton, a labourer's son who wrote poetry before he learned grammar, and became master of the village school before he passed to the Great Peace in the year of revolution, 1848; but a much greater man than he is associated with Teigh, for in the churchyard lies Anthony Jenkinson, first Englishman to enter Central Asia.

First Englishman in Central Asia

IT was of Anthony Jenkinson that Hakluyt uttered the proud boast, "Which of the kings of this land before her Majesty had their banners ever seen in the Caspian Sea? Which of them had ever dealt with the Emperor of Persia, as her Majesty hath done, and obtained for her merchants large and loving privileges?"

He must have been born about 1530; he was sailing as a youth to all the Mediterranean ports of Europe, Africa, and Asia Minor, and in 1553 received from Solyman the Magnificent written permission to trade with the Turks, whose dominions then extended over the greater part of Hungary and Transylvania.

In 1557 he sailed as captain-general of four Muscovy Company's ships for Russia, with sailors paid 2¼d a day, sleeping on the open decks wrapped at night only in canvas or blankets. Glowing chapters in Hakluyt enshrine the letters he wrote of his travels—magnificent pages of observation and narrative, which treat peril and tragedy as commonplace but glow with romance when he comes to the court of Ivan the Terrible.

Ivan took to Jenkinson, and sat him at a table opposite his own at a great banquet in "a fayre hall" at which were present ambassadors from divers nations, pagan and Christian, and an army of 2000 Tartars. "The Emperor sent me divers bowls of wine and mead, and many dishes of meat from his own hand, which were brought me by a duke, and my table served all in gold and silver. When the Emperor drinketh all the company stand up."

Three times Jenkinson went to Russia; he travelled far on foot, by water and by sledge. He reached Khiva and Bokhara; he penetrated to the Court of Persia. He saw wars and famine and pestilence, but survived all perils, won the friendship of rulers wherever he went, and created new trade for England.

The England of Elizabeth's early time was narrow and needy; and Jenkinson played a foremost part in bringing in the spacious days which glorified her later reign. He must have been one of the first to suggest the North-East Passage. He helped to fit out Martin Frobisher. It was as an old man that he came here to visit a friend, and here in 1611 he ended his marvellous career.

The Splendour of a Norman Arch

TICKENCOTE. It is one of the surprise villages of our smallest county, with a magnificent shrine from Norman England.

The chief glory of its famous church is the grand chancel arch, which, with the vaulting, is as the Normans left it. The arch is in five recessed divisions, all richly carved. The outer line has a foliage pattern only to be found here, it is said. The next has double zigzag. The third has 40 designs of foliage and moulding alternating with grotesques. Among the figures in this group are what appear to be two portraits in stone, possibly Robert Grimbold and his wife; he was a Justice of England, and may have built the chancel. Two crowned heads are thought to represent Stephen and Maud, rivals for the throne. In addition there are a muzzled bear, a fox with a monk's head in its mouth, a serpent issuing from the mouth of a woman, fantastic human faces, and heads of cats. The fourth division of the arch has an embattled moulding, terminating in a double zigzag; the fifth and innermost has beak-heads. The whole of this remarkable arch is marvellously preserved, happily left untouched by the 18th century restorers of the church.

The vaulting of the roof is magnificent Norman work; the only other example of the kind in England is in the choir of Canterbury. The six divisions of the vaulting are divided by massive ribs, ornamented by zigzag, the central boss being carved with a monk's head and two muzzled bears.

The 13th century font is worthy of its setting, a beautiful piece of work, its square bowl with interlacing arches and quaint faces. There is some old glass, one piece painted with the head of Christ.

A rare possession is a monumental wooden figure of a 14th century knight in armour, a tall thin man with his knees slightly bent so that the soles of his feet grip the little dog looking up at him. It is thought to represent Sir Rowland Daneys, who fought in the French wars of the 14th century and was lord of the manor here. He represented Rutland in the first Parliament. The Jacobean altar table was given by Lady Ann Beverly in 1627. There is a priest's chamber, not over the porch as usual but over the chancel.

Such is this wonderful little church, standing amid yews and great chestnuts, with Tickencote Hall in the distance and the River Gwash, which has ground corn for generations, flowing placidly by.

TINWELL. Its massive tower belongs to the days when this Norman church was looked to as a place of refuge. It has a saddleback roof, the only one in Rutland. Roses and fleur-de-lys are carved round the doorway. The nave arcade and the chancel arch are 13th century; the chancel and the clerestory are 15th century. In the chancel lies Elizabeth Cecil, sister of the great Lord Burleigh, Queen Elizabeth's great counsellor and founder of the House of Cecil. Her wall tomb, inscribed with three coats-of-arms, has cornstalks beneath it. The church has few possessions, but among them is a beautifully carved old chest.

The post office has an unusual doorway, shaped like a horseshoe.

TIXOVER. Its church stands aloof in the fields half a mile from a house, reached by a rough trackway. It is enclosed by yews and a primitive stone wall. The tower is almost as the Normans left it, but the embattled parapet is 15th century. There is a plain font looking like Norman, arcades of the 13th century, and a splendid old doorway. One of the 13th century windows has some ancient glass from the Continent.

The First of the Brownists

TOLETHORPE. It is but a cluster of houses, with Tolethorpe Hall among its fine old trees, a 14th century home with its original gatehouse.

Often there must have passed this impressive gatehouse a boy who was to give the hamlet its claim to fame, and to leave his name in the dictionary.

He was Robert Browne, born here about the middle of the 16th century, the first man to separate from the Church after the Reformation, and founder of the sect called the Brownists. His grandfather had the distinction of being allowed to wear his hat in the presence of Henry the Eighth; the grandson's distinction was that he thought out his own way in the world and attacked the Church so vehemently that he was compelled to flee to Holland. Men were hanged for printing or binding his books, and he was prosecuted again and again and committed to 32 prisons, some so dark that "he could not see his hand at noon."

In the end Robert Browne thought better of it all, and, reconciling himself to the Church, became master of Stamford Grammar School and a rector in Northamptonshire. But even in old age his energetic spirit was not subdued, for in a fit of rage he struck a constable who demanded a rate from him, and once more he went to prison. It was the last time, for, carried on a feather bed in a cart to Northampton Gaol, he quickly sickened and died.

"As for those which we call Brownists," wrote Francis Bacon, "being when they were at the best a very silly and base people, they are now suppressed and worn out so that there is scarce any news of them." The wisest, brightest, and meanest of men, as Bacon has been called, was not wise enough or bright enough to foresee that out of the Brownists were to grow first the Independents and then the Congregationalists, now widespread through the English-speaking world.

Its Fame is Round the World

UPPINGHAM. Perhaps we may say that its chief industry is the making of fine Englishmen and exporting them to the four corners of the world. This place so very small (though it is Rutland's second biggest town) has one of England's finest schools, equipped for 500 boys and with a reputation far beyond the borders of our land.

A pleasant little town with green fields everywhere, it has a few earthworks remaining from an ancient fortress on a hill which gives us views of Beaumont Chase and the blue hills of Leicestershire. Its great square (where we may often see a little group of boys in black jackets and pocketless trousers) has changed little since John Evelyn fell in love with it at first sight. One of its original school buildings stands in a corner of the churchyard, reminding the great modern buildings of their small beginnings. The great school of today, with its proud halls and fine courtyards, rises like a castle guarding the quiet town with the grey houses and the thatched cottages, and with the church looking down from a hill.

We see it from the square, its lovely spire rising from a handsome tower, both 14th century. In the churchyard are fragments of coffin stones and carvings from the Norman church, and there is an old timbered porch with a stone roof; but much of the. church is modern. The ancient font is hidden away in the tower, but a proud place is given to a pulpit that Uppingham must cherish as long as it lasts because Jeremy Taylor preached in it some of those brilliant sermons that are among the masterpieces of our pulpit literature. He came here soon after preaching his famous Gunpowder Plot sermon at Oxford, and he stayed three years talking to the small congregation of Uppingham, and to the boys of the school, of holy living and holy dying, in the language that has been familiar to many generations of readers. He has rarely been surpassed for pulpit eloquence. He was imprisoned in the troubled times of the Stuarts, and his life was in many ways full of sorrow, but he must always live in literature for his devotional writings, for his poetic sensitiveness to nature, and for his stately prose. It was at Uppingham that he wrote one of his best books; in this church he was married; and it was here that there came into his life the tragedy of the death of his little son.

All the world knows the moving page in Evelyn's diary which describes the death of little Richard Evelyn, and it was to the famous diarist that Jeremy Taylor wrote of the passing of his own little son:

I am in some little disorder by reason of the death of a little childe of mine, a boy that lately made me very glad, but now he rejoices in his little orbe, while we think and sigh and long to be as safe as he is.

The old school in the churchyard has windows with quaint shutters, and these inscriptions in Hebrew, Latin, and Greek:

Train up a child in the way he should go.
Suffer little children to come unto me.
Remember thy creator in the days of thy youth.

In this small room the first scholars of Uppingham met a few years before the Spanish Armada. The school was founded in 1584, by Robert Johnson, who founded Oakham school at the same time. For more than 250 years Uppingham school was carried on in this small room. Then about the middle of last century came the turning of the tide. Dr Thring became headmaster. He found the school with tiny rooms, two masters, and about 30 boys; he left it after 34 years equipped with magnificent buildings and with a place among the greatest public schools in England. He made it what it is, rebuilding the school, constructing noble rooms and houses, with a chapel, laboratory, workshops, a museum, and a gymnasium. He taught the boys not only English and the classics, but modern languages, and encouraged them to use their hands as well as their brains. He encouraged art and music and fostered humane and lofty ideals. He developed character as well as intellect and was the first to establish a public school mission to the poor of London. His energies unexhausted, he wrote much on education, founded the Headmasters Conference, and was a pioneer in higher education for girls. Here at Uppingham is his monument, but he is remembered far outside it, with Arnold of Rugby, as one of the energising forces in modern education.

Today his school has perhaps the biggest school playing fields in England, a splendid block of buildings, and a majestic tower with an arch crowned by a figure of the Founder, Robert Johnson, by Sir George Frampton. In the Memorial Hall, which has a magnificent roof, is preserved the original charter of the school with Queen Elizabeth's seal. It has been found in our own day after being lost for centuries. The school museum, which has treasures from all over the world, has a fine window telling the story of the school in eight panels, one of which shows Dr Thring bringing the school back from Borth, where he had removed it during an epidemic in 1876. In the school chapel Dr Thring himself sits in white marble; he sits in his chair smiling at the boys as they come in; there is a brass inscription with his favourite motto, reminding the scholars that they must have a ready hand and open heart to help each other in good work. He himself sleeps under a beautiful cross in the churchyard.

The chapel is rich with carving and full of light from its beautiful windows. The reredos has three scenes from the boyhood of Jesus, and the peace memorial shrine was designed by an Old Boy of Uppingham, Ernest Newton. It has a lead dome, a mosaic floor, a painted roof, and wooden angels looking down on the names of over 400 Uppingham boys who fell in the war. Four of them won the

V C and 88 the D S O. Thomas Maufe won his V C by repairing a telephone line under intense artillery fire and by preventing a tremendous explosion at an ammunition dump. Lieutenant Maling, R A M C, gave first aid to wounded for 25 hours, being flung down by one shell and half-buried by another, but calmly working on until he had dressed the wounds of more than 300 men. Captain Arthur Lascelles refused to have a wound dressed and went on defending his trench until taken prisoner, when he escaped to die a free man. Captain Collings-Wells with a few men held up the Germans for 90 minutes to allow the rearguard to retire in safety.

We found two interesting names of men of peace—that of Cecil Sharp, the famous collector of our folk songs, and that of Ernest Hornung, a fine writer of exciting stories widely read before the war and best remembered as the creator of Raffles, the gentleman burglar. He himself was with the Y M C A in France and Flanders through the war, but his only son fell on the battlefield and sleeps under one of those wooden crosses that were in his father's mind when he wrote these lines which may be taken as an Uppingham boy's tribute to so many Uppingham boys who lie in a foreign field for ever England:

The brightest gems of valour in the Army's diadem
Are the V C and the D S O, M C and D C M ;
But those who live to wear them will tell you they are dross
Beside the final honour of a simple wooden cross.

Margaret Beaufort's Screen

WHISSENDINE. The old manor house stands sturdy and charming, and in a field not far away two square moats (one still with water in it) tell of a glory that has passed away.

The 14th century tower is among the finest in the county, and the church has much splendid work from our greatest building centuries. The arcades are 13th and 14th century and have beautiful capitals with delicate carving. The clerestory and the roof are 15th century, but some of the roof timbers are older still. The roof is borne on finely carved figures. The font is about 600 years old. The stone pulpit, the oak stalls, the reredos, and the chancel panelling are all in memory of friends of the church in our time.

The great possession of Whissendine is the handsome screen in the south aisle. One of the sights of Cambridge for centuries, having been in St John's College there, it was made in Plantagenet England

and was given to the college by the famous Margaret Beaufort, mother of our first Tudor king, who lies near her in his famous chapel in Westminster Abbey.

A Wonderful Record

WHITWELL. The little 13th century church stands on a knoll, but its builders forgot the vagaries of a spring rising higher up the slope, the White Well from which the village was probably named. In rainy seasons the spring has overflowed into the church, and so at the foot of the chancel arch we find a drain by which the little flood can run away.

The oldest things in the church are the crudely carved font made about the year 1200, a gravestone which was once the altar stone, a primitive chest hollowed out of a solid trunk, and the chancel window with 14th century glass showing the Crucifixion; it is flanked by two delightful corbels with the faces of a man and a woman. There are two charming wooden figures of St Michael and St Gabriel.

Whitwell is one of the few Rutland villages with a bellcot in place of a steeple. It has two bells exposed to wind and rain, under a double gable. One of its rectors, Spencer Ellicot, was here for 60 years of last century, an unbeaten record for the county.

The Ancient Maze

WING. It has one of the oddest survivals of any English village, an ancient turf maze. Forty feet across, it is still preserved, an admirable example of the mazes that were once general in England. Here the maze is made up of little turf banks about a foot high, winding round and round.

In this rural setting is our ancient English way of reproducing the ancient mazes of Egypt described in Herodotus and, most famous of all, the Cretan labyrinth said to have been constructed by Daedalus, father of Icarus, whose legend tells us that he was the first victim of human flight. The tradition is that these old mazes were devised by the Church as a means of penance, the wrongdoer being put in them and left to find his way out.

The church, poised high above the road, has a Norman arcade rich with carving, but most of it is from the 13th and 14th centuries. There is an old font, and two medallions of ancient glass remain, one showing the head of a bearded man. A modern window is in memory of a rector here through nearly the whole Victorian Era.

LEICESTERSHIRE AND RUTLAND TOWNS AND VILLAGES

In this key to our maps of Leicestershire and Rutland are all the towns and villages treated in this book. If a place is not on the map by name its square is given here, so that the way to it is easily found, each square being five miles. One or two hamlets are in the book with their neighbouring villages; for these see Index.

LEICESTERSHIRE

RUTLAND

INDEX

This index includes all notable subjects and people likely to be sought for, and a special index of pictures appears at the beginning of the volume.

INDEX

Brasses—*continued*
  Stockerston, 195
  Swithland, 204
  Thurcaston, 209
  Wanlip, 217
  Wartnaby, 218
  Wymondham, 226
Braunston, 236
Braunstone, 41
Bray, Sir Reginald, 196
Breedon-on-the-Hill, 41
Brentingby, 44
Bridges, notable :
  Asfordby, 17
  Aylestone, 25
  Medbourne, 146
  Rearsby, 171
  Syston, 206
  Thrussington, 208
  Thurcaston, 209
Bringhurst, 44
Brooke, 236
Brooksby, 45
Broughton Astley, 46
Broughton-on-the-Hill, 48
Browne, Robert, 278
Buckminster, 47
Buddon Wood, 28
Bunyan, John, 104
Burbage, 47
Burley, 237
Burnaby, Frederick, 187
Burton, Robert, 82, 179
Burton, William, 82
Burton Lazars, 48
Burton Overy, 49
Byron, Lady, 93
Byron, Lord, 60

Caldecott, 240
Canning, George, 48
Cardigan, Lord, 45
Carey, William, 104
Carillon, 131
Carlton Curlieu, 49
Cartwright, Edmund, 76
Castles :
  Ashby-de-la-Zouch, 17
  Belvoir, 34
  Castle Donington, 50
  Hallaton, 80
  Kirby Muxloe, 93
  Leicester, 112
  Oakham, 262
Catlin, Robert, 31
Catthorpe, 53

Chadwell, 54
Chairs, notable :
  Barkeston, 28
  Bottesford, 40
  Goadby Marwood, 76
  Leicester, 117
  Long Whatton, 131
  Lutterworth, 139
  Nether Broughton,153
  Normanton, 258
  Stoke Dry, 271
  Woodhouse, 223
Chalice-case, old, 235
Chantrey sculpture, 238
Chapman, John, 134
Charles Stuart, links with :
  Ashby-de-la-Zouch,19
  Aylestone, 25
  Barrow-on-Soar, 29
  Belvoir Castle, 35
  Blaston, 38
  Burley, 237, 239
  Leicester, 107
  Lubenham, 137
  Mkt Harborough, 145
  Tur Langton, 54
Charles II, 30, 218
Charnwood Forest, 5, 27
Chaucer, 53, 99, 120
Cheselden, William, 48
Chestnut avenue, 181
Chests, notable :
  Ashby-de-la-Zouch,20
  Barrow-on-Soar, 29
  Belgrave, 127
  Brooke, 237
  Burton Overy, 49
  Catthorpe, 53
  Cosby, 63
  Evington, 69
  Hambleton, 250
  Hinckley, 84
  Ibstock, 88
  Kirkby Mallory, 94
  Leicester, 117, 121, 123
  Market Bosworth, 144
  Newbold Vernon, 154
  Normanton, 258
  Noseley, 160
  Oadby, 161
  Seagrave, 179
  Seaton, 269
  South Luffenham, 269
  Stoke Golding, 196
  Stonesby, 196
  Stretton, 273

  Swepstone, 203
  Theddingworth, 206
  Thurnby, 212
  Tinwell, 278
  Whitwell, 283
Church Langton, 54
Civil War, links with :
  Ashby, 19, 22
  Belton, 236
  Great Glen, 77
  Hemington, 81
  Leicester, 104, 124
  Lubenham, 137
  Mkt Harborough, 144
  North Luffenham, 259
  Wistow, 221
Clare, John, 247, 266, 268
Claybrooke, 55
Cleveland, John, 134
Clipsham, 240
Clocks, old, 122, 242, 257
Coal-mining, 7
Coalville, 57
Cobbett, William, 25, 95
Cold Overton, 57
Coleorton, 7, 58
Coleridge, 60
Collings-Wells, V C, 282
Constable, John, 60
Cosby, 63
Cossington, 63
Coston, 64
Cotes, Roger, 47
Cottesmore, 240
Crabbe, George, 36, 76, 152
Cradock, Joseph, 78
Cromwell letter, 145
Cromwell, Gregory, 97
Cromwell, Thomas, 97
Cropston Reservoir, 155
Crosses, notable :
  Asfordby, 17
  Ashby, 20
  Billesdon, 36
  Bottesford, 38
  Foxton, 72
  Frisby, 72
  Hallaton, 79
  Harby, 80
  Hathern, 81
  Knipton, 96
  Muston, 152
  Oakham, 261
  Ragdale, 168
  Rolleston, 171
  Rothley, 172

INDEX

U

INDEX

INDEX

Loudoun, Countess of, 20
Loughborough, 131
Lowesby, 136
Lubenham, 137
Lud, King, 176, 197
Luddite Riots, 14, 81, 134
Lutterworth, 137
Lyndon, 255

Macaulay, Lord, 11, 174
Maling, Lieut., V C, 282
Mammatt, Edward, 21
Manners family, 35, 38
Manton, 256
Market Bosworth, 143
Market Harborough, 144
Market Overton, 256
Marshall, Thomas, 27
Martival, Roger de, 159
Mary Queen of Scots, 18, 39, 122
Maufe, Thomas, V C, 282
Mawbey, Sir Joseph, 170
Maze, turf, 283
Mease, river, 4
Measham, 146
Medbourne, 146
Melton Mowbray, 147
Michel, Humphrey, 85
Milton's tutor, 26
Misterton, 151
Montfort, Simon de, 3, 10, 99, 113
Moore, Bishop John, 201
Moore, Sir John, 15, 159
Moore, Thomas, 53, 89
Morcott, 257
More, Hannah, 56
Mount St Bernard Abbey, 220
Mountsorrel, 151
Mowbray, Anne, 57
Muston, 152

Nailstone, 153
Naseby, links with :
  Ashby-de-la-Zouch, 19
  Belton, 236
  Great Glen, 77
  Lubenham, 137
  Mkt Harborough, 144
  Tur Langton, 54
  Wistow, 221
Nether Broughton, 153
Nevill Holt, 135
Newarke, 114
Newbold Verdon, 154

Newton, Gabriel, 99, 107, 118, 122
Newton, mother of Sir Isaac, 257
Newton Harcourt, 154
Newtown Linford, 154
Nicholls, John, 84
Noel family, 94, 161, 237, 244
Nollekens sculpture, 244
Normanton, 258
Normanton - le - Heath, 158
Normanville family, 243
North Kilworth, 158
North Luffenham, 259
Norton-by-Gaulby, 158
Norton-Juxta-Twycross, 159
Noseley, 159

Oadby, 161
Oak trees :
  from Boscobel oak, 49
  Chaucer's oak, 53
Oakham, 261
Oates, Titus, 261
Old Dalby, 161
Orton-on-the-Hill, 161
Osgathorpe, 162
Owston, 162

Packe family, 166
Packington, 162
Papillon family, 137
Papillon Hall, 137
Paten, medieval, 214
Patty of the Vale, 247
Paul, William, 24
Pearson, William, 190
Peatling Magna, 163
Peckleton, 164
Peters, Matthew, 96
Phillips, Ambrose, 183
Pickwell, 164
Pickworth, 265
Plungar, 165
Postman V C, 220
Potter, Thomas, 225
Preston, 266
Prestwold, 165
Pulpits, notable :
  Barrowden, 235
  Brooke, 237
  Castle Donington, 52

Empingham, 242
Great Casterton, 247
Leicester, 122
Lockington, 129
Loddington, 130
Lutterworth, 138
Market Overton, 258
Nevill Holt, 153
North Luffenham, 259
Peatling Magna, 163
Rotherby, 171
Saxelby, 177
Shepshed, 183
Thornton, 207
Thorpe Langton, 208
Uppingham, 280
Woodhouse, 224
Pulteney, John de, 151

Quarrying, 7, 230
Quenby Hall, 87
Queniborough, 166
Quorn, 167

Ragdale, 168
Ratby, 169
Ratcliffe Culey, 169
Ratcliffe-on-Wreak, 169
Ravenstone, 170
Rearsby, 171
Redmile, 171
Reredos, medieval, 189
Reservoirs, 5, 155, 207
Richard III, links with :
  Earl Shilton, 67
  Elmesthorpe, 68
  Leicester, 113
  Market Bosworth, 144
  Stapleton, 192
  Sutton Cheney, 199
  Woodhouse, 224
Richardson, Benjamin, 48, 186
Ridlington, 267
Robin-a-Tiptoe, 48
Rogers, Samuel, 60
Rolleston, 171
Romans in Leicestershire and Rutland :
  Bardon Hill, 27
  Barrow-on-Soar, 28
  Burley, 237
  Caldecott, 240
  Cottesmore, 240
  Great Casterton, 246
  High Cross, 56
  Hinckley, 83

INDEX

INDEX